IMAGES
of America

PAWTUXET VALLEY VILLAGES

HOPE TO NATICK TO WASHINGTON

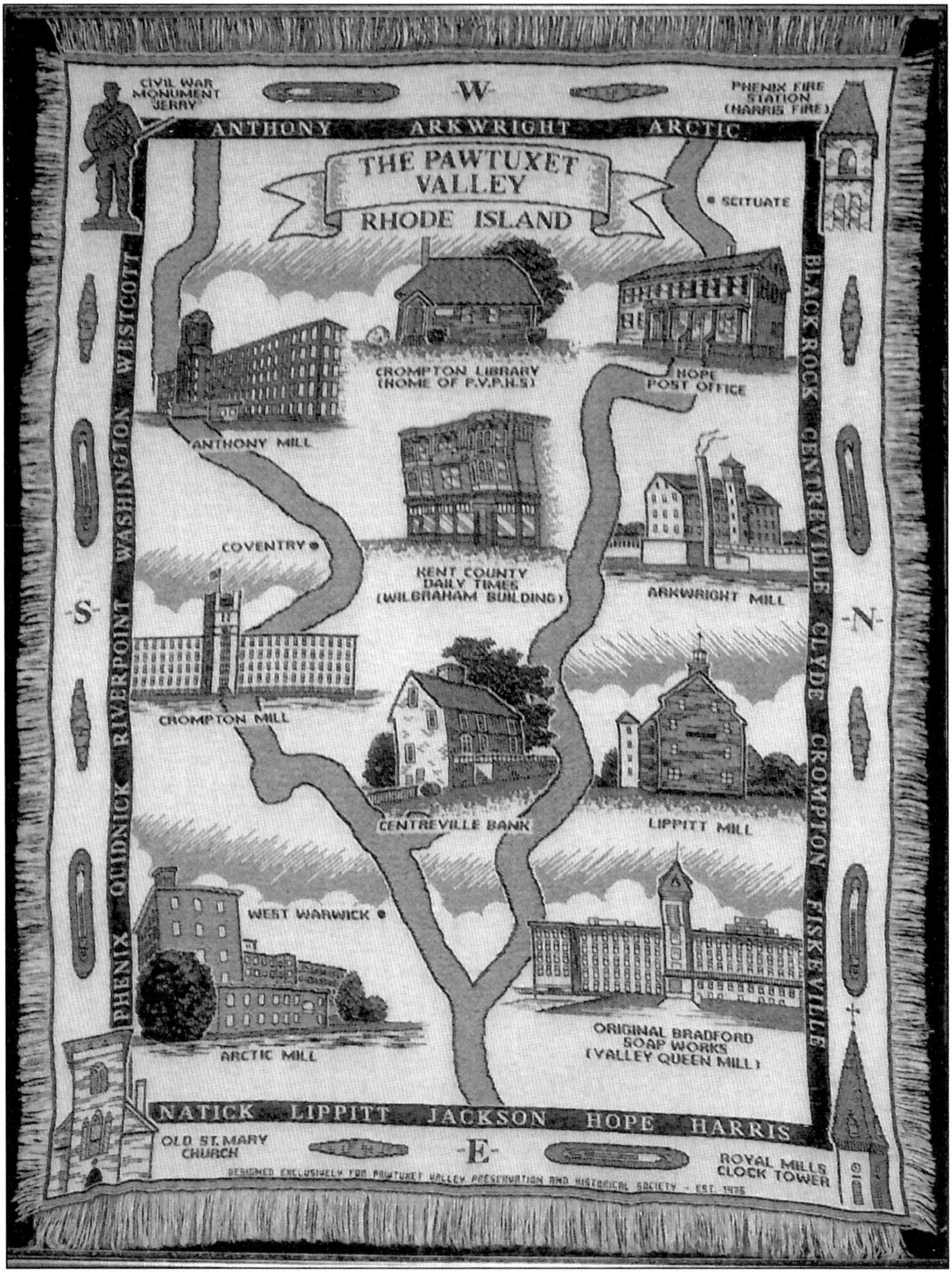

This framed throw hangs in the Centreville Bank in Arctic. It was produced for, and is sold by, the Pawtuxet Valley Preservation and Historical Society, located in Crompton. Starting in the top left corner and listed clockwise, the villages in the Pawtuxet Valley are Anthony, Arkwright, Arctic, Black Rock, Centreville, Clyde, Crompton, Fiskeville, Harris, Hope, Jackson, Lippitt, Natick, Phenix, Quidnick, River Point, Washington, and Westcott. (Author's collection.)

On the Cover: William and Richard Anthony built this company store in 1807. It was located opposite their mill on the corner of Main and Anthony Streets. It has since been torn down and is now home to a World War I monument, seen on page 106. (Courtesy of Donald Carpenter.)

IMAGES
of America

Pawtuxet Valley Villages

Hope to Natick to Washington

Raymond A. Wolf

ARCADIA
PUBLISHING

ISBN 978-0-7385-9752-2

Published by Arcadia Publishing
Charleston, South Carolina

Printed in the United States of America

Library of Congress Control Number: 2012937000

For all general information, please contact Arcadia Publishing:
Telephone 843-853-2070
Fax 843-853-0044
E-mail sales@arcadiapublishing.com
For customer service and orders:
Toll-Free 1-888-313-2665

Visit us on the Internet at www.arcadiapublishing.com

To my mom, Helen O. Larson, who chose to build her home and raise her children in the Pawtuxet Valley Village named Hope

Contents

ACKNOWLEDGMENTS

The reason I have written yet another book is in memory of my mother, Helen O. Larson. As I stated in *West Warwick*, she shopped in Arctic for over 60 years. She traveled there from the village of Hope on the Pawtuxet Valley bus lines, and on December 21, 1957, she married the bus driver, Ivar E. Larson.

I wish to thank the Pawtuxet Valley Preservation and Historical Society, the Foster Historical Society, and the Hope Historical Society for opening their archives to me. Without their cheerful assistance, this book would not have been possible.

As usual, local historian Donald Carpenter loaned his collection and provided his extensive knowledge of the area. He also proofread the entire book for historical facts. Thank you so much, Donald; I really appreciate it. I also want to thank Jenn Carnevale, my resident proofreader. She started with *The Lost Villages of Scituate* followed by *The Scituate Reservoir*. She cheerfully accepted reading *West Warwick*, then *Foster*, and now, *The Pawtuxet Valley Villages*. Jenn, you are the greatest.

A special thank-you goes to Richard Siembab for giving me access to his large collection of material on the valley. Also, the following people provided a helping hand in the creation of this book: Barbara Auger, Samuel Brown, Jean DeGraide, Charles Despres, Patsy Frost, Gerard H. Heroux, Gerard J. Heroux, Hope and Jackson Fire Company, Richard Hughes, Arlene Moan-Leyden, Dennis Picard, Lawrence G. Soucy, Gary St. Onge, Leo St. Onge Jr., Kathy Swanson, Gerard Tellier Jr., and Betty Thurn.

Again, I wish to express my appreciation to Richard Blodgett of Providence Water for providing unique photographs of the Pawtuxet River in 1921 and during the flood of 1936.

In conclusion, I wish to thank the super team I worked with at Arcadia Publishing: Lissie Cain, acquisitions editor; Chanler Jeffers, sales and marketing specialist; Jennifer Pratt, regional sales and marketing manager; and all the people behind the scenes who make the Images of America series so great.

Unless otherwise noted, all images appear courtesy of the Pawtuxet Valley Preservation and Historical Society.

Introduction

Pawtuxet Valley Villages is a companion book to *West Warwick*. There are over 200 new images covering all 18 villages, shown on the throw on page 2. Emphasis in this book is placed on the nine villages not covered in *West Warwick*.

The North Branch of the Pawtuxet River begins as it exits the Scituate Reservoir dam. It then travels through the villages of Hope, Jackson, Fiskeville, Arkwright, Harris, Phenix, Lippitt, and Clyde on its way to River Point.

The South Branch of the Pawtuxet River flows from the flatlands of Coventry and through the villages of Washington, Anthony, Quidnick, Crompton, Centreville, and Arctic to River Point. River Point is where the two branches join together to flow as the Pawtuxet River around the village of Westcott and through the village of Natick on its way to Narragansett Bay.

Together, they flow through the towns of Scituate, Coventry, and West Warwick, and the village of Natick; in Natick, it is the dividing line between West Warwick and Warwick. The area surrounding the branches of this river has become known as "the Valley."

There were a dozen mills built on the Pawtuxet River from 1806 to 1821, which created small villages all along its banks. Nine of the villages are covered extensively in *West Warwick*. For over 100 years, the mills were a thriving industry. They provided a source of income for the families that lived in the valley and the immigrants that moved here looking for a better life. Some of the businesses that sprang up were hotels, stables, blacksmiths, tailors, and cobblers, along with banks, general stores, and drugstores. Eventually, the railroad came to the valley, followed by the trolley in the late 1880s.

In 1988, Gerard H. Heroux was commissioned to write "West Warwick Queen of the Valley," a poem commemorating the 75th anniversary of West Warwick. The following verses are from his poem: "Take a walk with me by the bank of the river, / As the evening Sun goes down. All orange and black, / the old railroad track, / Where we lift up our voices in the praise of our town. O West Warwick Queen of the Valley, / River Pawtuxet, flows through your heart. / Like castles from a dream, all the cotton mills seem, / To be watchful and sheltering as each new day starts. / From Phenix, to Arctic, Natick, to Crompton, River Point, Westcott, Lippitt, and Clyde. / From Prospect Hill to Old Centreville, can we make this renewal, one of promise and pride."

If West Warwick is "queen of the valley," then surely the Pawtuxet River is "king of the valley." The Pawtuxet is what gave life to the mills, and in turn, employment to the villagers.

A large portion of the valley resides in West Warwick, and the town will proudly celebrate its centennial in 2013. However, Scituate, Cranston, Warwick, and Coventry all claim a portion of it.

There is a tremendous amount of history in the Pawtuxet Valley. Your journey begins in the village of Hope and follows the North Branch of the Pawtuxet River downstream, through a number of villages to River Point, and then on to Natick. Your journey then reverses and follows the South Branch upstream, visiting villages all the way to Washington.

As in his previous books, the following poem by the author's mother, written in 1992 at the age of 81, will serve as an introduction:

The *Pawtuxet Valley Daily Times* (now the *Kent County Times*)
By Helen O. Larson

This local paper has been published
One hundred years
It carries good news and bad news
The bad news brings tears

I look forward to the *Times*
When the day is through
First I read the headlines
Then the weather too

And I always read
Every obituary through
To see if any person who passed away
Was someone that I knew

Then I read someone marries
And is happy as can be
This part of the paper
Brings joy to me

If you are a sports fan
And many are I know
There are several pages
I know this to be true

Then there's Dear Abby
Giving her advice
I always read her column
Sometimes I read it twice

And the Poetry Corner
I read when my work is done
For many of my poems
Are published one by one

Then there's the Town Meeting
Folks can tell what's on their mind
I call now and then
Weekends any time

I read the Classifieds
Not to skip them I try
It brings much happiness
Many beautiful things I've been able to buy

I always look at the want ads
Those I always read
I do this all the time
Though a job I do not need

I look at news of the markets
I do this with out fail
I always like to know
What items are on sale

I read the *Times* through again
Before I lay it down
To see if I have missed
Any news of my home town

So keep on publishing the *Times*
Though it isn't free
It makes the end
Of a happy day for me

When the paper boy comes
Sometimes he's early, sometimes late
But faithful he comes
Every evening through my gate

One

Hope and Jackson

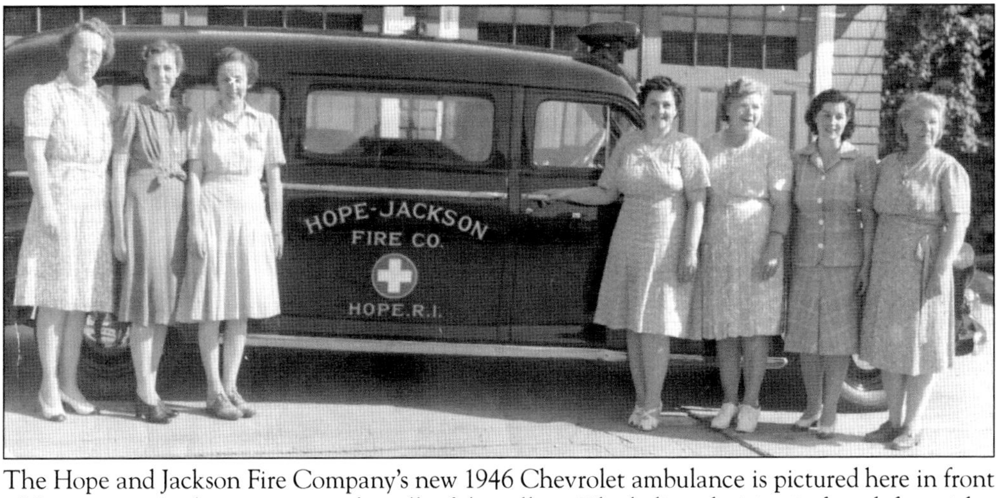

The Hope and Jackson Fire Company's new 1946 Chevrolet ambulance is pictured here in front of the station. At the time, it was the talk of the village. The ladies admiring it, from left to right, are Lillian Brown, Lucille Gardner, Hazel Durand, Mabel Hutchins, Lillian Remington, Violet Gresty, and Lottie Luther. (Courtesy of Jean DeGraide.)

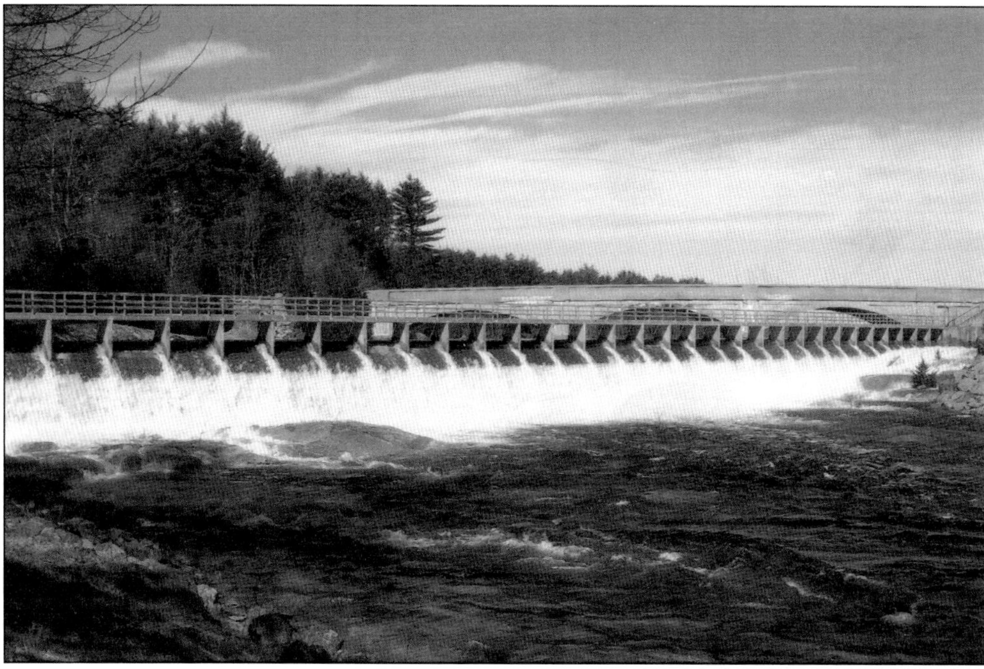

The valley was carved out of the landscape by the Pawtuxet River as it flowed to Narraganset Bay. Today, the north branch begins as it pours out of the dam of the Scituate Reservoir, including over the spillway shown above, and follows the same route. This was the scene in March 2010 at 11:30 a.m. Even though two sets of flashboards are in place, 601 million gallons of spillage is taking place every day. The first obstruction it encounters is the Hope Dam, shown below on the same day. The Hope Furnace forge was located on the hillside to the right of the Hope Furnace Dam. It operated from 1765 to 1815 (see page 19). (Both, author's collection.)

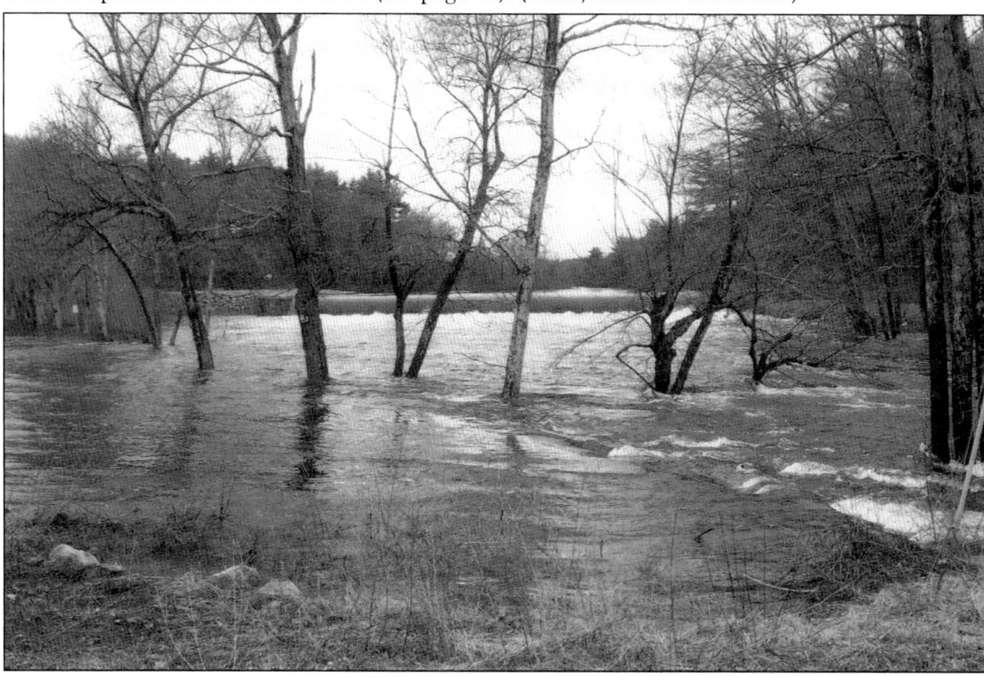

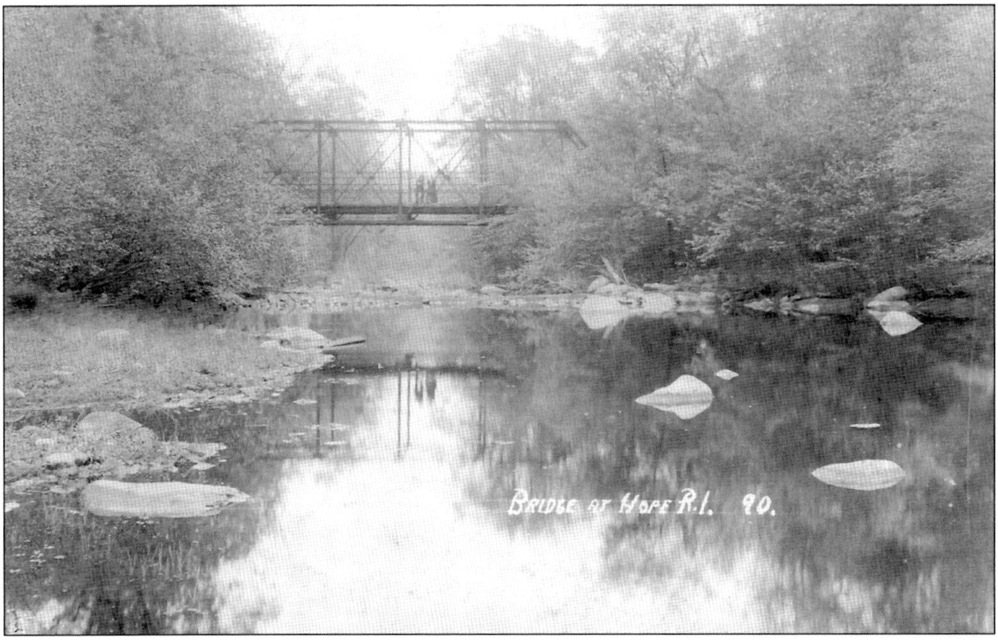

This postcard shows the area below the Hope Dam, looking downstream. The steel bridge was replaced with a concrete bridge in 1929. At the same time, the road was constructed to go straight to the Coventry line. (Courtesy of Donald Carpenter.)

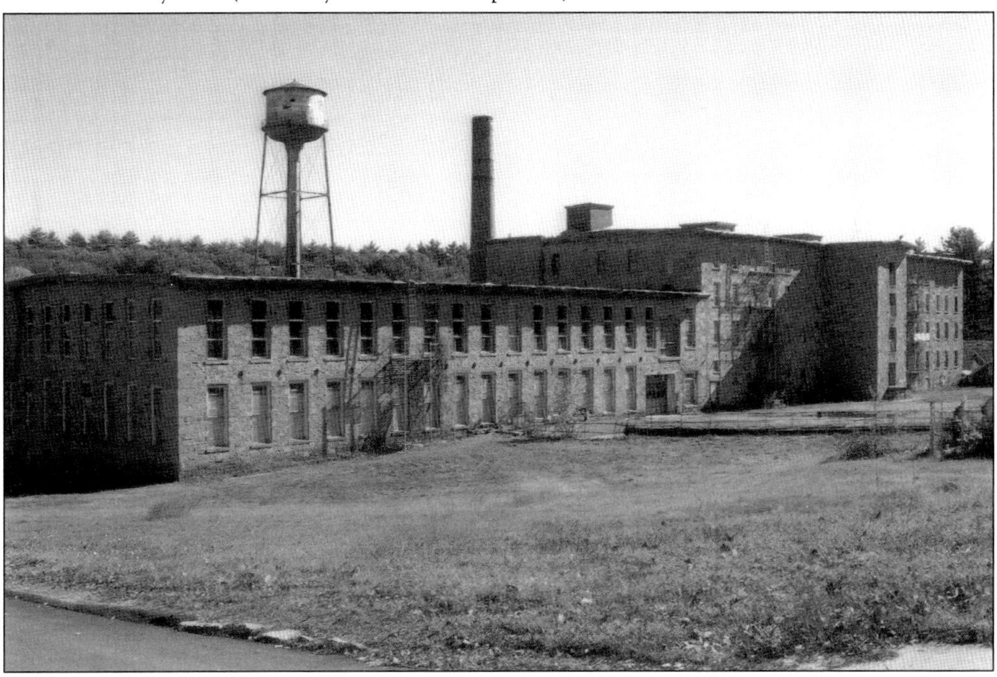

The original Hope Manufacturing Company mill was built of wood in 1806 by Sylvanus Hopkins. It burned in 1843 and was bought by John Carter Brown, Moses B. Ives, and Robert H. Ives in 1844. They erected the large stone mill on the right that same year. With anticipation of the railroad, the owners constructed a major addition in 1871, shown on the left. The original trench was diverted to the new addition and is clearly seen on page 12. (Author's collection.)

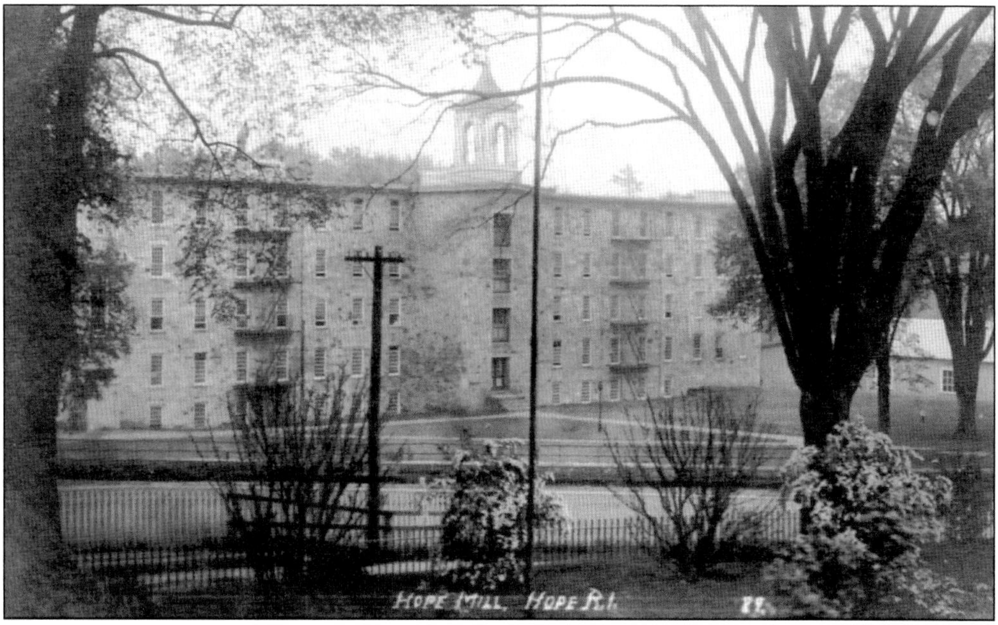

Elizabeth J. King of 101 Main Street mailed this postcard on September 25, 1913. It shows the reconstructed trench entering the north wing addition. It also was taken before a one-story brick addition was constructed at the south end of the mill in 1916. The Hope Company was incorporated in 1847 and operated until 1944. (Courtesy of Foster Historical Society.)

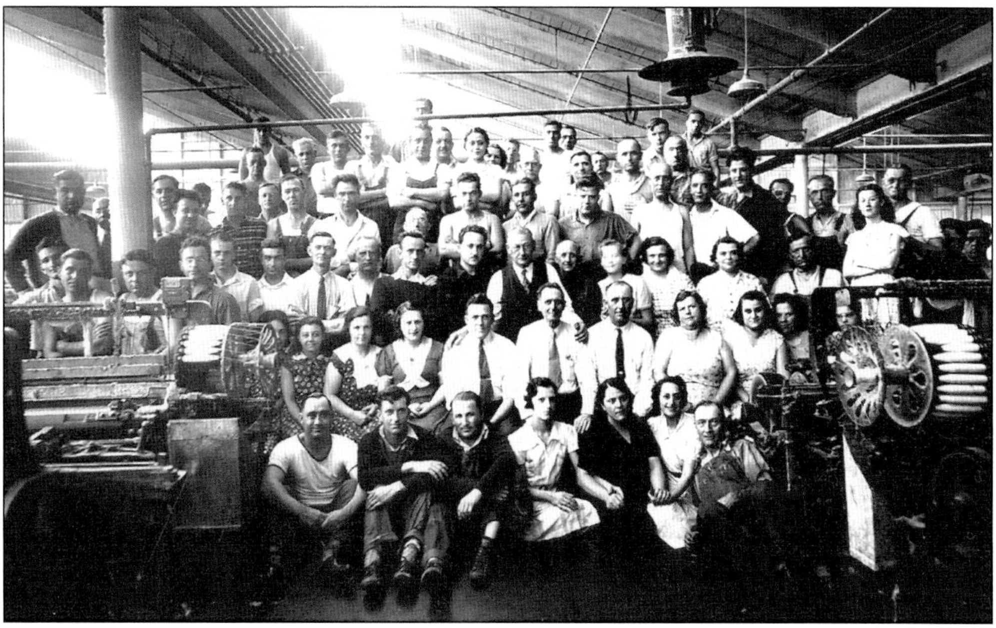
This group of workers is pictured in the weave shop of Hope Mill in the 1940s. The only workers identified are Albert W. Wolf, the author's father (first row; first on left); William Gifford (second row, fifth from left); boss Edward Fryer (second row, sixth from left); John Trunk (third row, man wearing glasses third from left); John Craig (third row, tenth from left); Nathanial Hopkins (third row, eleventh from left); Walt Smith (fourth row, short man sixth from left); and Albert "Big Boy" Berube (fifth row, man with an arrow over his head). (Courtesy of Donald Carpenter.)

This 1940s photograph proudly displays the Moan Brothers Express fleet of trucks. They are lined up in the yard at the north side of Hope Mill. Wally Moan's daughter Arlene relates, "Dad used to pile us kids in whichever truck was available and off to church we would go." (Courtesy of Arlene-Moan Leyden.)

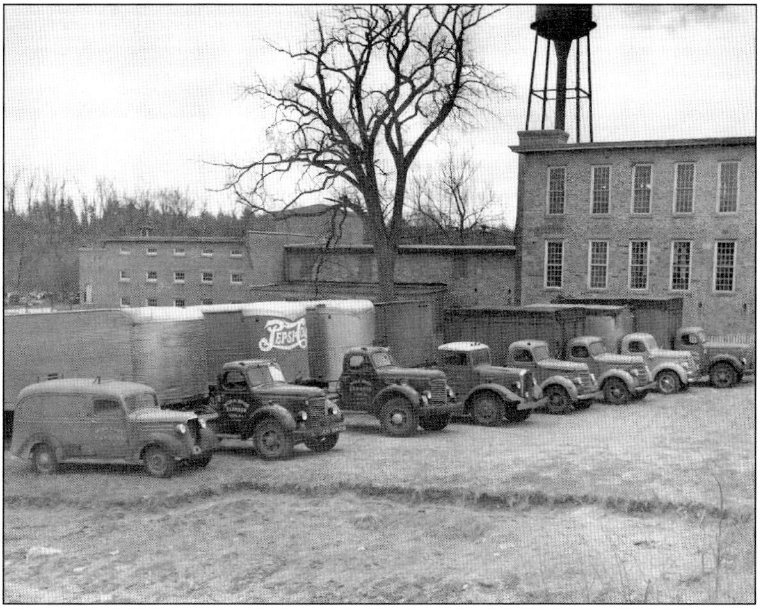

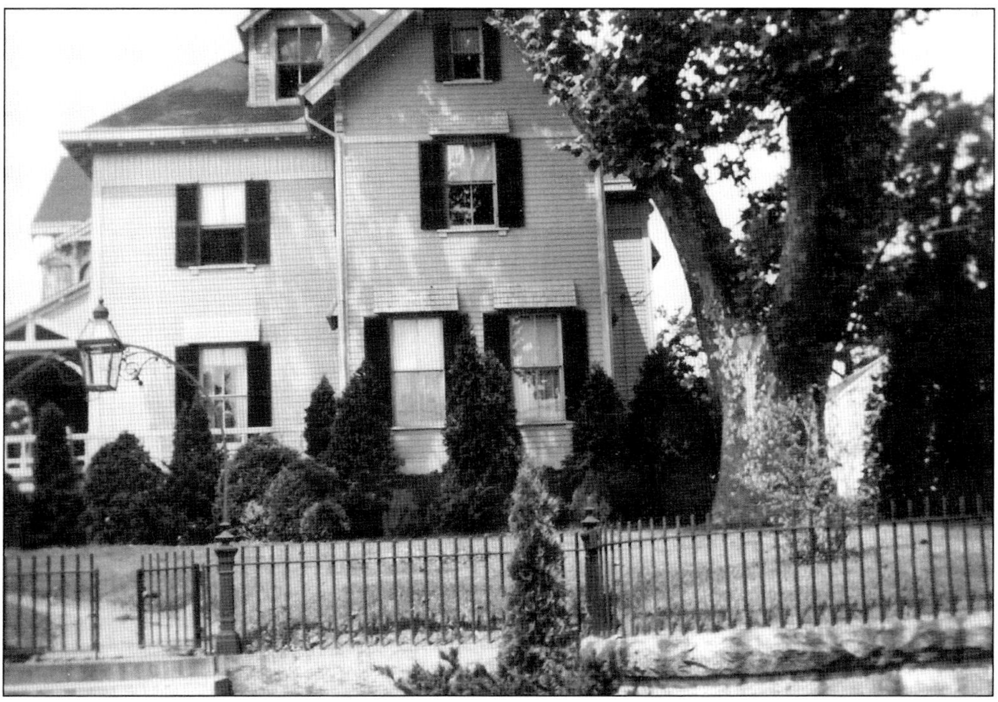

The Hope Company built this large house for Supt. Samuel G. Allen. Pictured here in 1950s, it was designed by Providence architects Stone and Carpenter in 1880 and is located across the street from the mill. The Hope Furnace was previously located on this property (see pages 10 and 19). (Author's collection.)

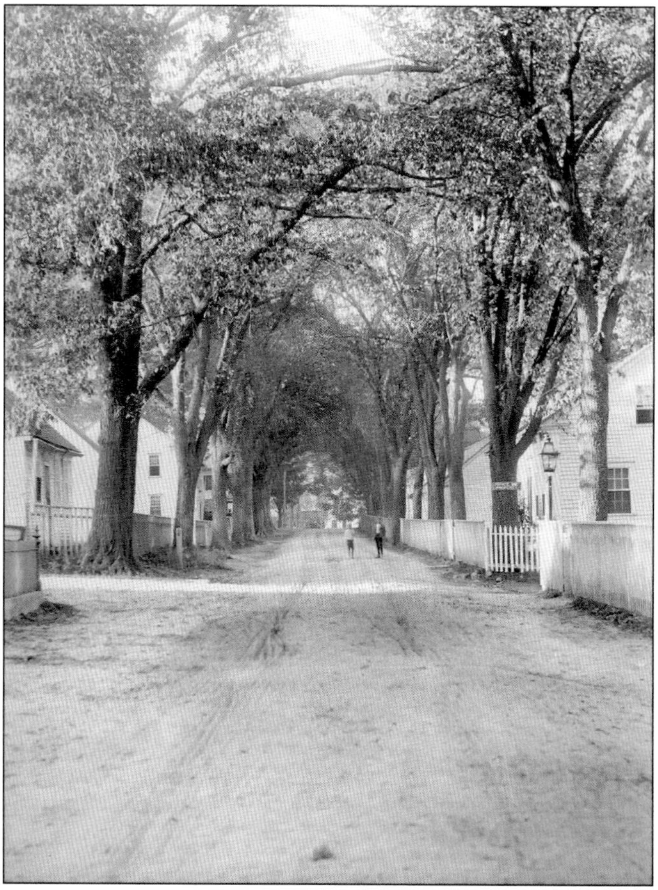

This postcard of Main Street, facing north towards the old post office, was mailed September 1, 1909. Mill Street is on the right by the lamppost. The sign attached to the tree announces "private property." Telephone poles have not yet come to the village. The hitching post at left can be seen below in the image taken from the opposite direction. (Courtesy of Kathy Swanson.)

This postcard was mailed June 25, 1913. The photograph shows Main Street, facing Hope Mill, after Hope Church was built. The two women pictured, Mary Carter (left) and Bertha Brayton, may have been out for a stroll. The trolley tracks have not been laid, but the poles are in place (at right), with the arm that will support the electric lines. (Courtesy of Patsy Frost.)

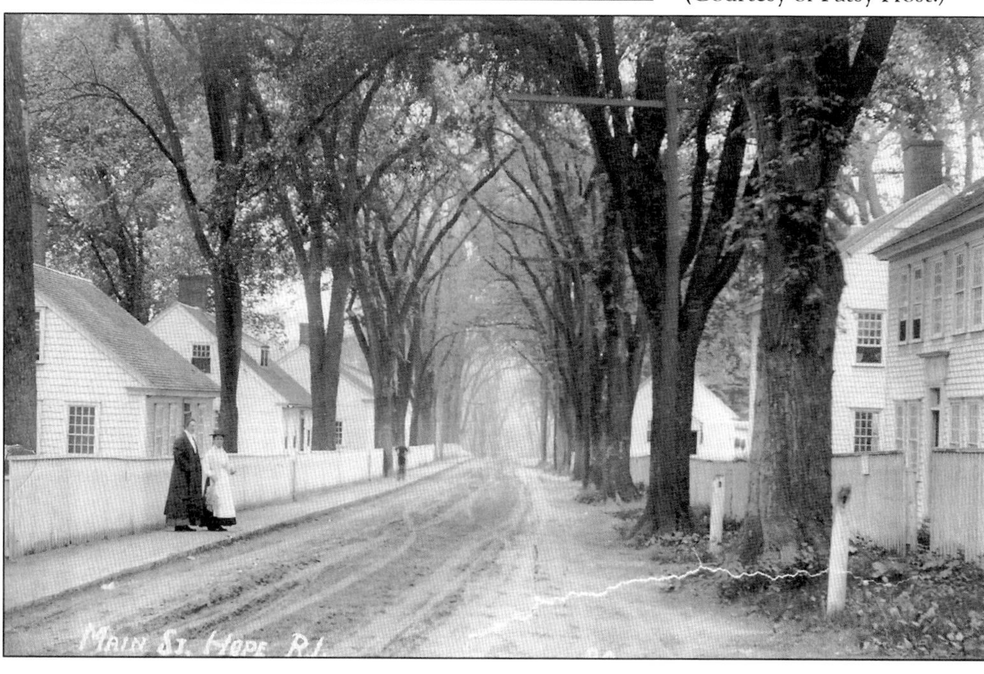

The Hope Methodist Church, designed by Stone and Carpenter of Providence, is pictured right in 1913. The church was built in 1874 for the Hope Mill Company. The village library was established on the lower level. Alice Howland was appointed librarian in 1896 and served in that position for 50 years. The organ, seen below, was installed in 1913 and is emphasized by the intricate truss work supporting the roof. In the 1970s, the congregation joined with the Phenix Methodist Church. They built a new church in Hope and named it Shepherd of the Valley. (Right, courtesy of Richard Siembab; below, courtesy of Donald Carpenter.)

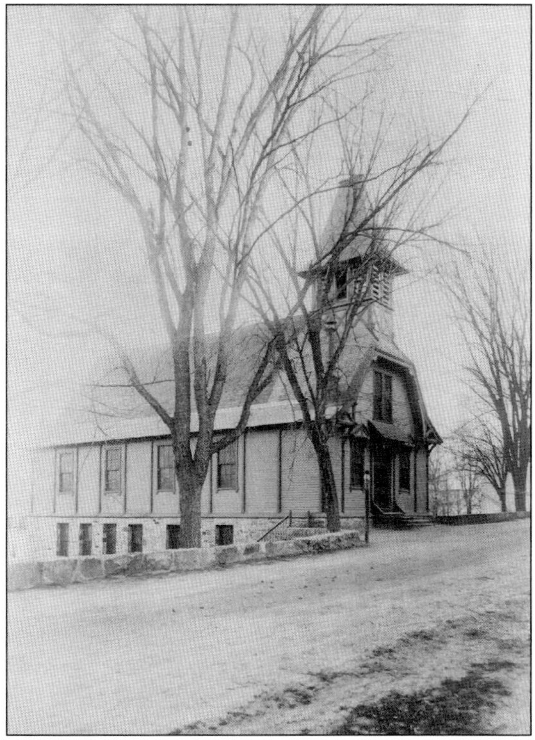

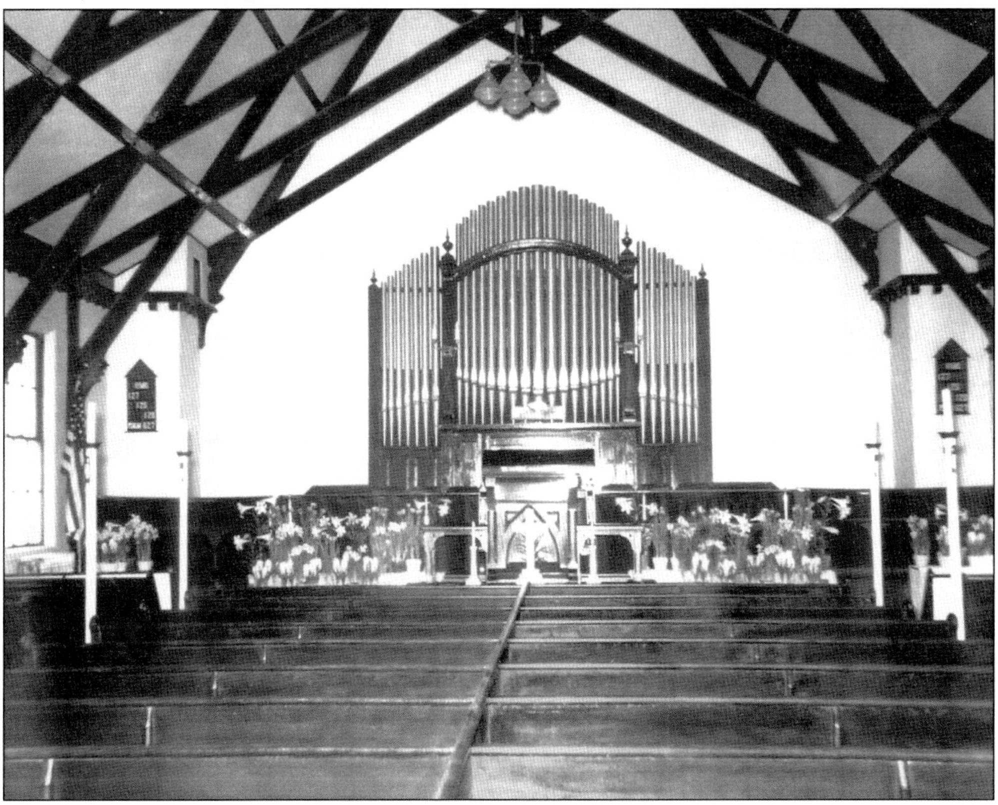

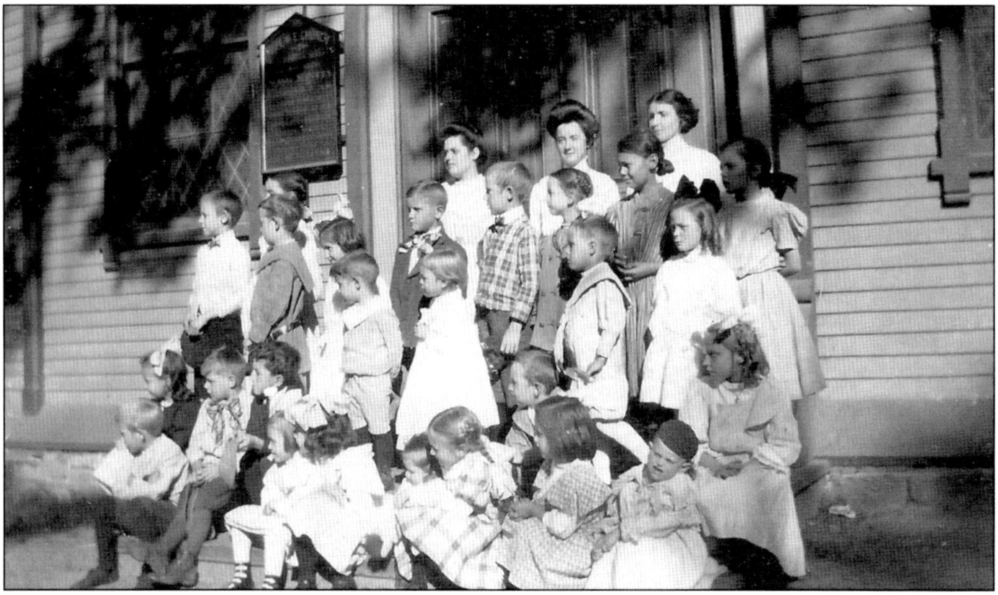

This Sunday school class is gathered in front of Hope Methodist Church around 1910. In the back row, Mary Lyons is on the left with her sister Ruth on the far right. The following verse is from "The Greatest Story Ever Told," written by Helen O. Larson in 1999 at the age of 89: "The greatest story ever told, was about a baby boy born one day / There was no room at the inn, so He was born on the hay." (Courtesy of Patsy Frost.)

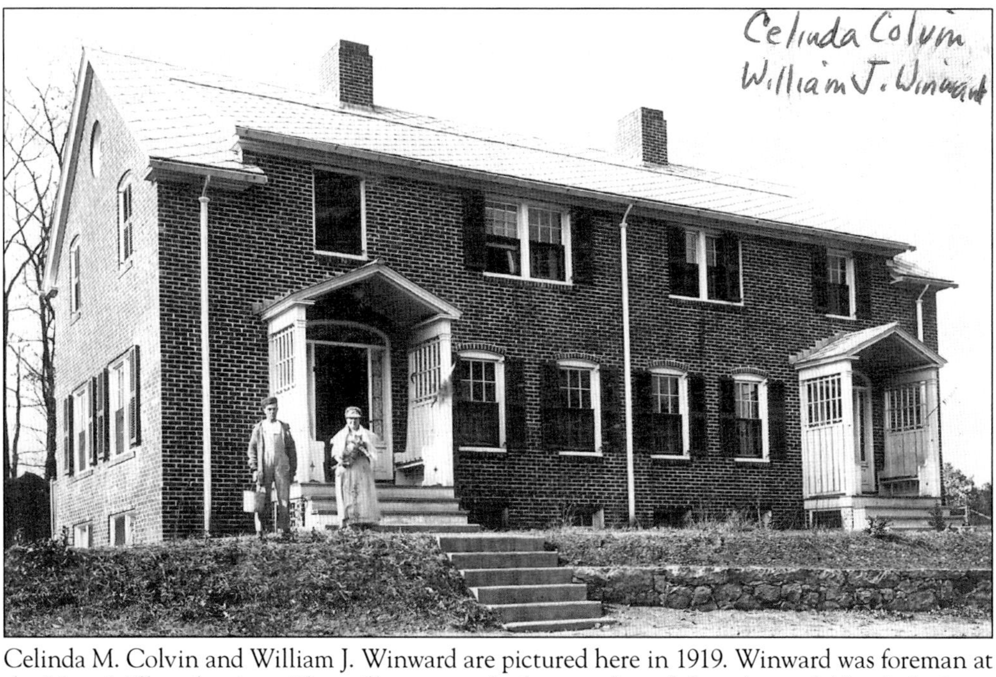

Celinda M. Colvin and William J. Winward are pictured here in 1919. Winward was foreman at the Hope Mill at the time. The mill company built a number of these beautiful brick duplexes on Goddard and Ives Streets. (Courtesy of Patsy Frost.)

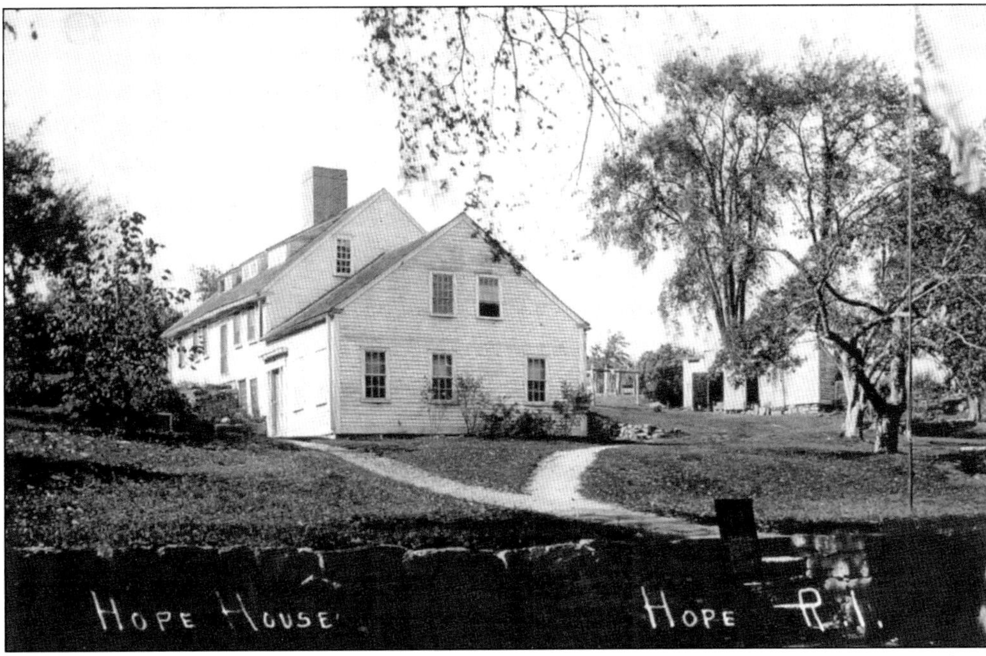

Daniel Fiske built this home, also known as the Hope House, in the mid-1700s. Alice Howland (see page 15) lived here from the late 1800s to the mid-1900s. This view faces west from Main Street. (Courtesy of Kathy Swanson.)

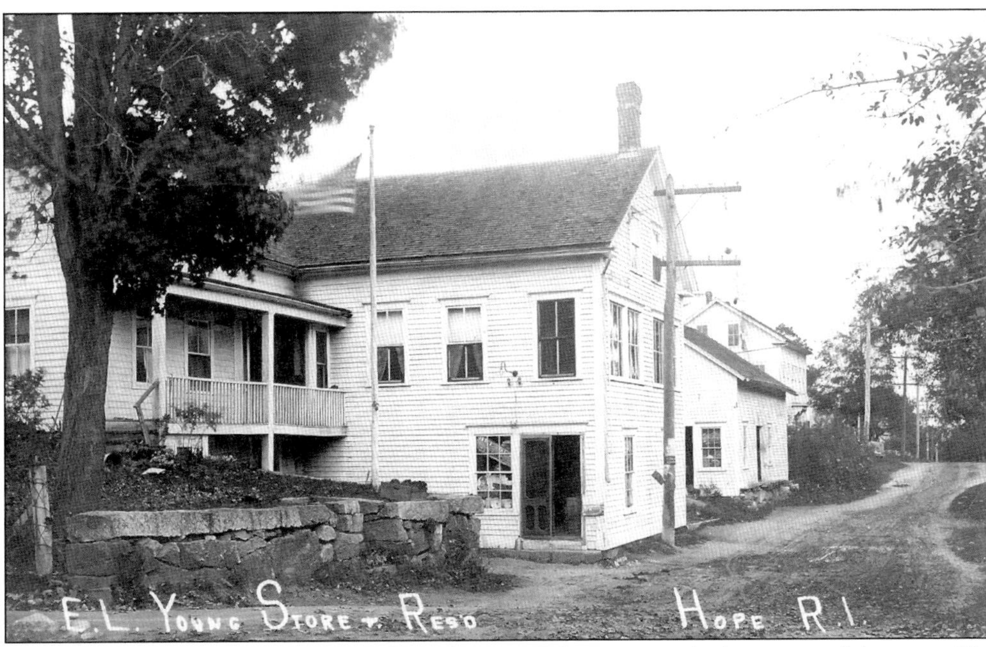

Eugene L. Young maintained his residence here, with his store in the basement of the wing. The wing has since been removed, as has the barn behind it. At this time, High Street, pictured here, was just a dirt lane as it approached North Road. (Courtesy of Patsy Frost.)

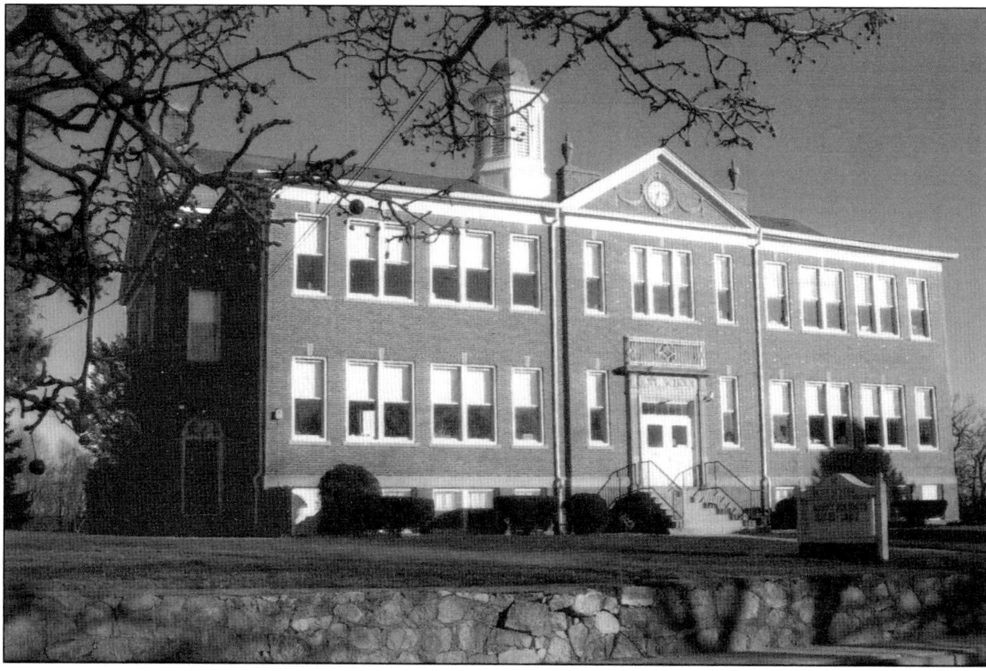

The grand entrance of Hope School is pictured here in December 2011. It was built in 1928 with additions in 1972 and 1990. Notice the girls' entrance on the left, while the boys had their entrance on the right of the building. (Author's collection.)

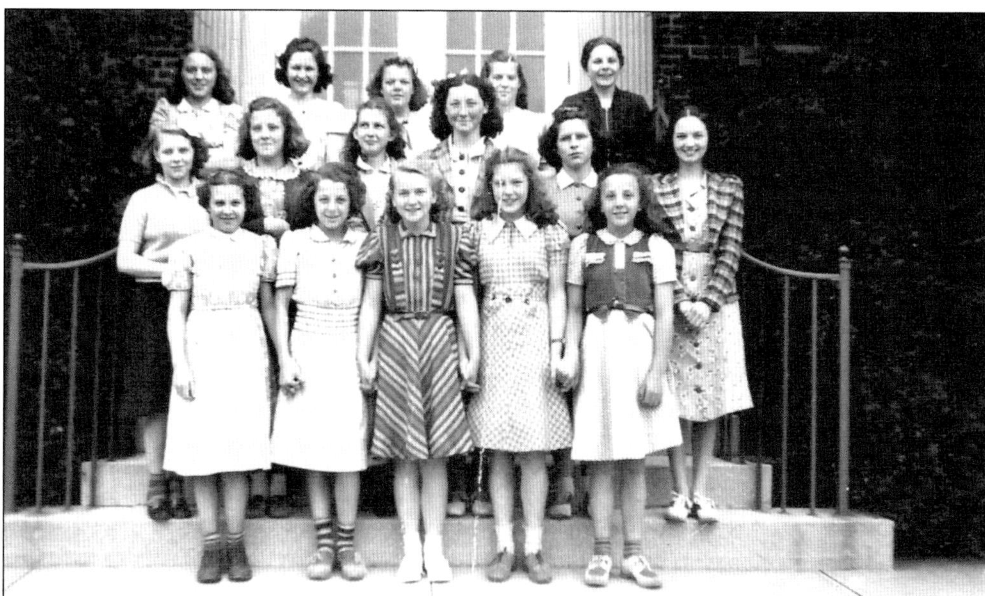

This group of girls stands on the Hope School steps in 1942. From left to right are (first row) Helen Dodd, Winfrid Anit, Virginia Remington, Lillian Winward, and Gladys Howard; (second row) Audrey Spencer, Virginia Howard, Esther Spaulding, Shirley Needom, Cora Lamourx, and Barbara Cole; (third row) Emily Ide, Helen Swan, Betty Spencer, Ruth Clark, and Barbara Thornton. (Courtesy of Patsy Frost.)

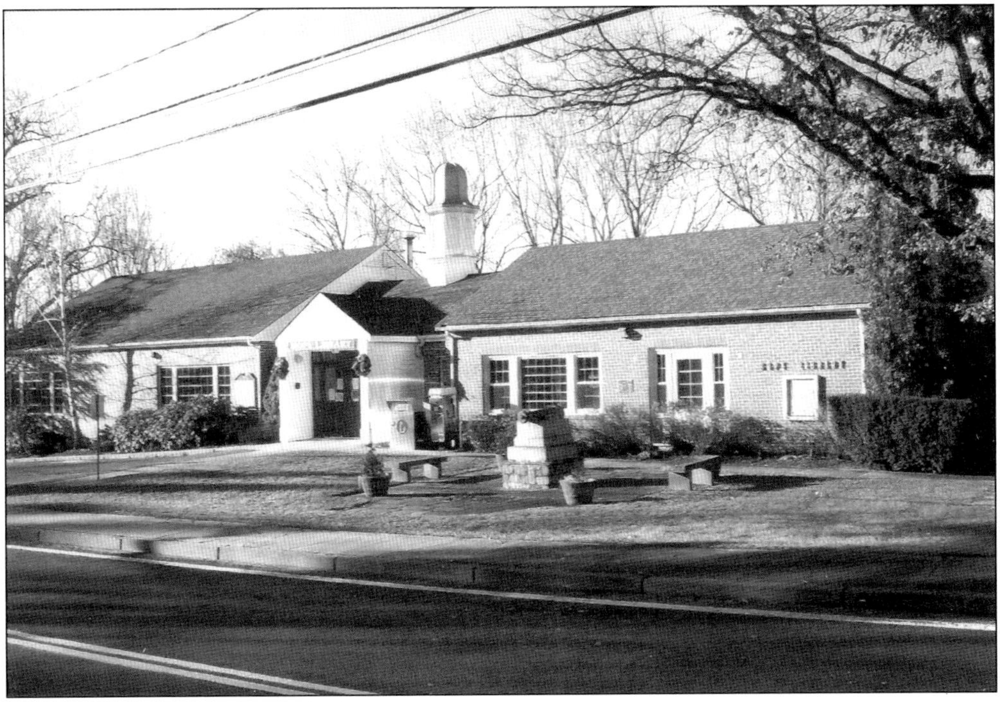

This January 2012 photograph shows the north section of Hope Library on the right, built in 1966, and the south addition of 1989 that doubled its size. The cannon located in front was originally beside the Crompton School in the village of Crompton, West Warwick. It can be seen on page 75 of Images of America: *West Warwick*. (Author's collection.)

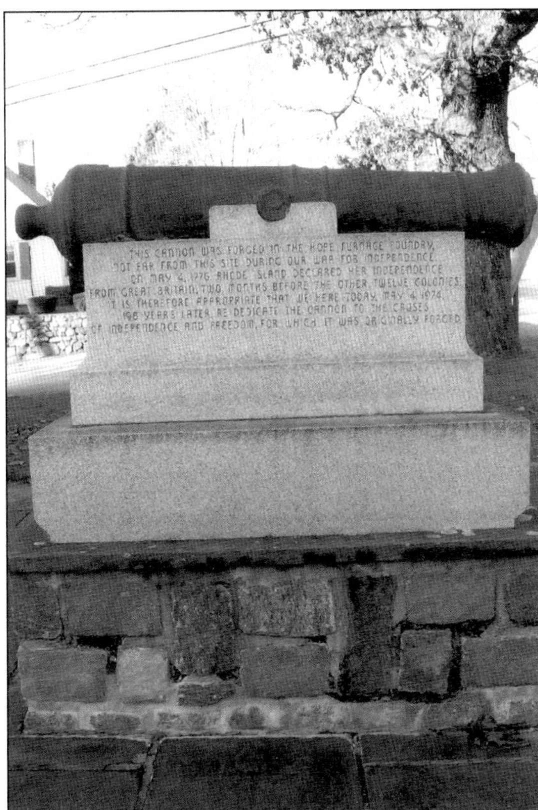

The inscription on the side of the monument reads, "This cannon was forged in the Hope Furnace Foundry, not far from this site, during our war for independence. On May 4, 1776, Rhode Island declared her independence from Great Britain, two months before the other twelve colonies. It is therefore appropriate that we here today, May 4, 1974, 198 years later, re-dedicate the cannon to the causes of independence and freedom, for which it was originally forged." (Author's collection.)

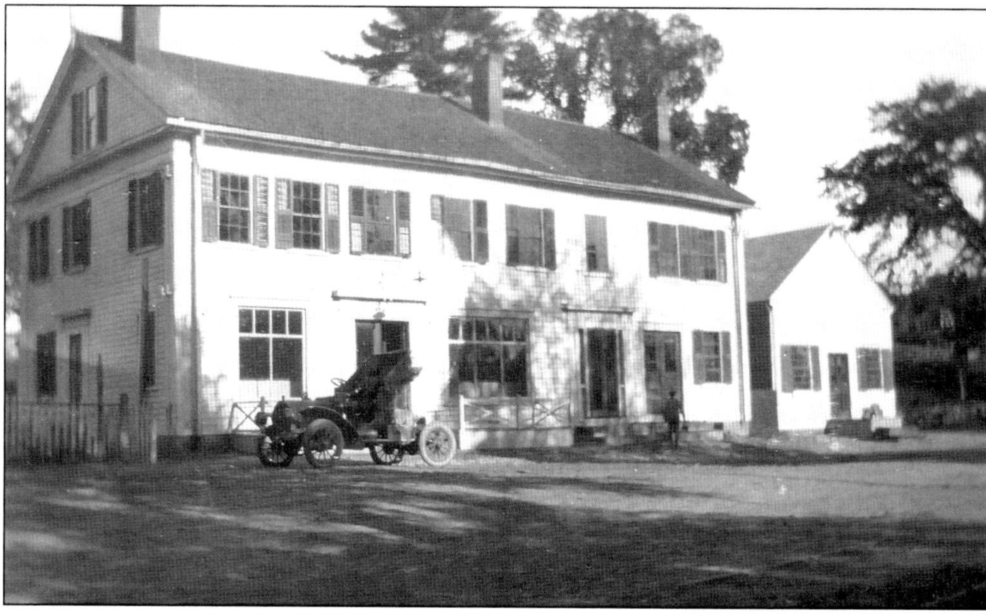

The Welcome Matteson Tavern and Hotel was built in the 1830s. It has been a stagecoach stop, housed variety stores, and was home to the US post office. Today, the first floor stands vacant. (Courtesy of Donald Carpenter.)

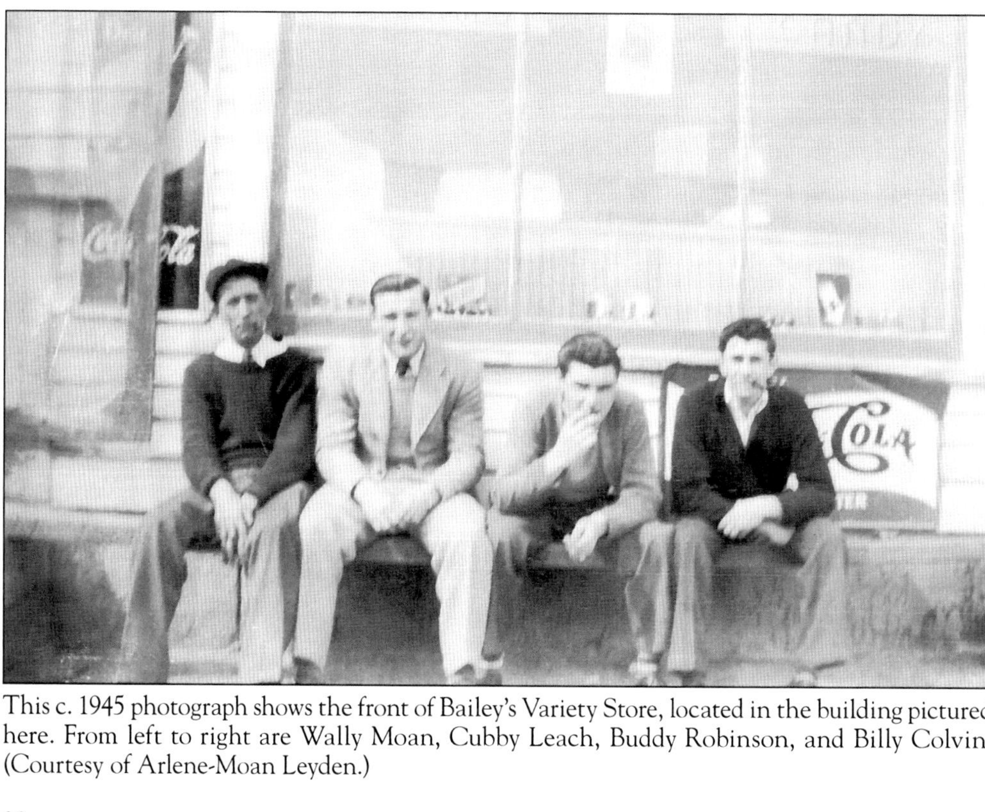

This c. 1945 photograph shows the front of Bailey's Variety Store, located in the building pictured here. From left to right are Wally Moan, Cubby Leach, Buddy Robinson, and Billy Colvin. (Courtesy of Arlene-Moan Leyden.)

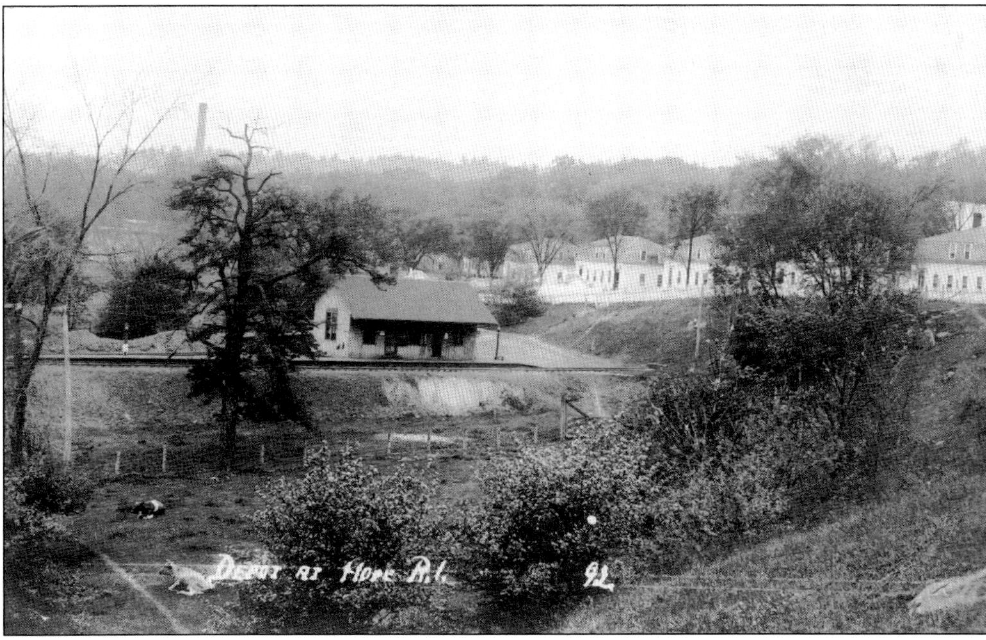

In 1874, the Pawtuxet Valley Railroad Company ran a three-mile spur off the main line in River Point. It ran parallel to Main Street and came to a dead end just short of Mill Street. The tracks curved to the left and continued only to service Hope Mill. In 1875, the line was leased to the trustees of the Hartford, Providence & Fishkill Railroad. The depot on the postcard above was built by Nathan Bennett in 1874. Below is a ticket to attend the Acc't Preparedness Parade in Providence. It was only good for the special train leaving Hope on June 3, 1916 at 1:00 p.m. and returning at 6:45 p.m. (Both, courtesy of Donald Carpenter.)

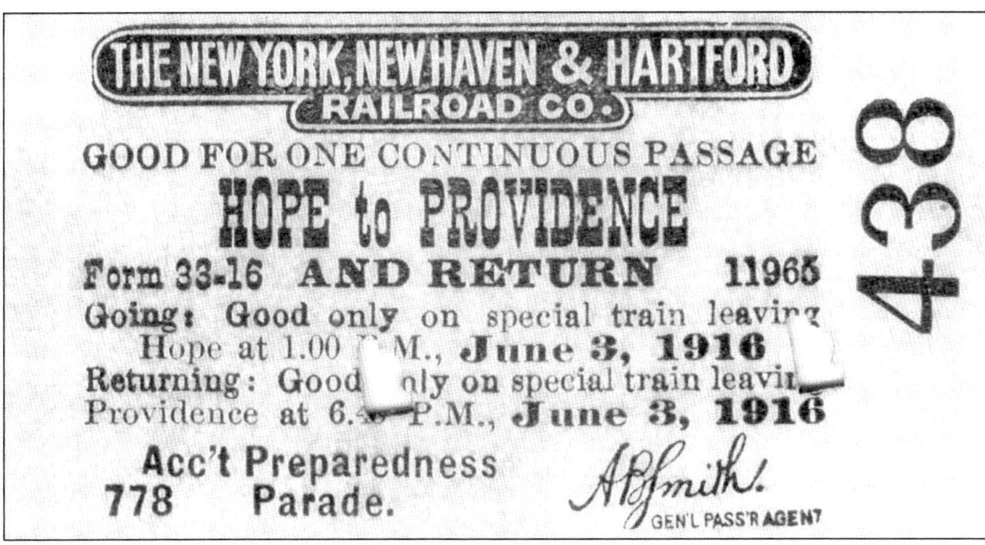
THE NEW YORK, NEW HAVEN & HARTFORD
RAILROAD CO.
GOOD FOR ONE CONTINUOUS PASSAGE
HOPE to PROVIDENCE
Form 33-16 AND RETURN 11965
Going: Good only on special train leaving
Hope at 1.00 P.M., June 3, 1916
Returning: Good only on special train leaving
Providence at 6.45 P.M., June 3, 1916
Acc't Preparedness
778 Parade.
A.B. Smith
GEN'L PASS'R AGENT
438

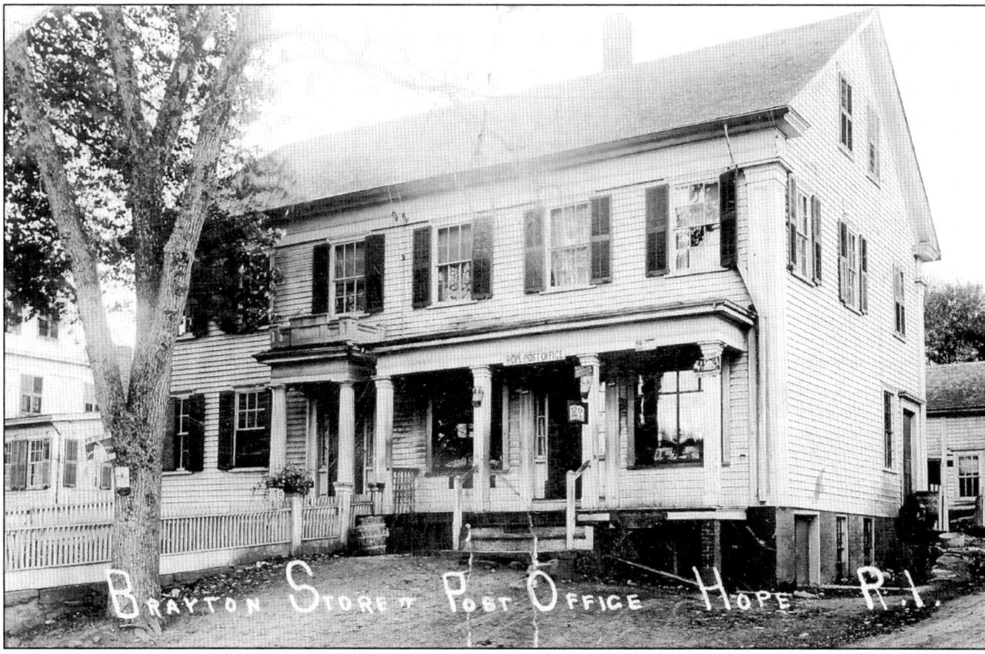

This 1919 postcard shows the Brayton Store and post office on the corner of Main and Hill Streets. Bertha Brayton ran the store and was postmistress for over 30 years. It would later become Bob's Variety Store, operated by Robert Abramson. Today, it has been remodeled and converted to apartments. The little building to the right was a barbershop. (Courtesy of Patsy Frost.)

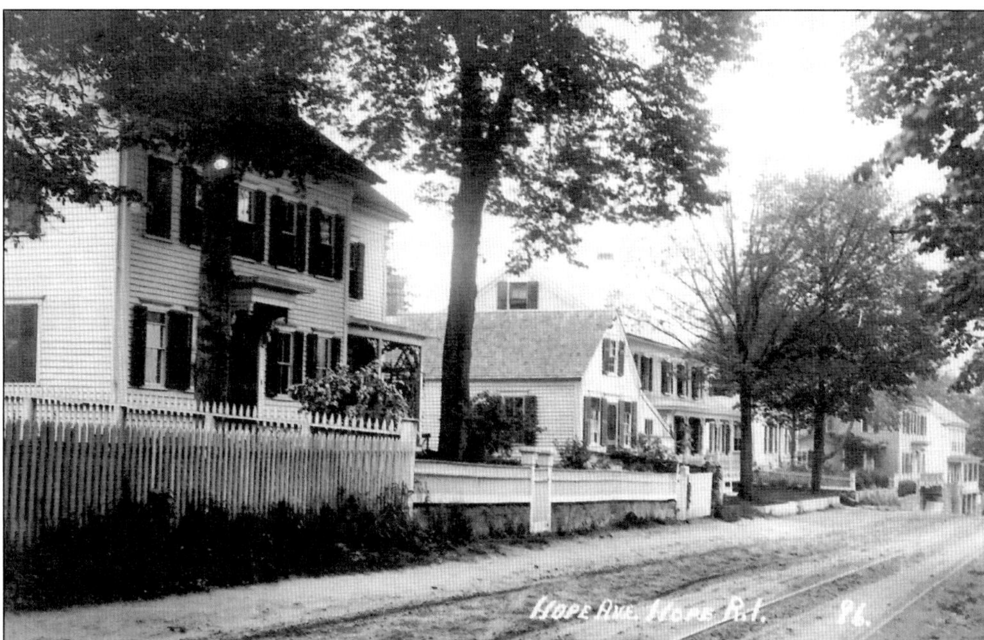

The trolley tracks are pictured here, facing east on Arthur Lowell Johnson owned the first house on the left. It was built in the 1860s and remained in the Johnson family for over 80 years. (Courtesy of Foster Historical Society.)

Hope residents used to bring their film to Lemoi's Market to have it developed. Here, the author wanted two jumbo prints of 12 negatives at a cost of $1.08. Lemoi's would send them out to the Bell & Wood Photograph Service, and in about a week, the prints would be delivered. (Author's collection.)

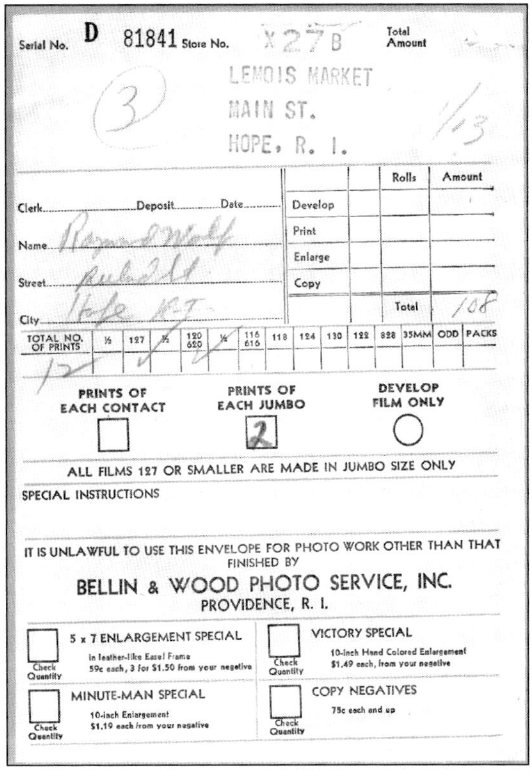

Serial No. D 81841 Store No. X 27 B Total Amount

LEMOIS MARKET
MAIN ST.
HOPE, R. I.

Clerk...... Deposit...... Date......

Name......

Street......

City......

	Rolls	Amount
Develop		
Print		
Enlarge		
Copy		
Total		108

TOTAL NO. OF PRINTS	½	127	½	120 620	¼	116 616	118	124	130	122	828	35MM	ODD	PACKS
12														

PRINTS OF EACH CONTACT — PRINTS OF EACH JUMBO 2 — DEVELOP FILM ONLY

ALL FILMS 127 OR SMALLER ARE MADE IN JUMBO SIZE ONLY

SPECIAL INSTRUCTIONS

IT IS UNLAWFUL TO USE THIS ENVELOPE FOR PHOTO WORK OTHER THAN THAT FINISHED BY

BELLIN & WOOD PHOTO SERVICE, INC.
PROVIDENCE, R. I.

5 x 7 ENLARGEMENT SPECIAL
in leather-like Easel Frame
59c each, 3 for $1.50 from your negative
Check Quantity

VICTORY SPECIAL
10-inch Hand Colored Enlargement
$1.49 each, from your negative
Check Quantity

MINUTE-MAN SPECIAL
10-inch Enlargement
$1.19 each from your negative
Check Quantity

COPY NEGATIVES
75c each and up
Check Quantity

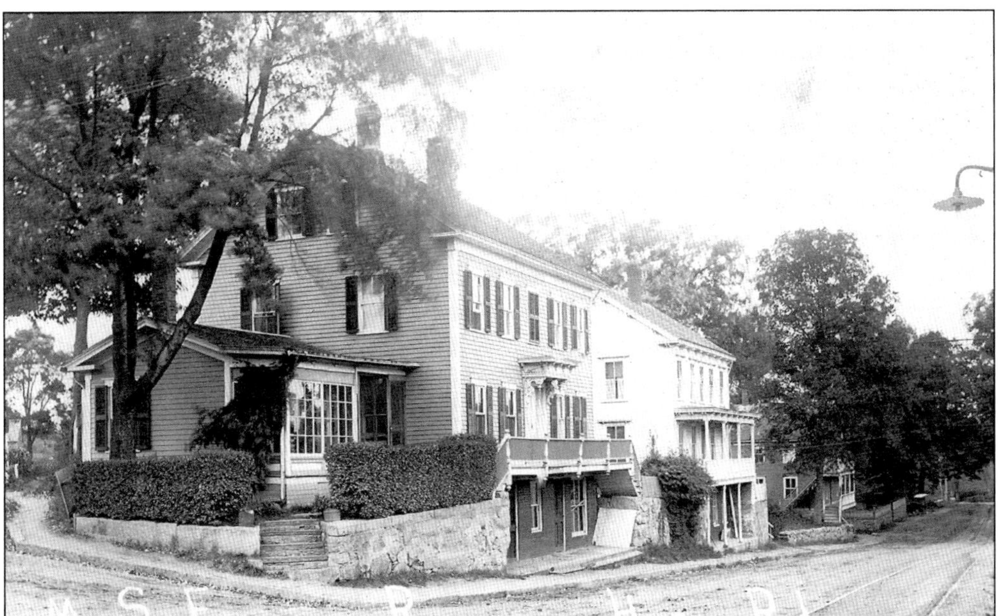

M.S. Francis lived in this house on the corner of Harrington Avenue when this photograph was taken. The building was constructed in 1885 and would later be bought by Arthur Lemoi Sr. and his wife, Laura. They raised three children here: Arthur Jr., Norman, and Loretta. (Courtesy of Lawrence G. Soucy.)

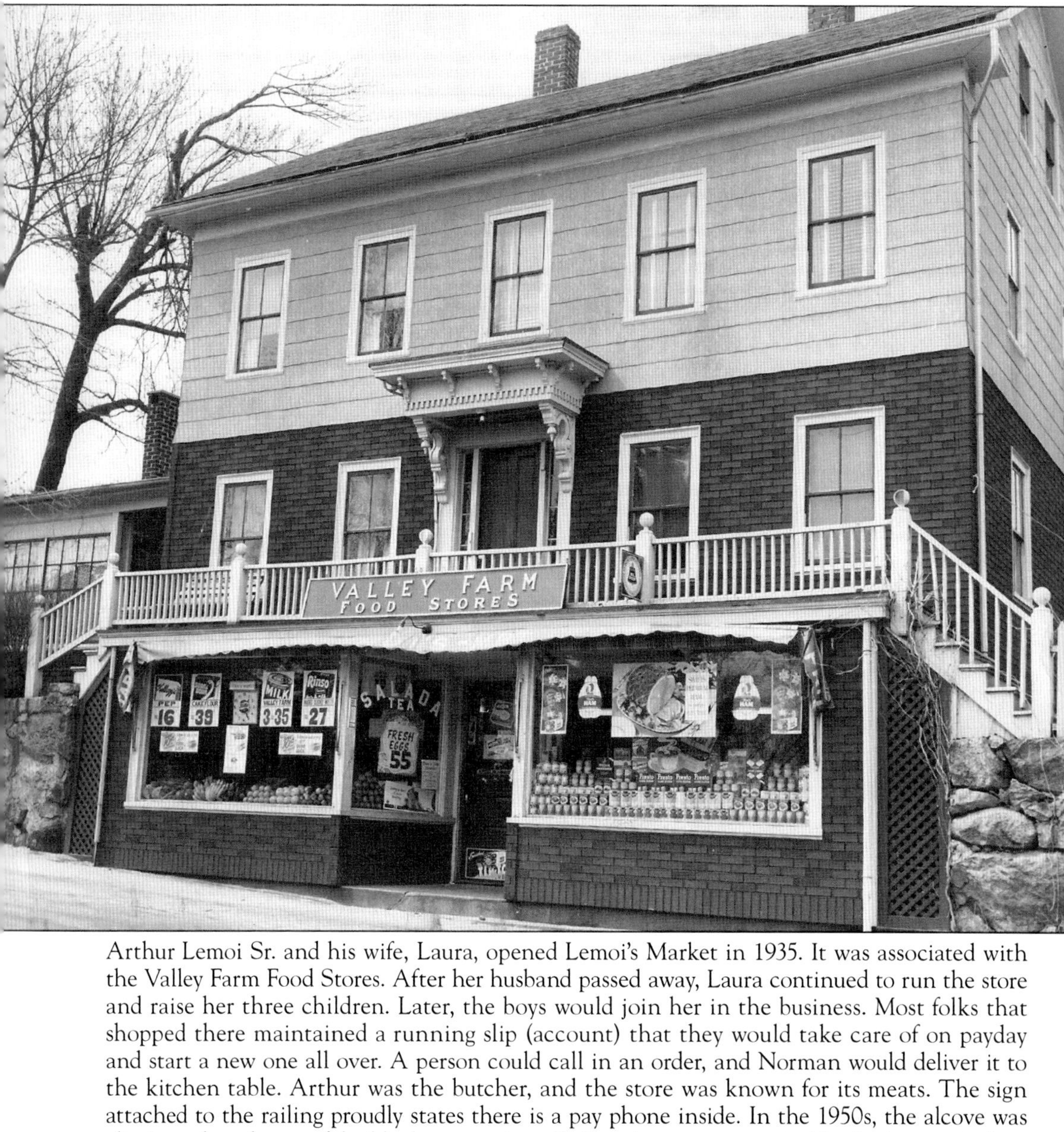

Arthur Lemoi Sr. and his wife, Laura, opened Lemoi's Market in 1935. It was associated with the Valley Farm Food Stores. After her husband passed away, Laura continued to run the store and raise her three children. Later, the boys would join her in the business. Most folks that shopped there maintained a running slip (account) that they would take care of on payday and start a new one all over. A person could call in an order, and Norman would deliver it to the kitchen table. Arthur was the butcher, and the store was known for its meats. The sign attached to the railing proudly states there is a pay phone inside. In the 1950s, the alcove was eliminated, and a set of double doors was installed to give more room inside. A picture window, or a large plate-glass window, also replaced the two windows on the second floor left of the door. The bread man and milkman delivered before the store opened and left their goods on the curb. If a person needed break or milk, they just took it and called the store later to have it added to their slip. The store closed in 1985.

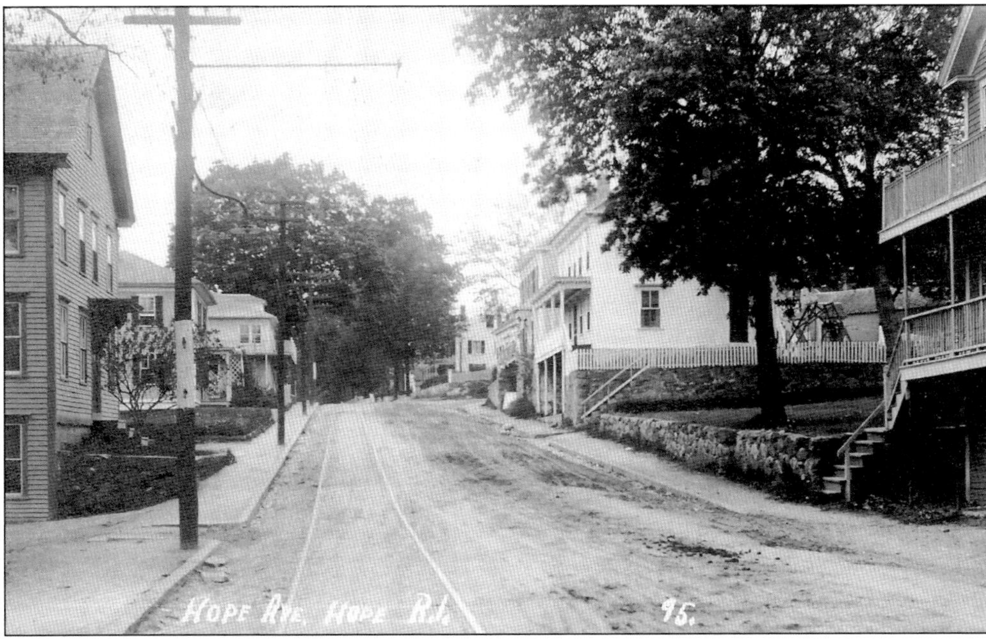

Mildred Colvin of Coventry sent this postcard to Flora Harris in Providence on September 26, 1913. Laura's Lunch was located in the basement of the building seen here on the right (as well as below on the left and on page 28) in the 1940s. Joseph D. Noel lived in the tenement above the restaurant. He was killed while serving his country in Vietnam in January 1967. (Courtesy of Foster Historical Society.)

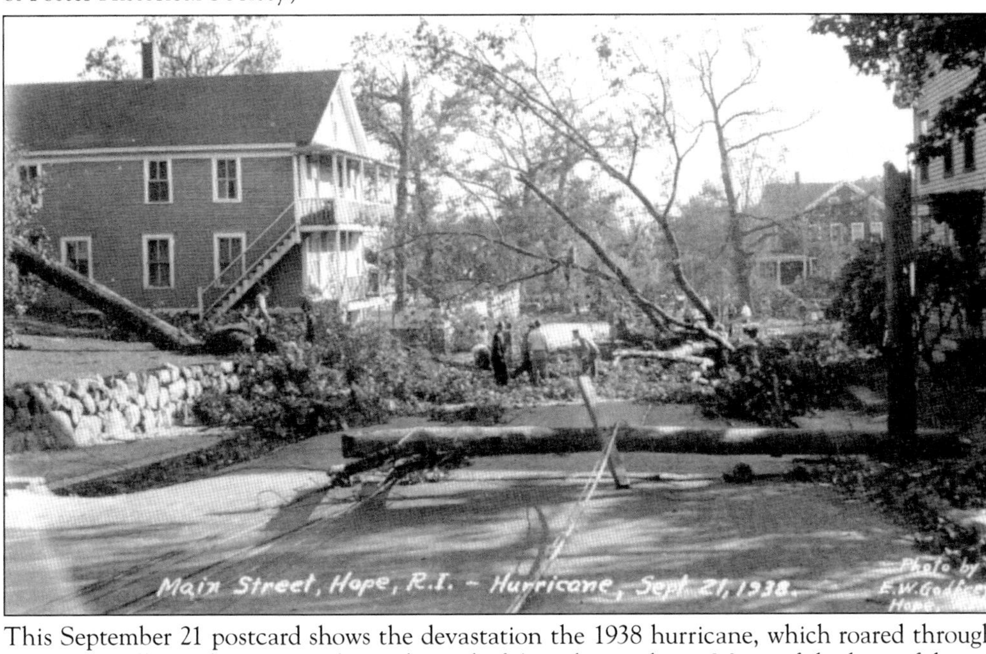

This September 21 postcard shows the devastation the 1938 hurricane, which roared through did to the village of Hope at a forward speed of 50 miles per hour. Many of the beautiful trees that lined the quiet streets in the village were uprooted and destroyed forever by the maximum sustaining winds of 120–125 miles-per-hour range. Originally, the forecast had predicted that the storm would turn out to sea.

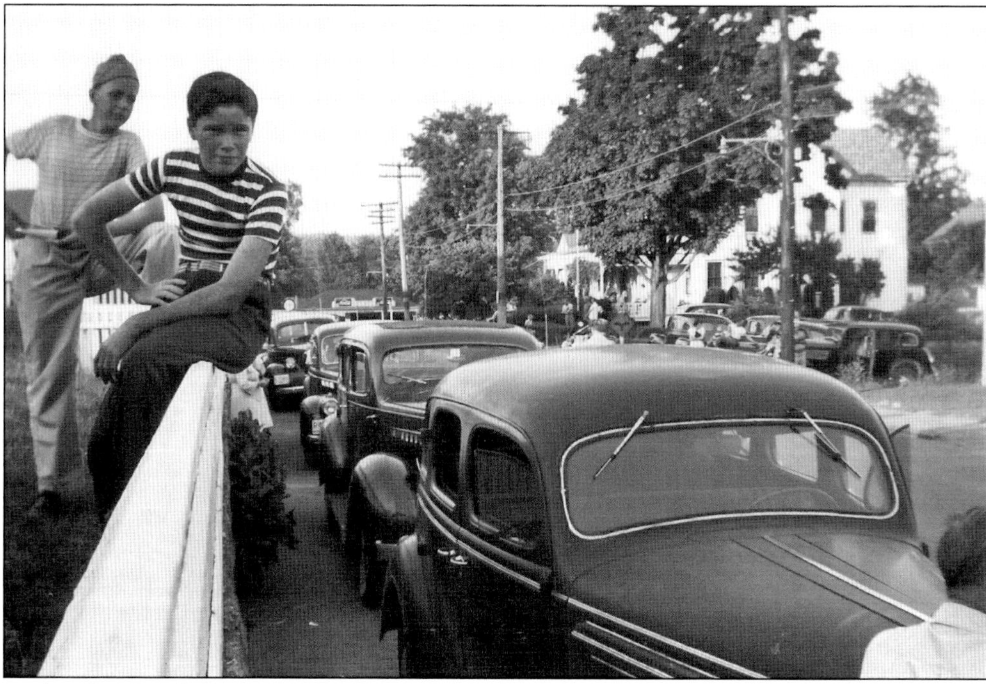

In the photograph above, the author's uncle Harry Groves, left, and Donald Leach relax on the community house fence. They are watching a parade pass on Main Street in 1948. D. Noel's Service Station can be seen in the distance, as well as on page 32. Below, the American Legion post in West Warwick used to send their train to participate in the Hope parades. This one is pictured in the 1950s. The local blacksmith shop was established in the 1800s and located in the ground floor basement of the house pictured on the left, also seen on page 29. The next house was built in the mid-1880s for the Gardiner family. (Both, author's collection.)

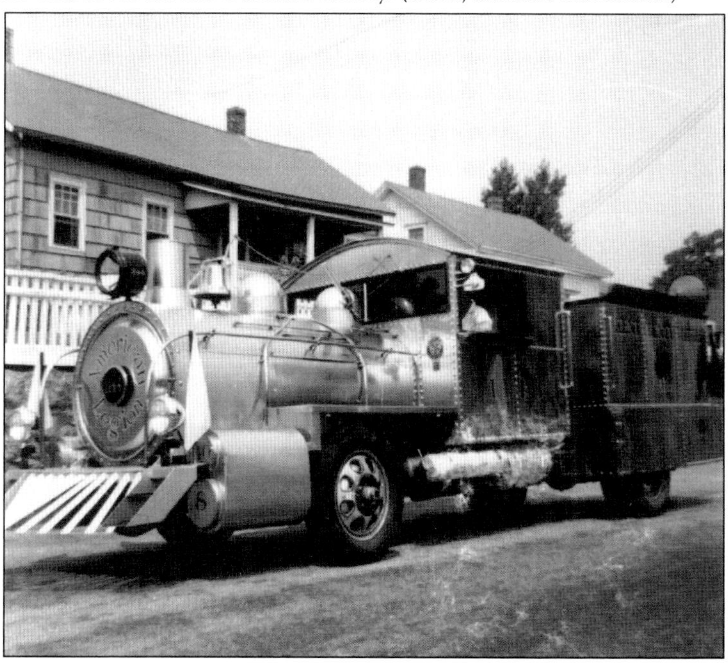

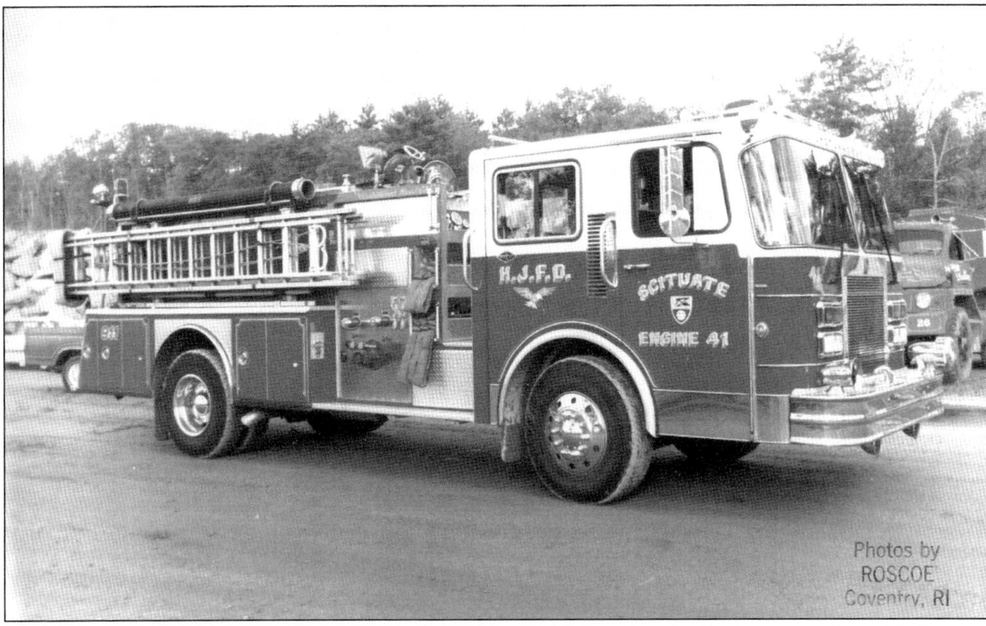

This 1986 American Eagle Pumper truck took over lead position when it joined a 1954 Maxim and the 1931 Maxim pictured below. The new truck cost over $100,000 and holds 1,000 gallons of water. It is still in service today. (Courtesy of Hope and Jackson Fire Company.)

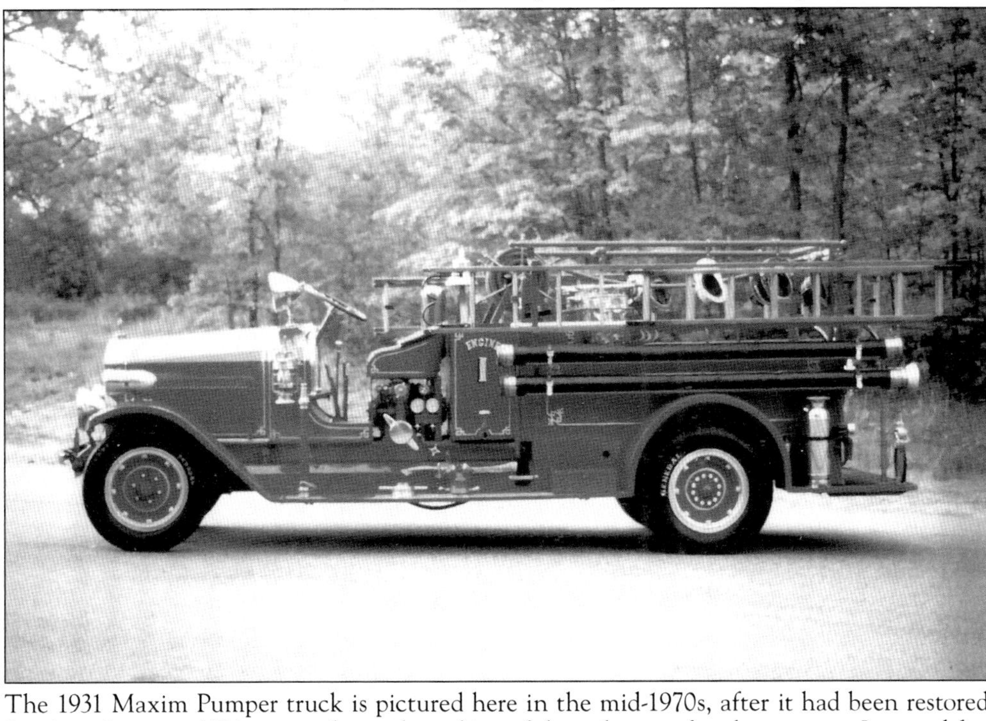

The 1931 Maxim Pumper truck is pictured here in the mid-1970s, after it had been restored. Purchased new in 1931, it was the pride and joy of the volunteer fire department. It served fine until it was retired in 1971. The cost new was $7,500 and held a whopping 50 gallons of water. It was later changed to a 100-gallon tank. It still is grand to see when it cruises in parades. (Courtesy of Hope and Jackson Fire Company.)

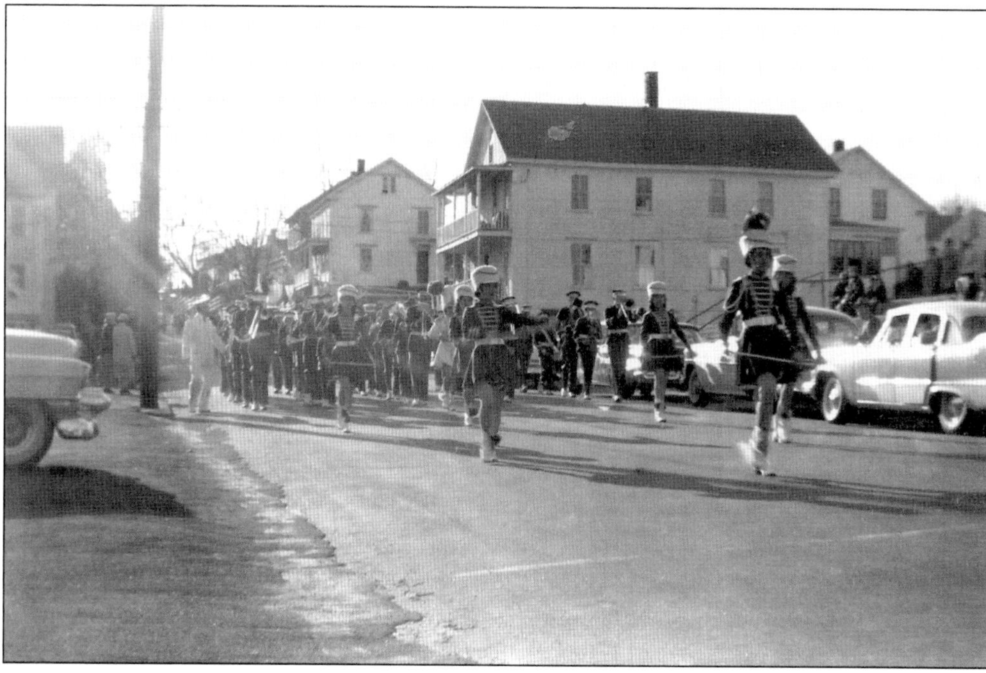

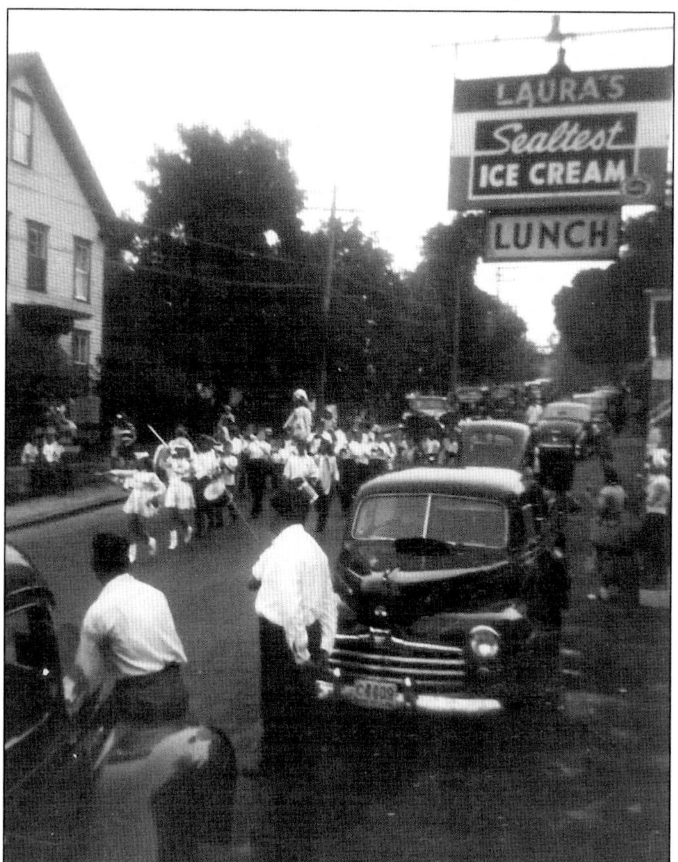

The photograph above shows the Coventry majorettes leading their high school band. Coventry was participating with Scituate in this 1959 Memorial Day Celebration. Laura's Lunch, pictured left, was located in the first floor of the three-story building in the foreground. The following verses are from "The Unknown Soldier" by Helen O. Larson: "There's a grave in Arlington, where an unknown soldier lies / His name is known only to God, as he sleeps beneath the skies. He went off to war so proudly, for his country he did fight / Amid the shooting and the bombing, he laid down his life one night. He was some mother's son, who shed tears when he went / He left his comfortable home, he spent his nights in a tent." (Both, author's collection.)

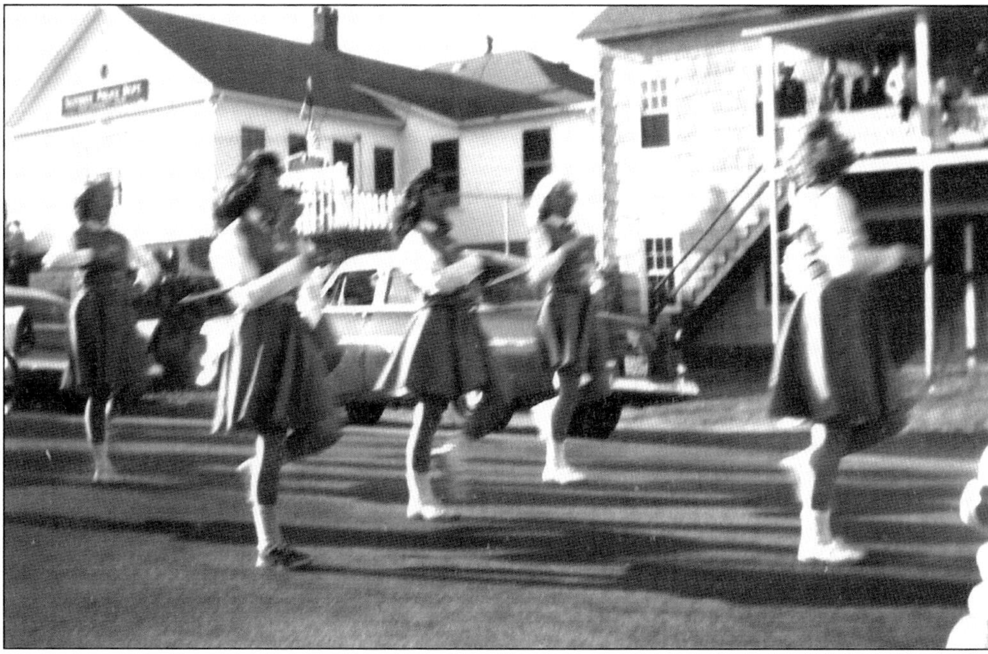

The Scituate Spartans majorettes lead this holiday parade in 1959. They are, from left to right, Carole Kettelle, Patricia Finnegan, Elayne Francisco, Bonnie Lee Baker, and head majorette Sharon Latschar. They are marching past a 1954 Ford Customline parked in front of the building that housed the blacksmith shop in the basement during the 1800s. Below is a photograph of the community house in 1948. It was taken after it was the Hope Grammar School and before the Scituate Police Department consumed the entire building, as seen above. To the right and in the rear is the home the author grew up in. To the left is Chris Noel's barn, and behind it is Steven Walker's house. (Both, author's collection.)

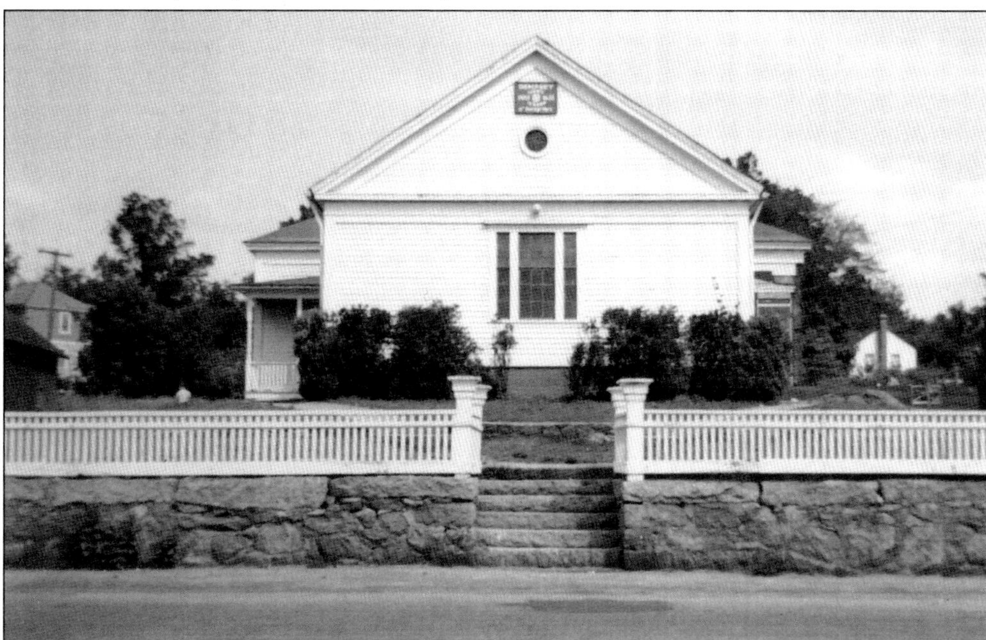

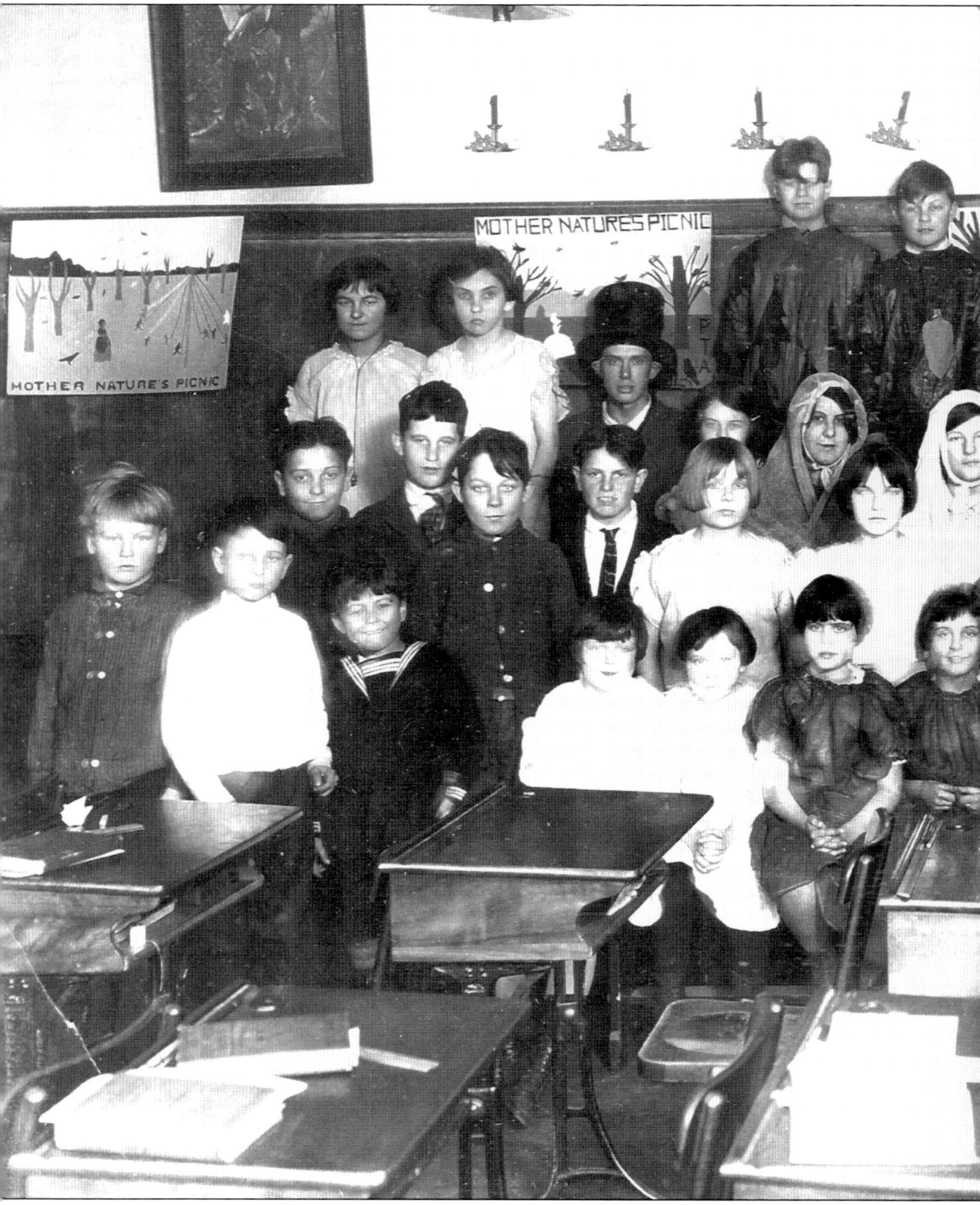

This c. 1925 photograph shows students at Hope Grammar School. The building is now occupied by the Scituate Police Department. The students had just completed a Christmas play and are taking a moment to pose for the camera. They are, from left to right, (first row) Axel Johnson, Harry Simmons, unidentified, Lucy Gifford, Hazel Brayton, three unidentified, Mildred Bowlin, unidentified, Virginia Cassidy, Ellen Dempsy, Mary Whitford, and unidentified; (second row)

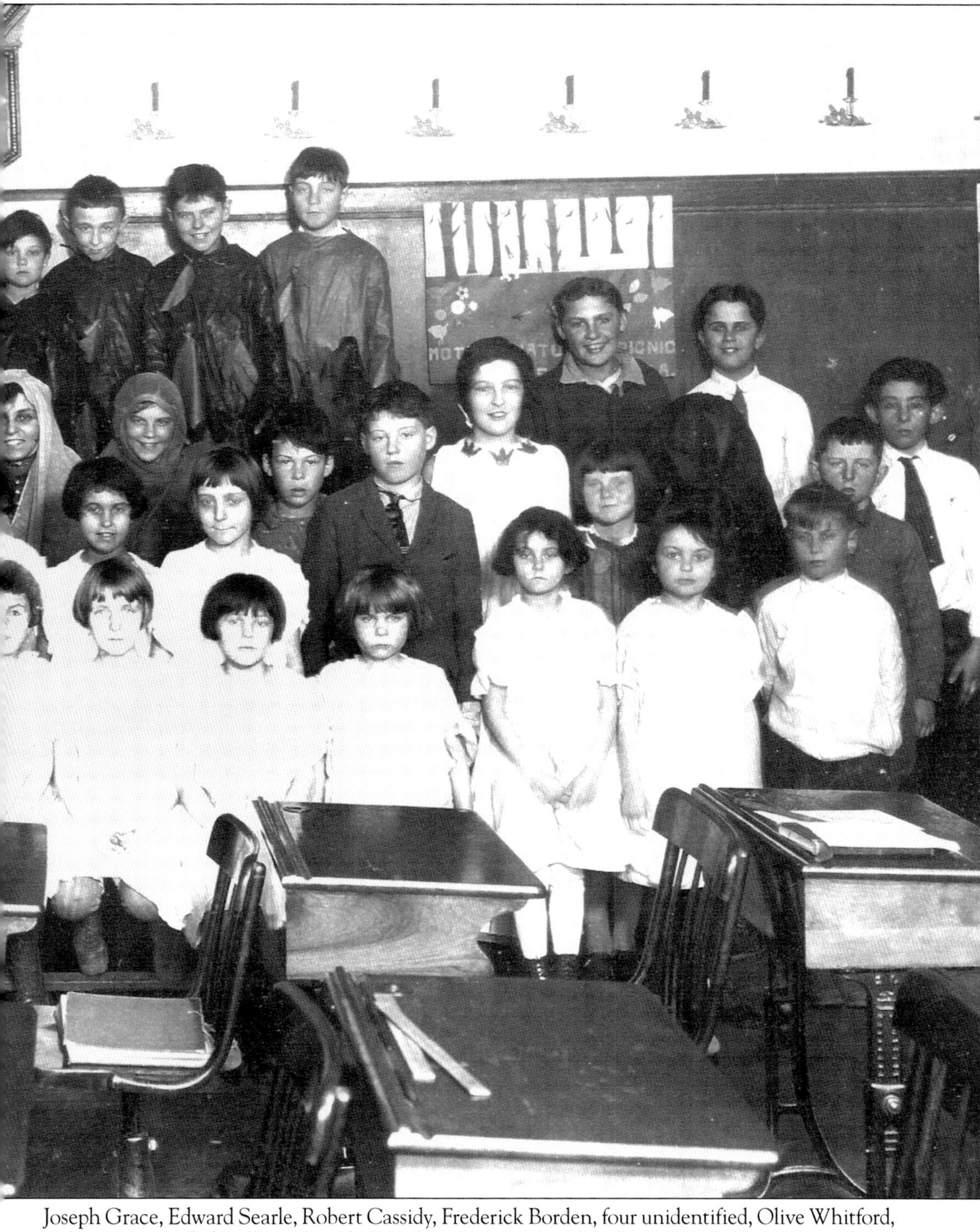

Joseph Grace, Edward Searle, Robert Cassidy, Frederick Borden, four unidentified, Olive Whitford, Robert Brayton (behind), unidentified, Barbara Brayton (small girl), and Thomas McShane; (third row) unidentified, Helen Colvin, two unidentified, Palma Cote, Ruth Henry, unidentified, Eva Brayton, Doris Clark (tall girl), and three unidentified; (fourth row) Otis Luther, Charles Henry, two unidentified, Nathan Colvin, unidentified, and Richard Colvin. (Courtesy of Betty Thurn.)

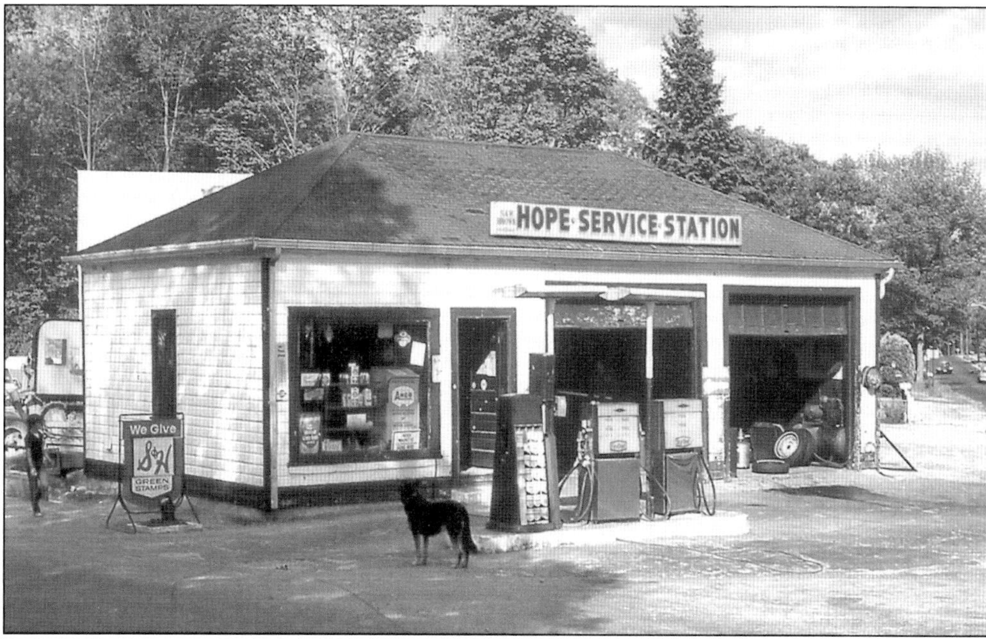

The service station, pictured above, was operated by Donat Noel as D. Noel Service through the 1940s and 1950s. His brother Chris was the mechanic. Sam Brown and Jess Miller bought the station in 1965 and renamed it Hope Service Station. Later, Brown would obtain sole ownership. A wall for the replacement of this station can be seen above the roof at the rear of the building in the photograph above. The new station, built in 1973, can be seen below. The small station was later demolished. (Both, courtesy of Samuel Brown.)

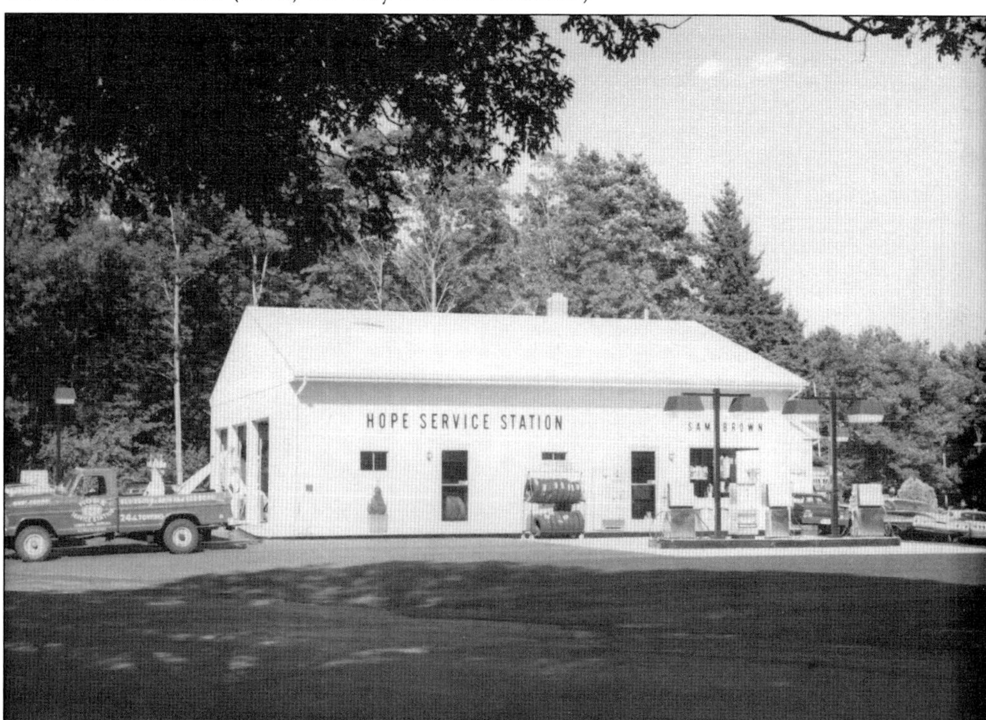

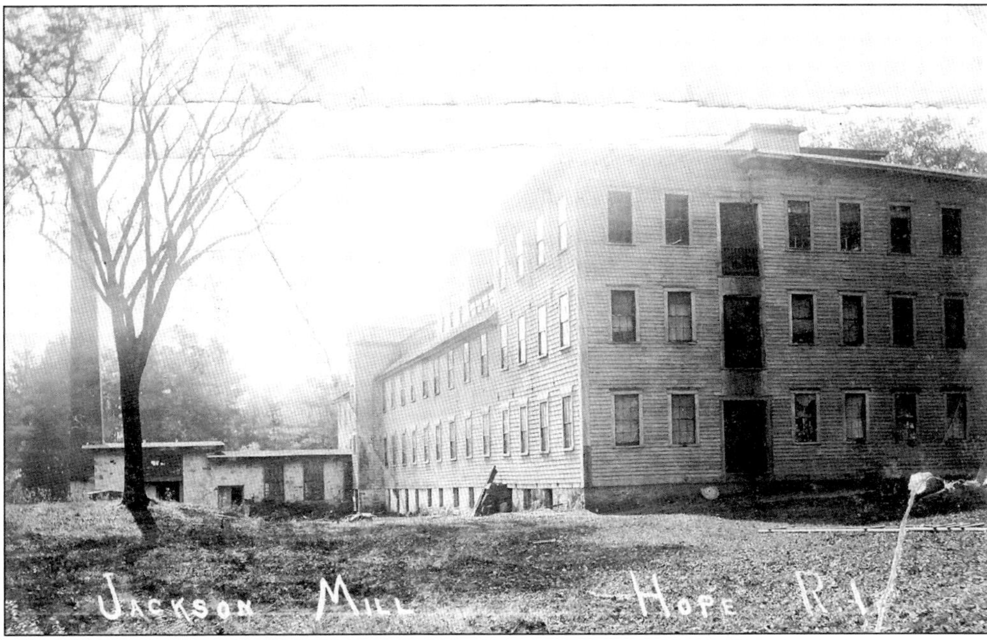

Caleb Fiske built this mill on the Pawtuxet in 1828. He later sold it to Charles Jackson, governor of Rhode Island. Jackson named his mill the Jackson Mill, and the area became the village of Jackson. In later years, it was one of B.B. and R. Knight's holdings. The mill was destroyed by a fire in 1938. (Courtesy of Lawrence G. Soucy.)

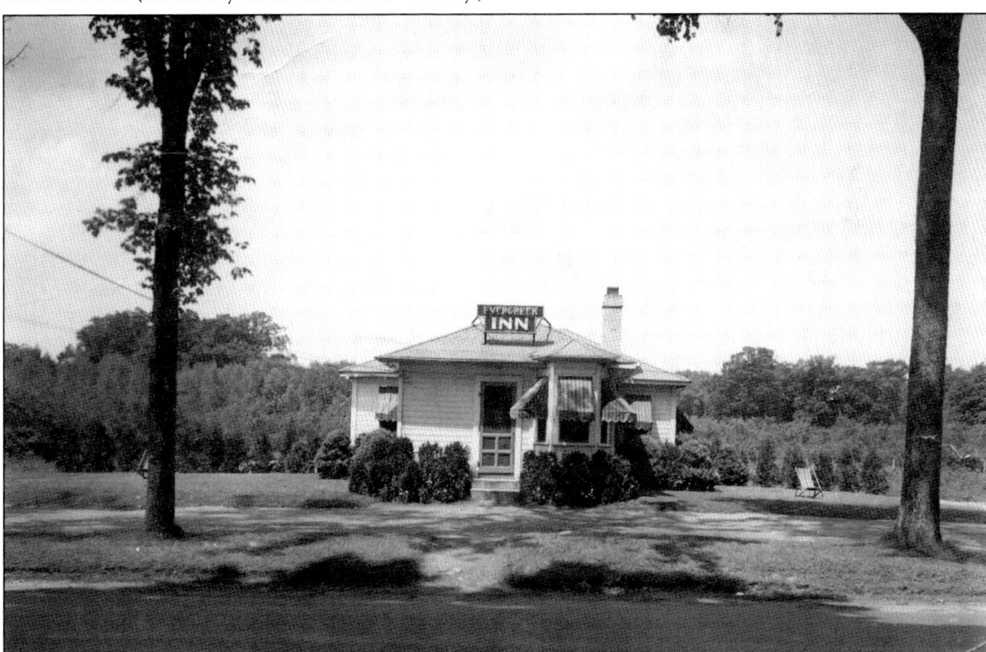

Charles Campbell owned and operated the Evergreen Inn on Jackson Flat Road through the 1920s and 1930s. In the 1940s, he leased it to the Caniglia family. Every Fourth of July, it was tradition to have a huge bonfire in the area left of the building. The only other tavern in town was the Jackson Tavern, located across the bridge on Colvin Street. (Courtesy of Barbara Auger.)

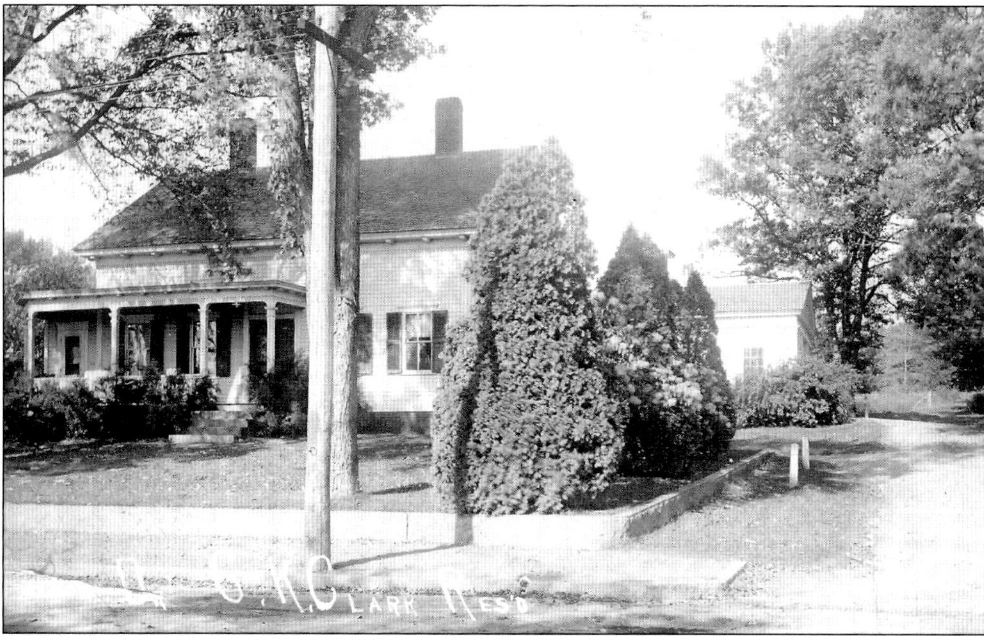

Dr. Charles K. Clarke was born in Fiskeville in 1851. He later resided here on Jackson Flat Road with his wife, Mary . Their son Daniel A. and his wife, Mary Craig Clarke, would later reside in the family homestead. Daniel would run his business, Red Oak Nursery, while Mary would teach in the Scituate school system. (Courtesy of Lawrence G. Soucy.)

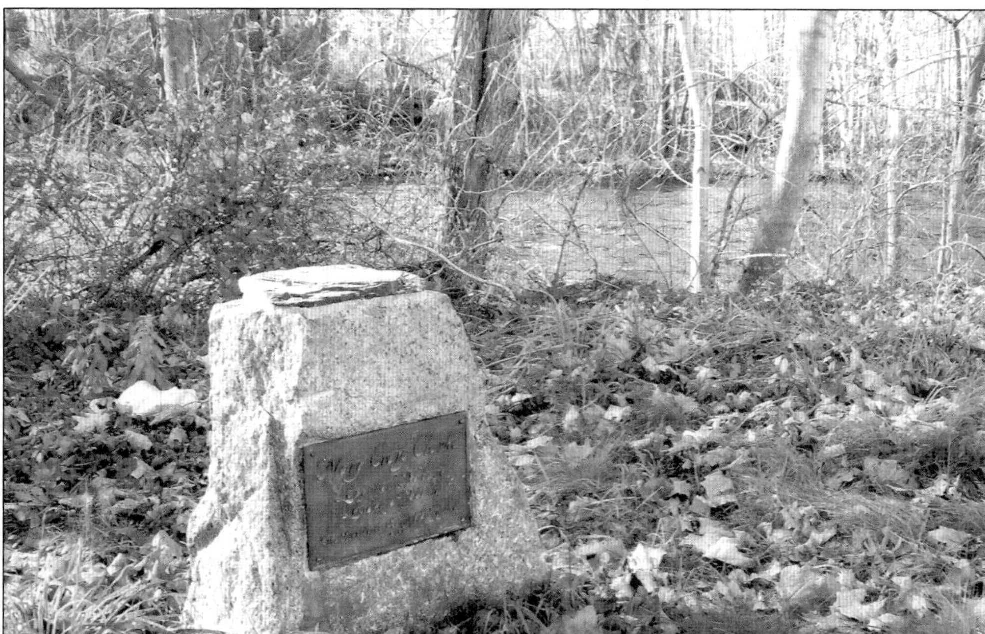

This small monument is located in a peaceful grassy area beside the Harris Fire Station as the Pawtuxet River quietly flows by behind it. It was placed there by the Providence County Garden Club in 1939 in honor of member Mary Craig Clarke. It is inscribed: "Lover of Nature, Leader of Youth." (Author's collection.)

Two

Fiskeville and Arkwright

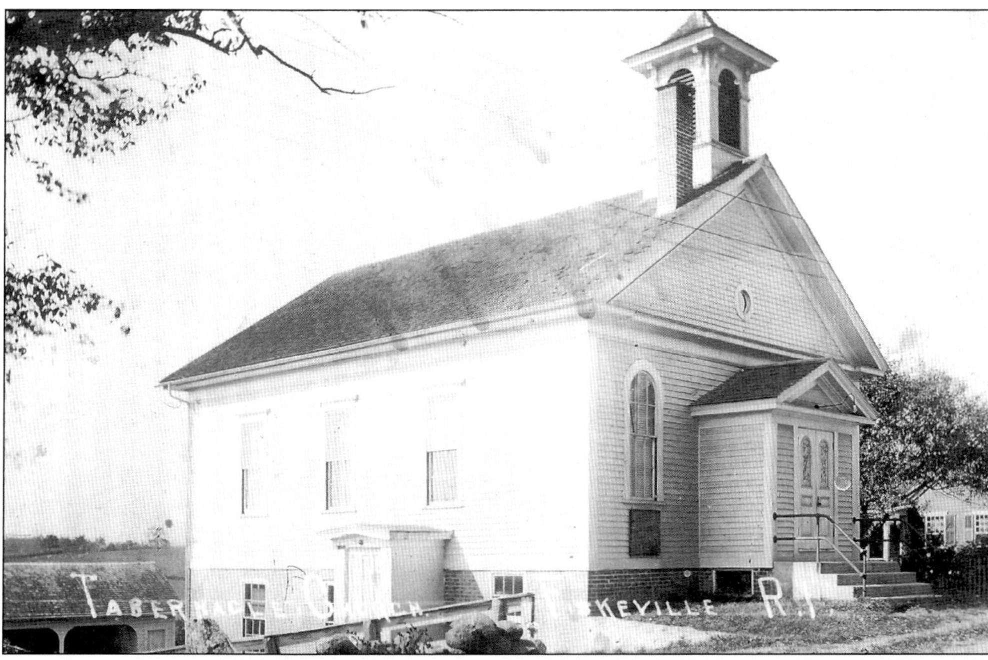

Albert Hill built the Fiskeville Tabernacle Baptist Church in 1873 on a lot on Seven Mile Road, donated by Peleg A. Walton. Rev. Benjamin B. Cottrell served as pastor for 23 years. The wagon shed in the rear burned down in 1924. The congregation still maintains services after 140 years. (Courtesy of Lawrence G. Soucy.)

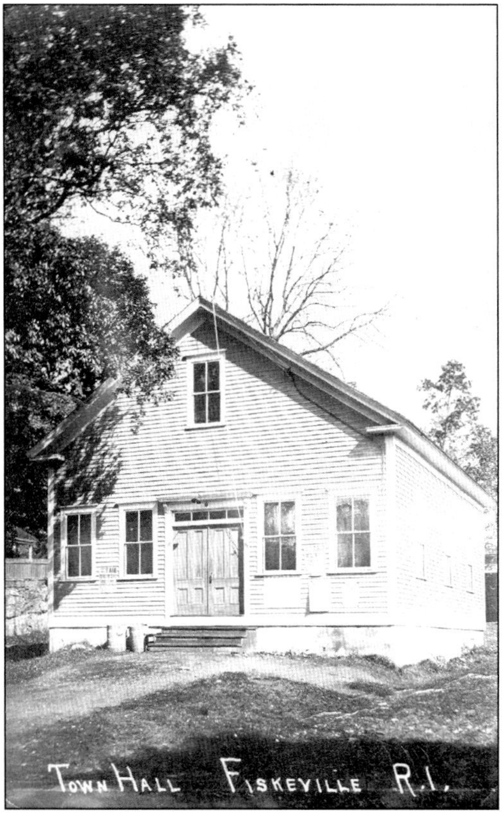

This postcard shows the Fiskeville Town Hall, even though Fiskeville was only a village. At this time, Fiskeville wanted to break away from Cranston to be its own town, but history records indicate that it never happened. To the left of the entrance, between the windows, is a sign the Fiskeville Fire Co. No. 1 will be at the fair. The first Fiskeville Fair was held in the lot to the right of the town hall building. (Courtesy of Lawrence G. Soucy.)

Wilfred Provosts' Variety Store is behind the automobile in this photograph. The store also maintained gas pumps for the convenience of his customers. The Provost family lived in the house to the far right. It later was converted to tenements. In the 1940s, Louis Magiera took over the store and named it Everybody's Market. In 1948, he moved the store down the street near where the post office is currently located. (Courtesy of Donald Carpenter.)

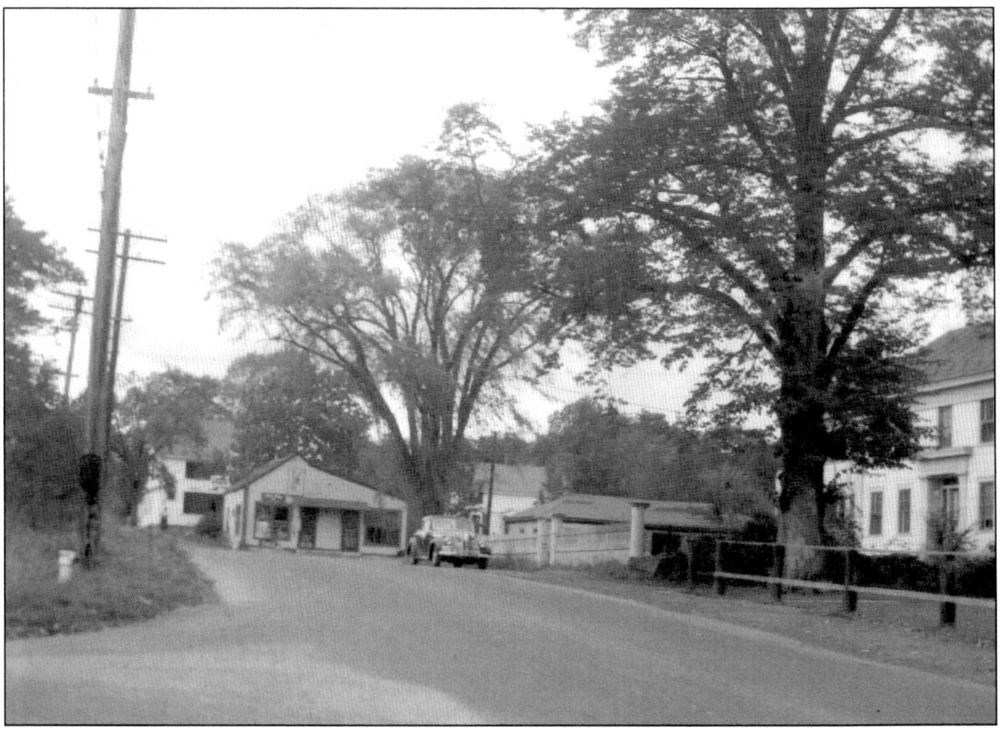

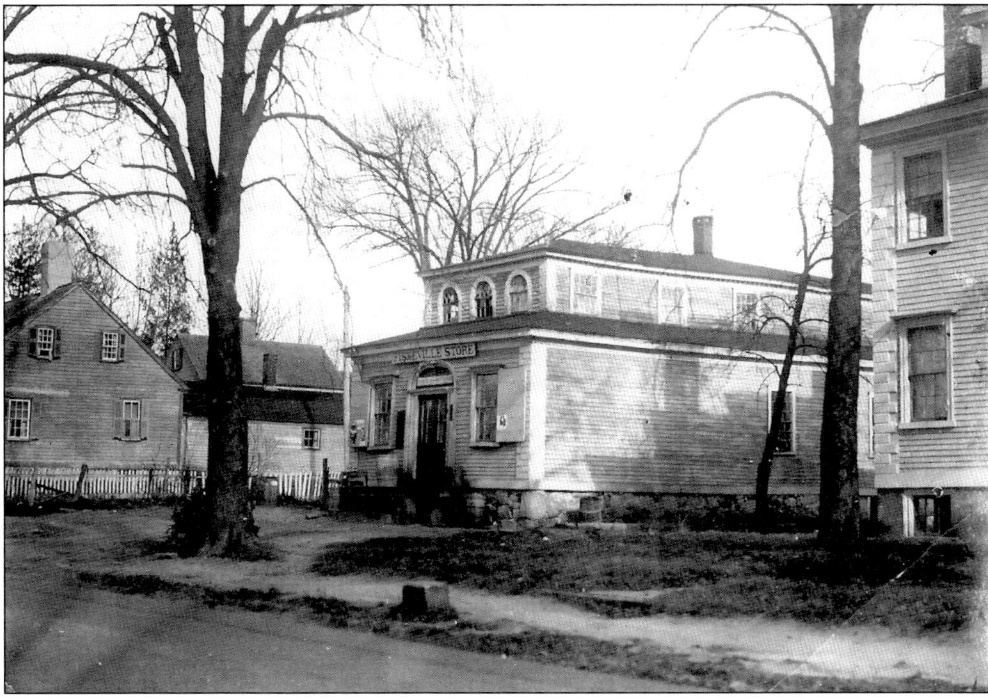

The Fiskeville branch of the US post office was originally located at the corner of Hope Road and Main Street. It then moved down Main Street to the Fiskeville Store, pictured above, operated by Westgarth Trayner. Later, it moved to a three-decker beside Dewey's Store and then to the Schofield family home. Lillian Schofield-Salisbury started helping her mom in 1944 and continued when they moved to the new post office, pictured below, on Labor Day weekend in 1954. From 1970 to 1984, she maintained the title of postmaster. (Above, courtesy of Donald Carpenter; below, author's collection.)

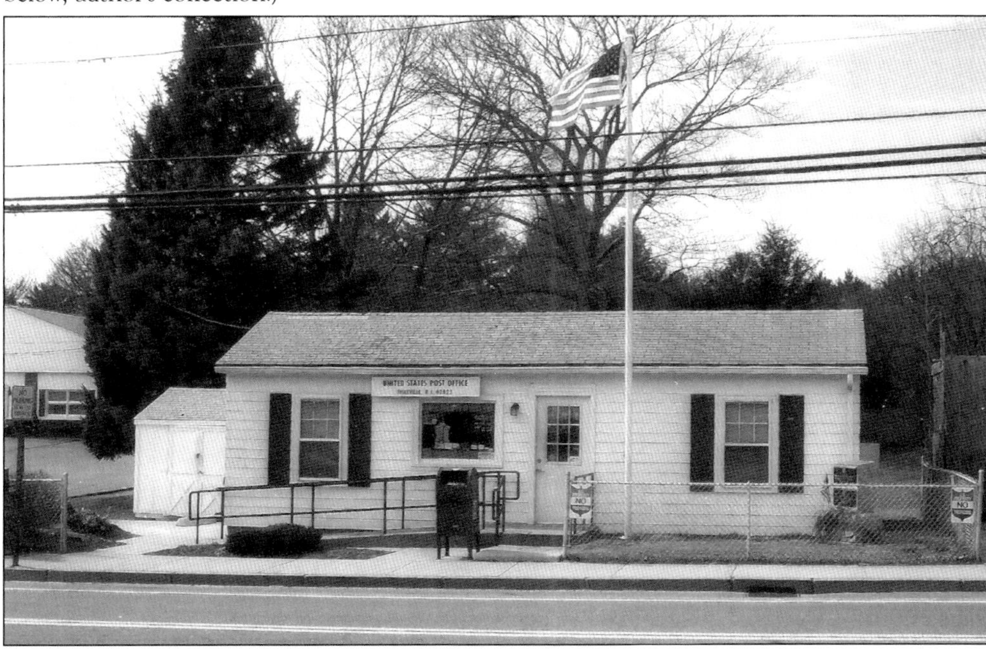

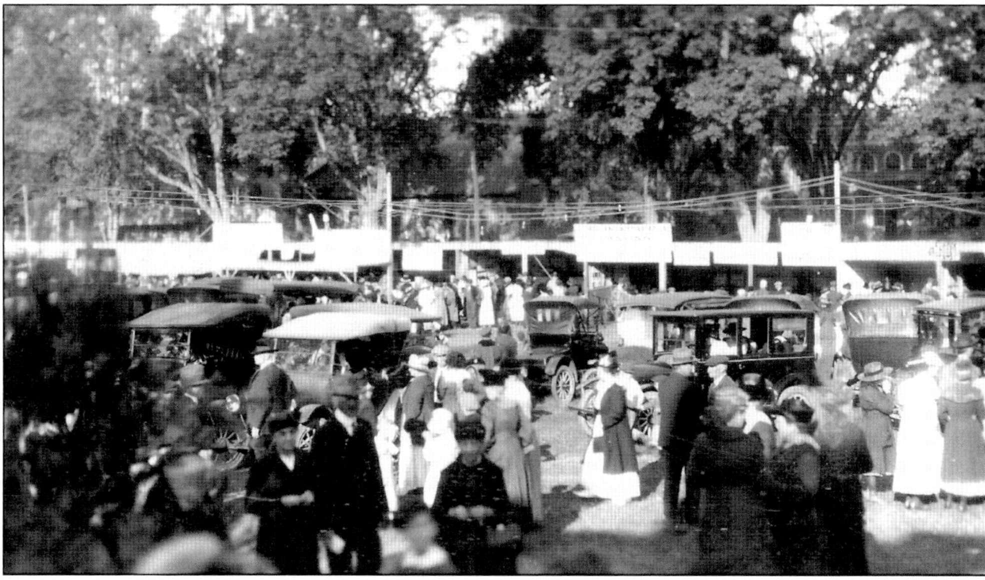

The Fiskeville Fairgrounds are pictured here in the early 1900s. The fair was organized by the local Grange and the Ladies Aid Society under the leadership of Minnie Shippee. Minnie is pictured below with Israel W. Brayton Sr. at a fair in 1920. This was a time when horse and carriage was still a means of transportation. In May 1927, the Pawtuxet Valley Agricultural Association purchased the land they had been leasing for the fairgrounds for the sum of $12,000. The Fiskeville Store can be seen through the trees in the upper right corner (also, see page 37). Note that Fiskeville became Hopeville on January 7, 1854; however, it was changed back to Fiskeville on November 5, 1858. (Both, courtesy of Donald Carpenter.)

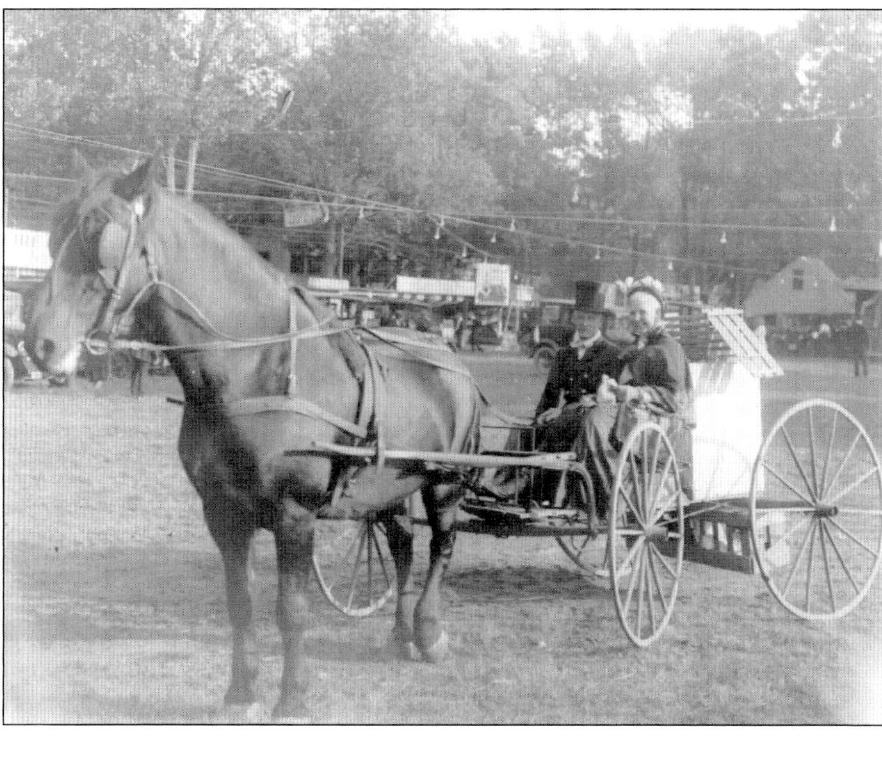

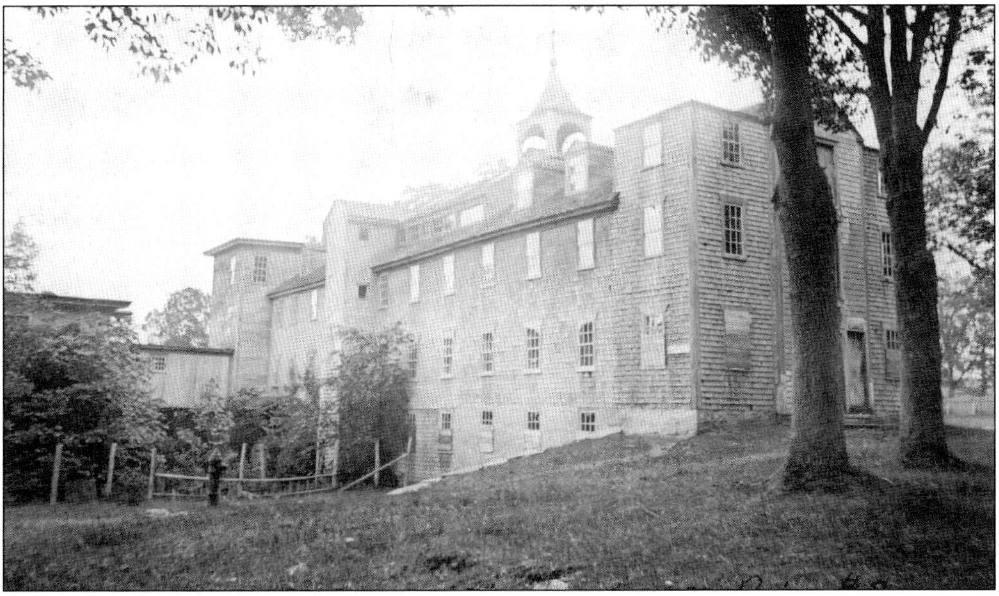

This c. 1910 photograph shows Fiskeville Cotton Mill, built in 1812 by Dr. Caleb Fiske. In the early 1900s, it was bought by the B.B. and R. Knight Company. The mill was destroyed by a fire on February 8, 1914. This site would become the Fiskeville Fairgrounds and home to the Pawtuxet Valley Fair, shown below and on the opposite page.

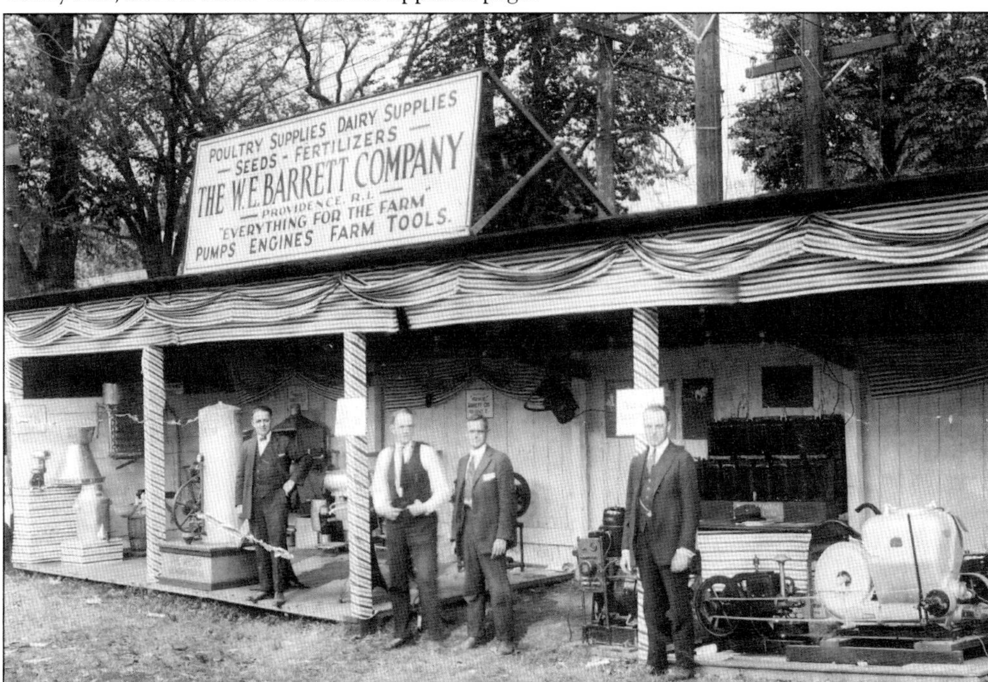

The fair was so popular at this time that people attended from all over the state. Pictured here is the booth of the W.E. Barrett Company of Providence, Rhode Island. They advertised they had "Everything for the Farm." On October 30, 1943, the Fiskeville Fairgrounds was sold at public auction by the Phenix Trust Company, ending the village fair. (Courtesy of Richard Siembab.)

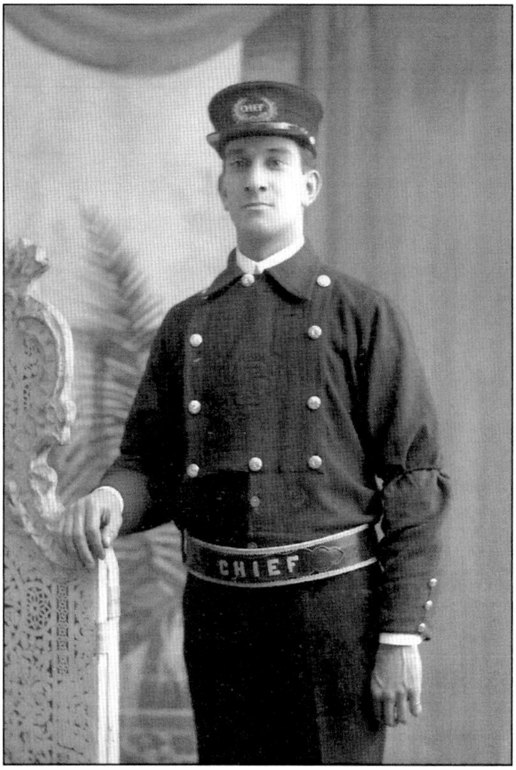

This is a portrait of Chief Everett Fiske of the Fiskeville Fire Company No. 1. The following verse is from "Dedicated to Firemen," written by Helen O. Larson in 1980 at the age of 70: "These men are right on the job, whenever there's a fire / Though it's icy cold, the firemen are right there."

Below, Chief Everett Fiske, seated fourth from left, is surrounded by his volunteers. The banner on the right reads, "One Hundred Fiftieth Anniversary of the Incorporation of the Town of Cranston June 14, 1904, Reel Contest won by Fiskeville Fire Co." The following verse is from "Dedicated to Firemen," by Helen O. Larson: "So when the weather is nice, let's honor all these men / Because all kinds of weather, so dedicated they've been."

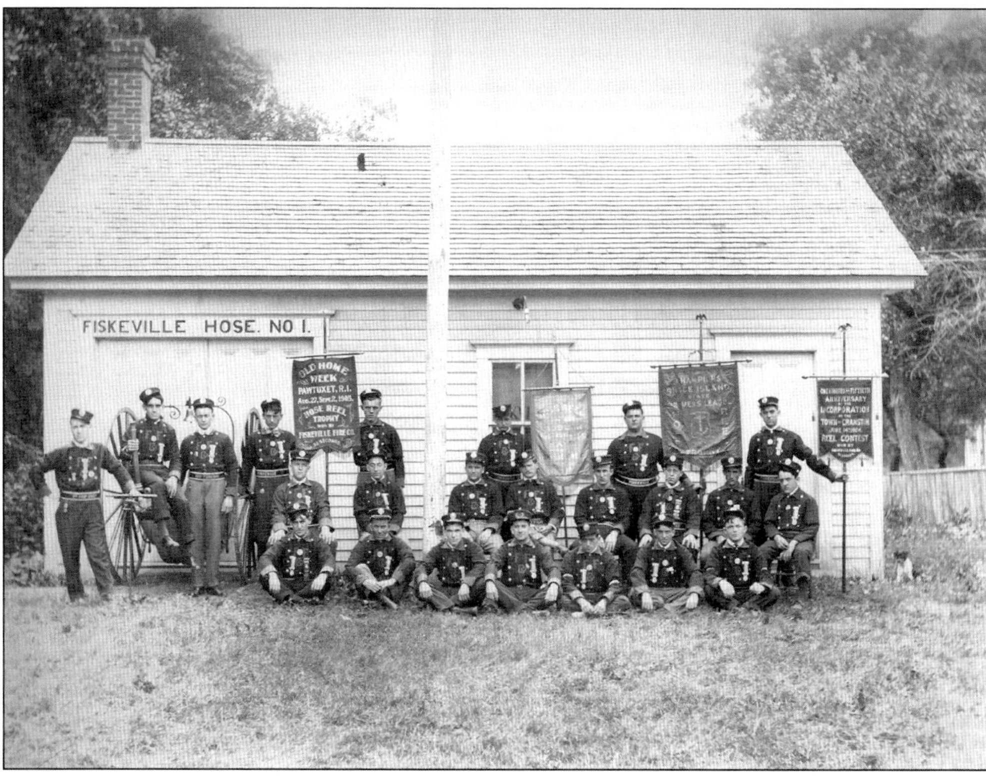

The Fiskeville Hose and Reel team is practicing for competition in 1900. The third banner from the left in the photograph at the bottom of the opposite page reads, "Champions, Rhode Island State, Firemen's League, Hose and Reel Trophy."

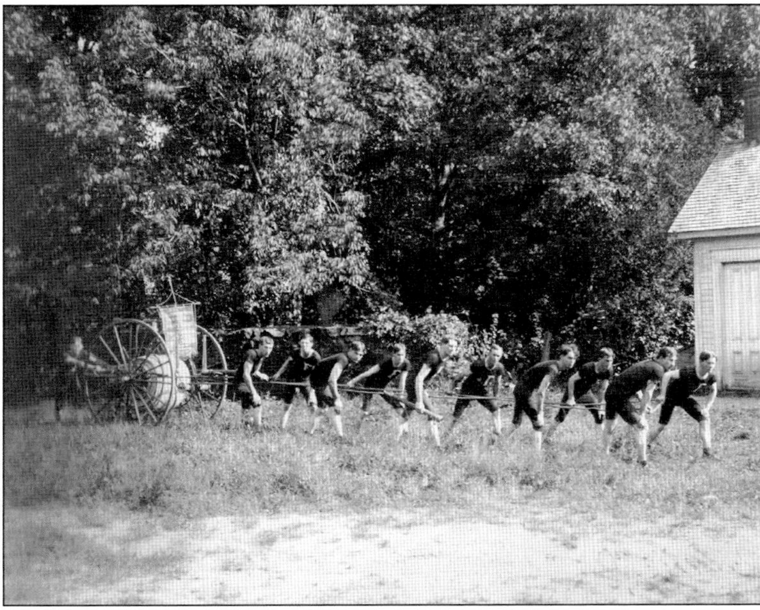

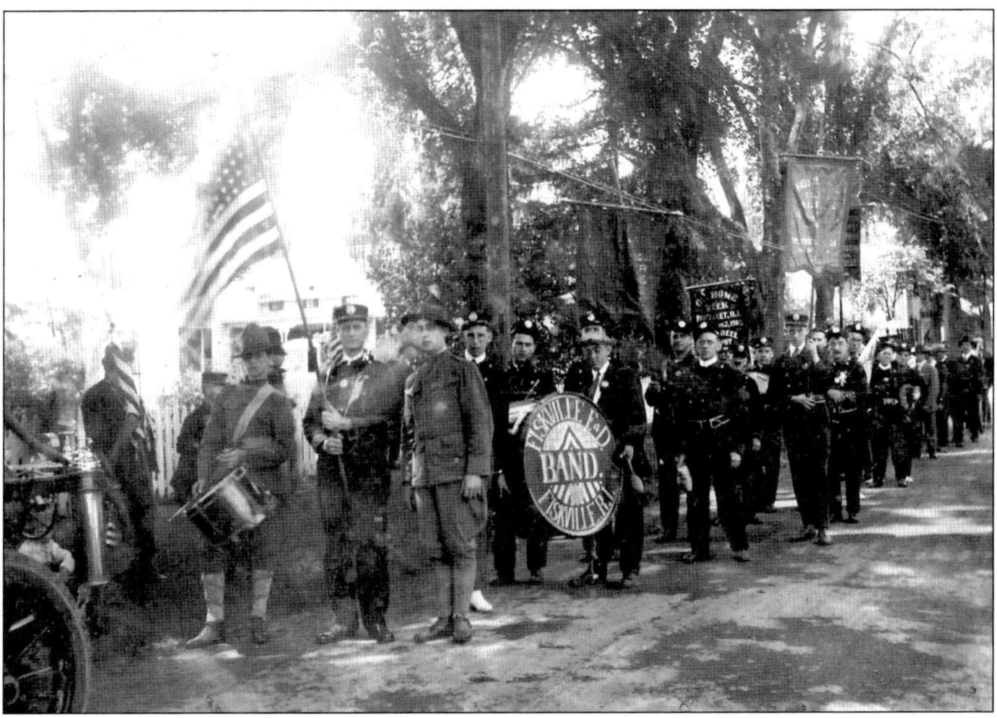

The Fiskeville Fife and Drum Band are pictured here in 1905. It could be a celebration parade. The small banner being carried, also seen as the first on the left on the opposite page, reads, "Olde Home Week, Pawtucket, R.I., Aug. 27, Sept. 2, 1905, Hose Reel Trophy, Won by Fiskeville Fire Co., 33 Seconds."

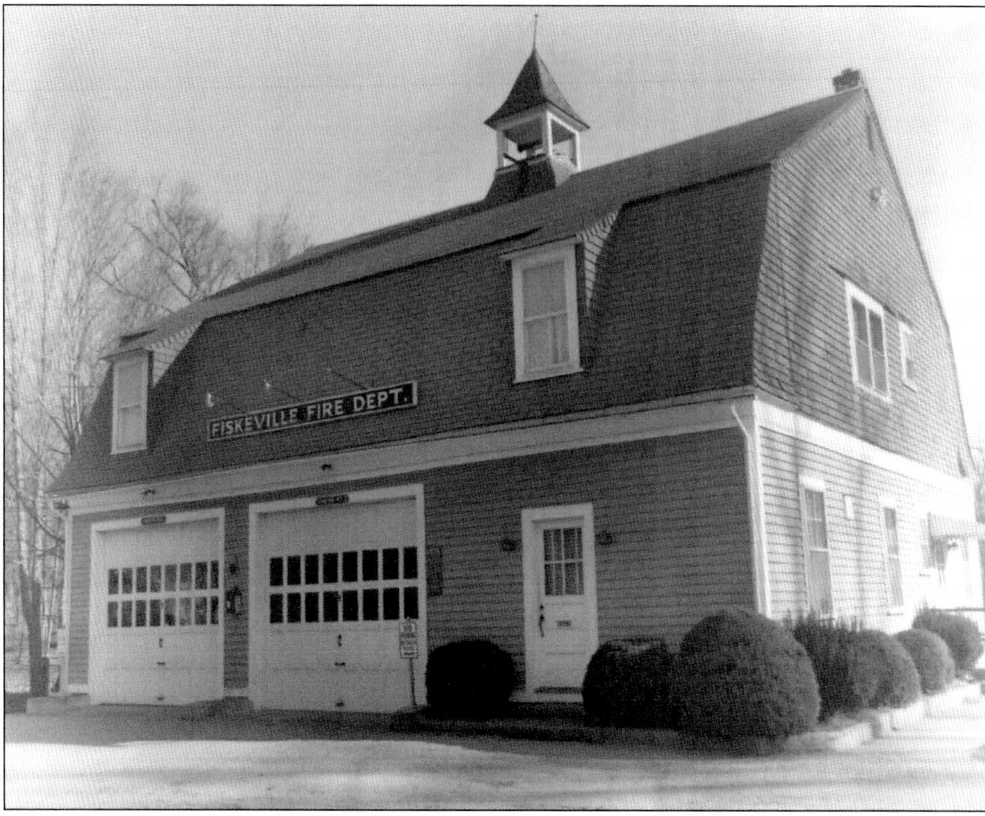

The Fiskeville Fire Department building was originally a carriage barn located on Arkwright Mill property. Arkwright sold the building to the fire company for $1 on November 5, 1950, and moved it to this new location on Main Street. The bell, built by Henry Hooper Company in 1855, was originally located at the Harris Mill. In 1950, it was placed in the belfry of the new station. It can be seen alongside the walkway to the entrance of Arkwright Manufacturing offices. The plaque reads, "Dedicated by the Fiskeville Fire Company #1 Inc., To commemorate their dedication and service to the community, 1900–1995." (Above, courtesy of Gerard Tellier Jr.; below, author's collection.)

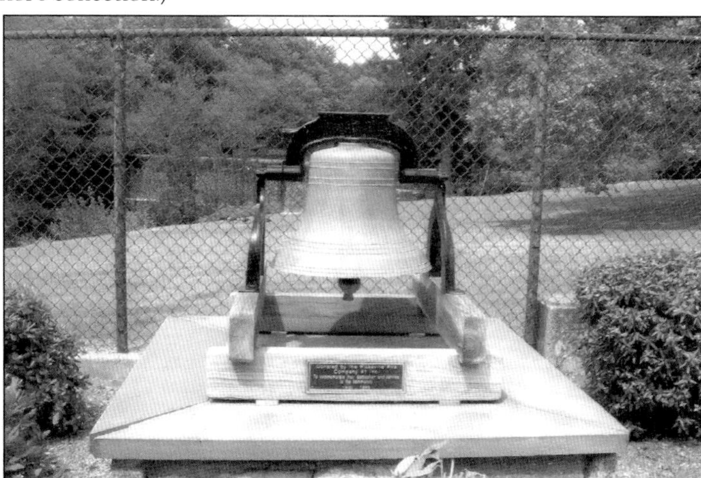

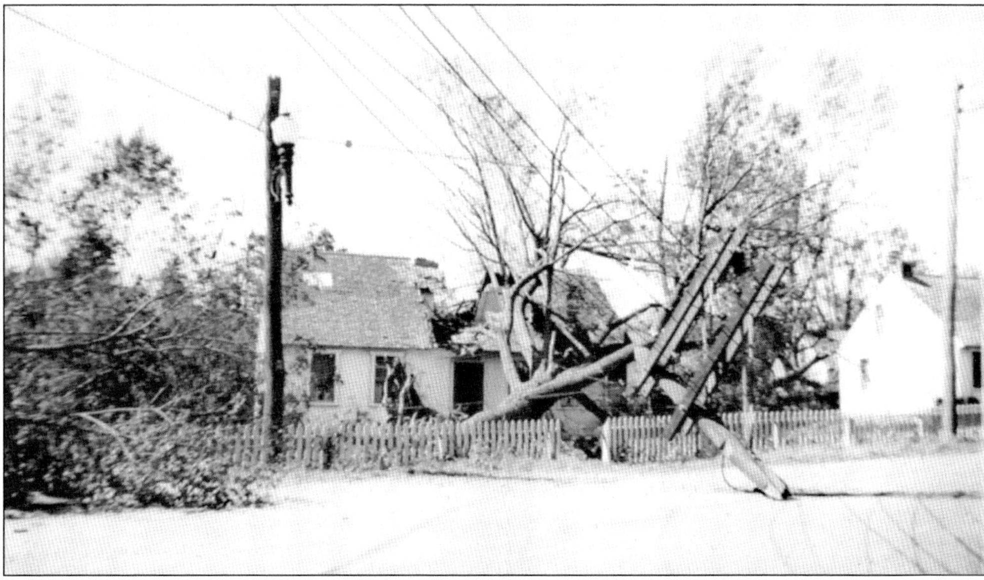

This is a sample of the devastation that the Hurricane of 1938 left behind after it struck Rhode Island. The house is located at the bend of Main Street opposite the fire station. Note the old-fashioned streetlight fixture. The following verse is from "The '38 Hurricane" by Helen O. Larson: "There were floods, water everywhere / A tree down in one place, another one over there." (Courtesy of Gerard Tellier Jr.)

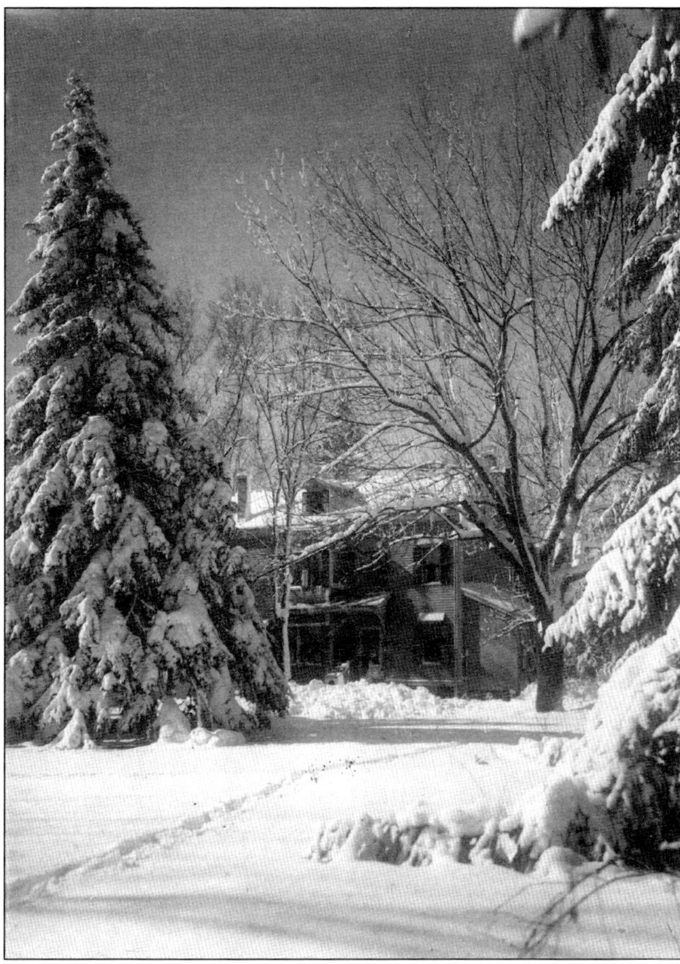

This house, pictured on a winter day, was named Brunleigh. It still stands across the street from the Arkwright Bridge and was the home of James Gee, the first superintendent of Arkwright Mill. In 1913, the home was occupied by his son Robert.

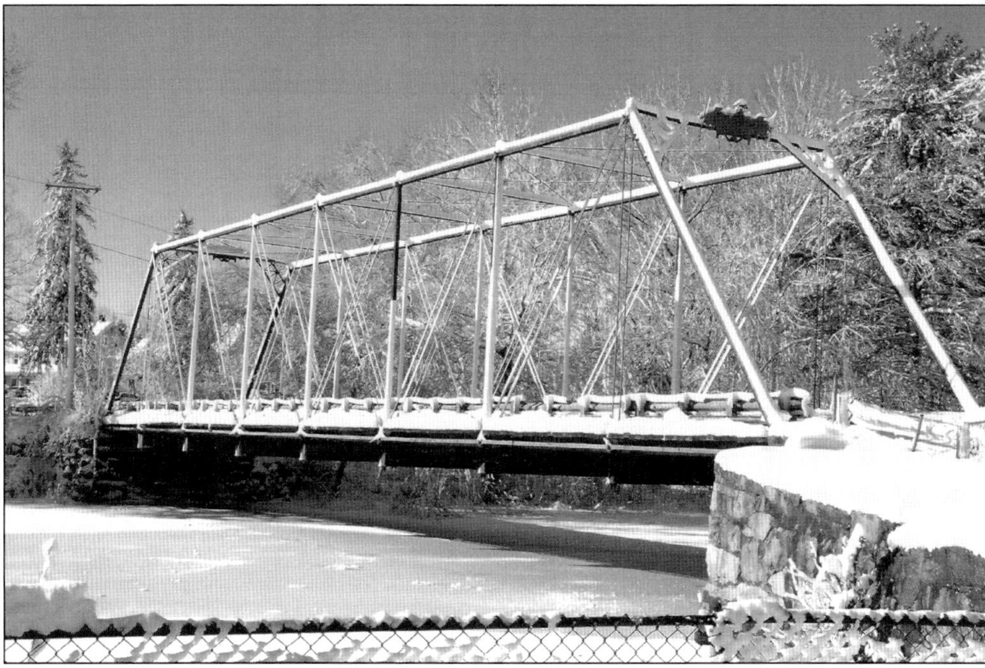

Arkwright Bridge is pictured here on January 13, 2011. Built in 1888, it is a 125-foot Pratt Truss Bridge. By the end of 2011, the bridge was closed to traffic and now awaits dismantling. This is the last of this type bridge on the Pawtuxet. (Courtesy of Gerard Tellier Jr.)

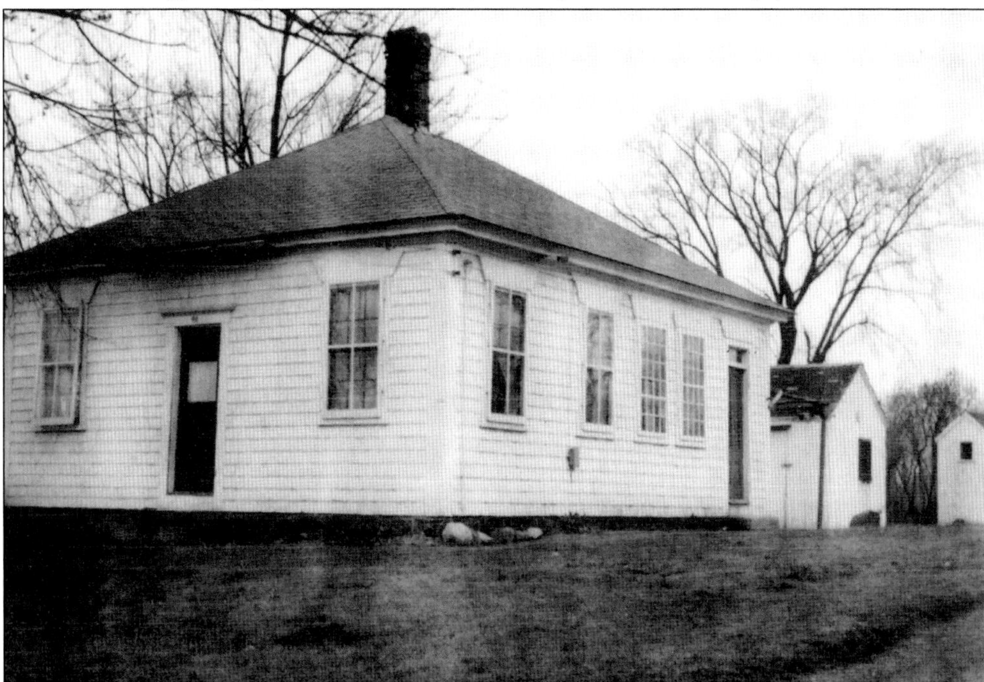

Arkwright School House is pictured here in the 1970s, just before it was burned down by the local fire company as a training exercise. Three other homes nearby were also taken down to create room for a parking lot for Arkwright Mill. (Courtesy of Gerard Tellier Jr.)

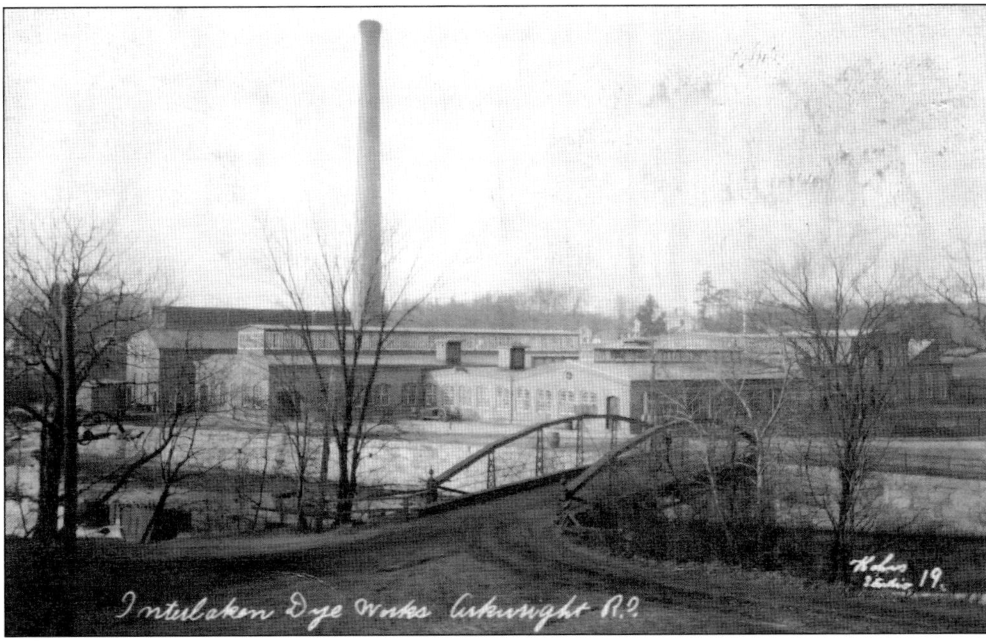

The first Arkwright Mill was built in 1810. A second building was added in 1822. They were both located on the south side of the Pawtuxet River. The present mill, shown here, was built on the north side but not until 1883. The bridge is a 100-foot-long, single-span, lenticular truss bridge. Built in 1855, it is the only lenticular bridge to survive in Rhode Island today.

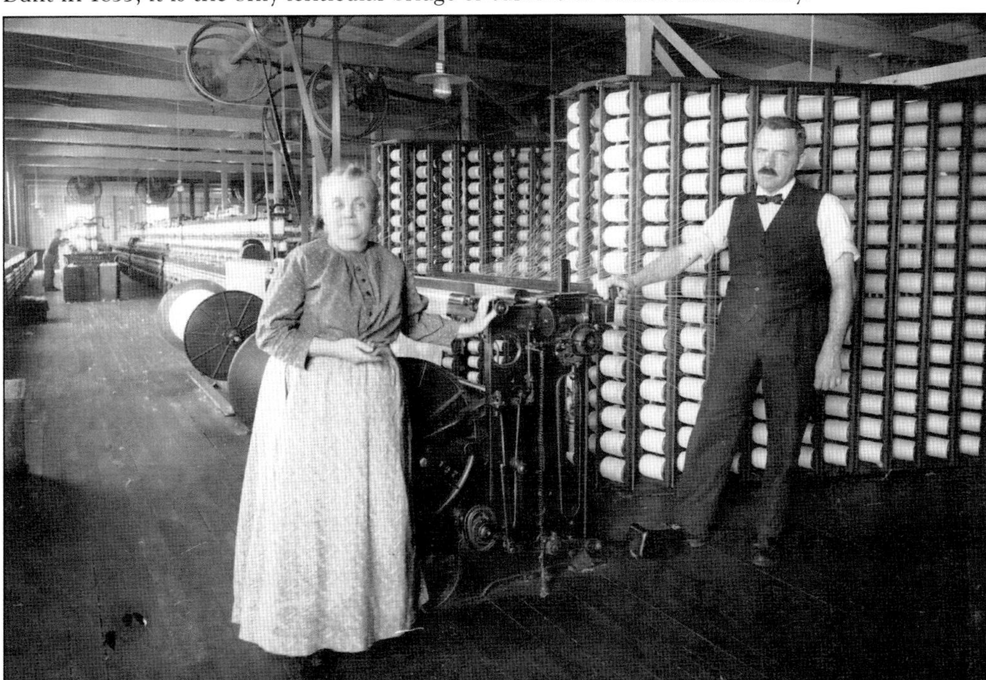

This c. 1914 photograph shows Jacqueline Kirchoff with her husband, Alan. They pause during their busy day at Arkwright Mill to pose for the camera. Alan is also seen on page 50 working at the Harris Mill. The Harris Mill Complex was bought by Arkwright Interlaken Mills in 1900.

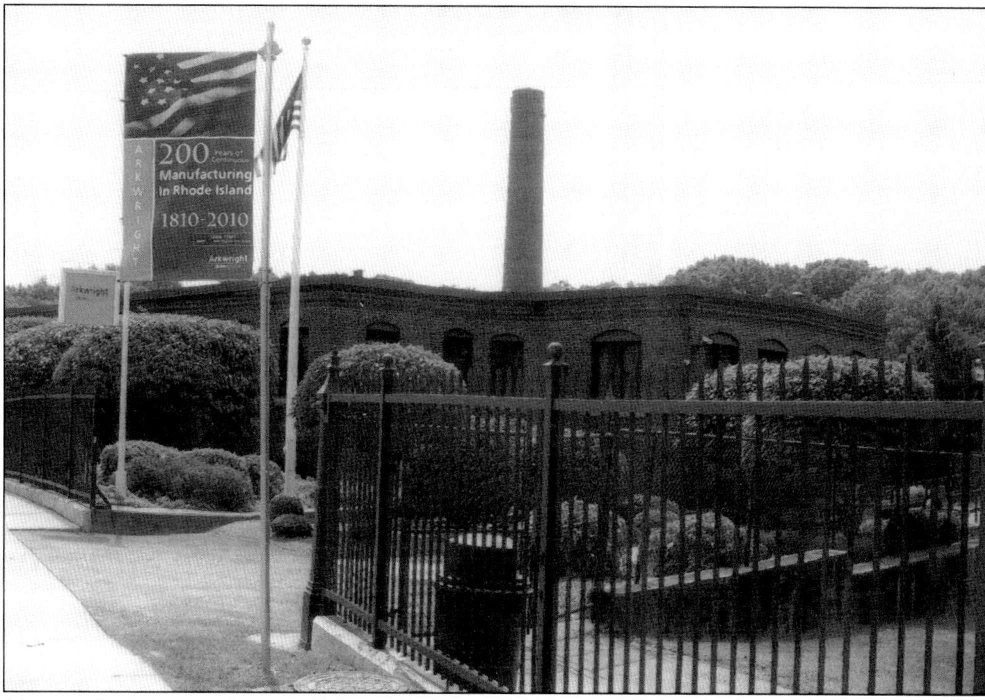

2010 marked the 200th year of continuous manufacturing by Arkwright in Rhode Island. This September 9, 2010, photograph was taken during the celebration party. It shows the entrance walkway to the main building and offices. (Author's collection.)

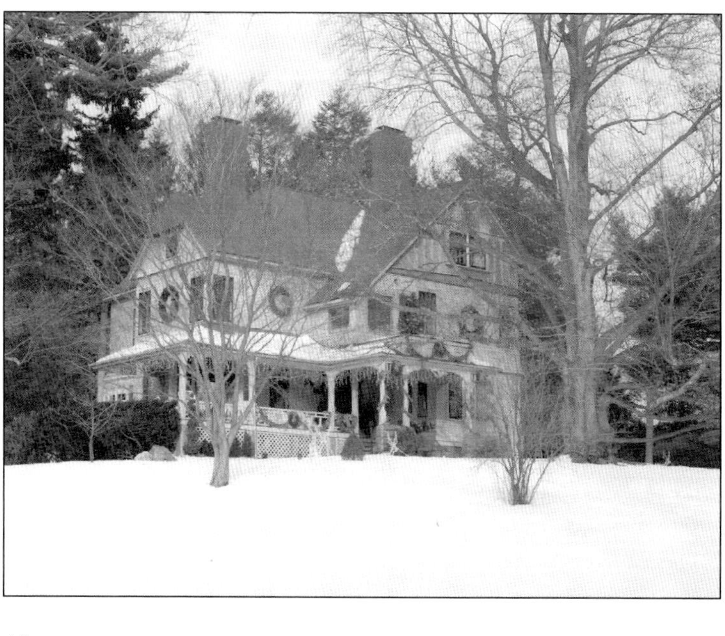

Christopher Rhodes Greene and his wife, Maria, lived in this Queen Anne–style house, which was built in 1882 and designed by architects Stone and Carpenter. It is located on the corner of Main Street and Potter Court and overlooks the Pawtuxet River. Greene lived here until his death on March 13, 1885. His father, Simon, died one month later on April 26, 1885. (Courtesy of Gerard Tellier Jr.)

Three

HARRIS AND PHENIX

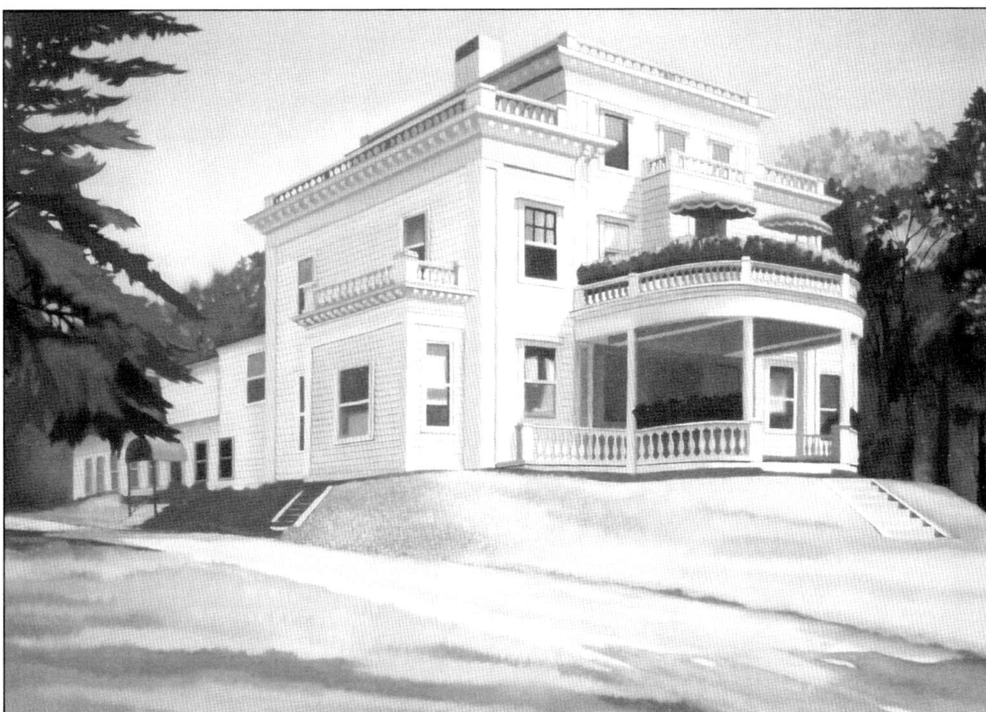

This painting shows the large mansion that Elisha Harris, owner of the Harris Mill, built in 1840 in what was then Harrisville. It overlooked the Pawtuxet River, and therefore, he named it Riverview. Harris died in 1861 as governor of Rhode Island. Harris's son-in-law Henry Howard moved into the mansion that same year. Howard would also go on to be elected governor of Rhode Island in 1873. In later years, it became the Riverview Nursing Home. (Courtesy of Riverview Nursing Home.)

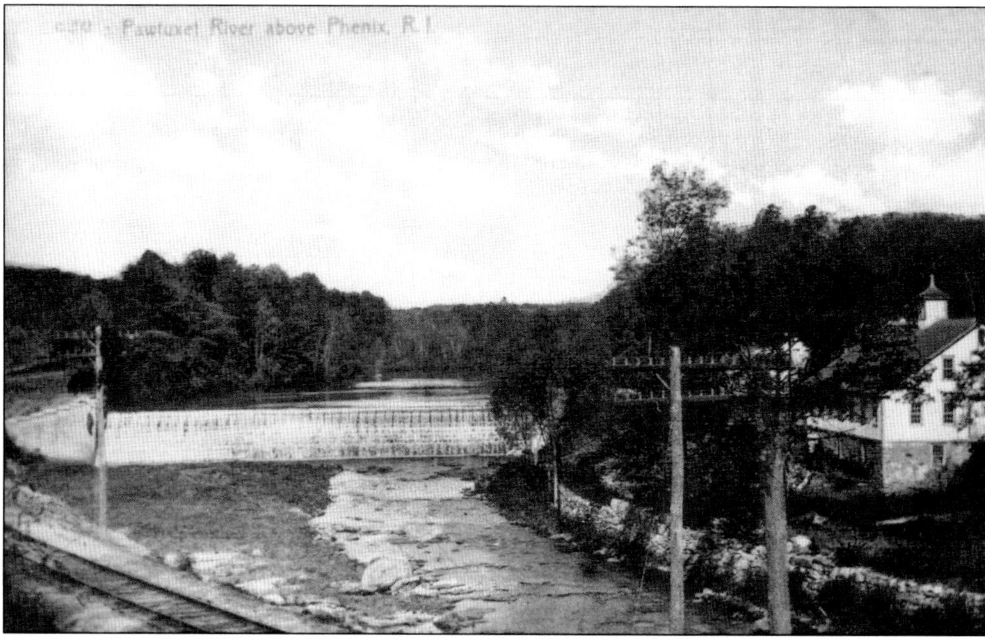

The Harris Dam is pictured here in 1910. The stone dam was built by Rowland Lovell in 1861 for the Harris Manufacturing Company, pictured below. After the flood of 1886, it needed to be rebuilt. The c. 1890 photograph below was taken from the railroad track looking downstream. The mill pictured was constructed in 1822 by Gov. Elisha Harris but was taken down in 1902. The new Harris Mill was built across the street where it stands today. The nest of small cottages along the bank of the Pawtuxet River was mill housing. (Below, courtesy of Donald Carpenter.)

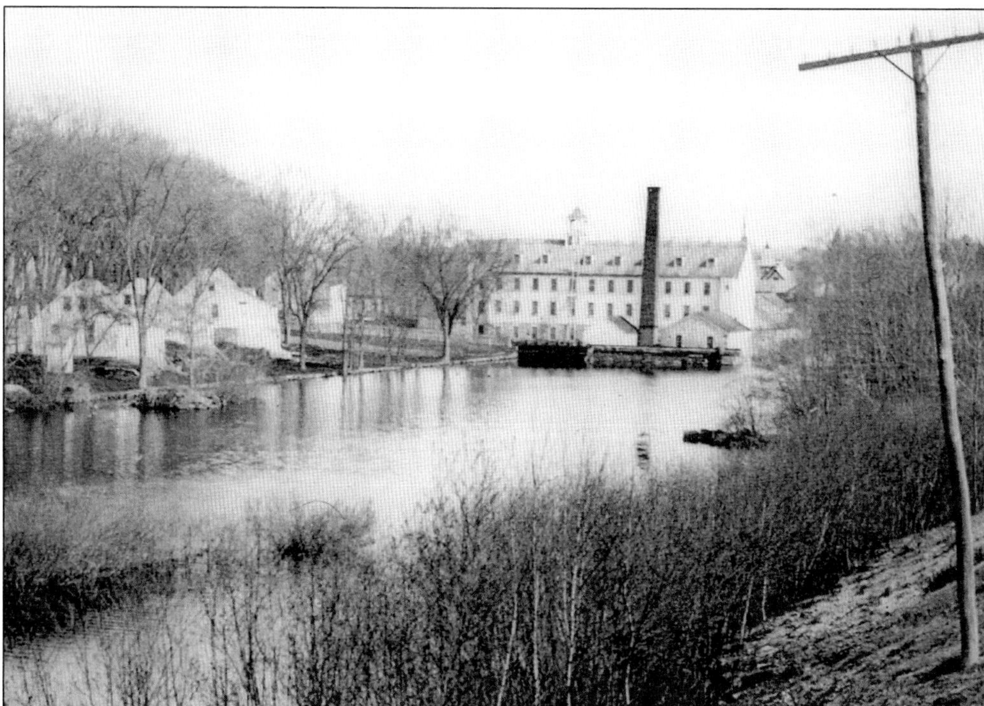

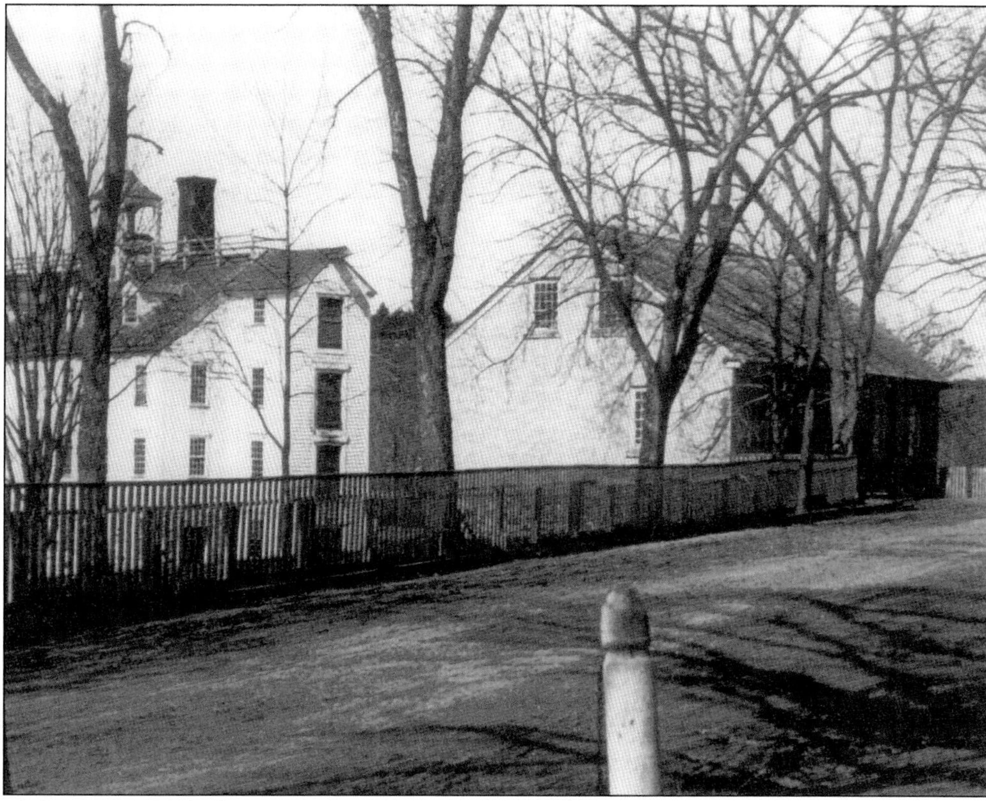

Elisha Harris built the first Harris Mill in 1822. It was located between the river and Main Street. Also visible is the Harrisville Company Store. In 1851, Harris erected a second mill across the street. By 1902, the first mill was no longer occupied and was torn down. (Courtesy of Donald Carpenter.)

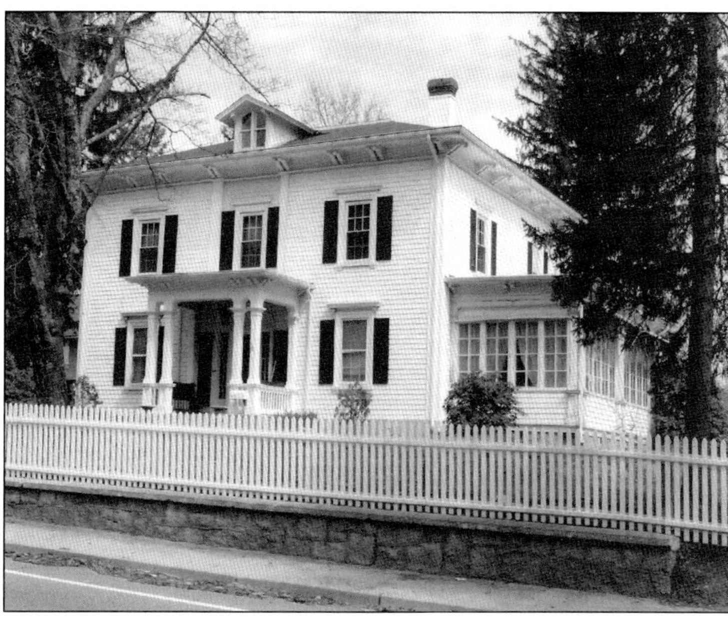

Elisha Harris's brother David built this house on Main Street at the corner of Harris Street. The Harris Manufacturing Company closed in 1953. (Courtesy of Gerard Tellier Jr.)

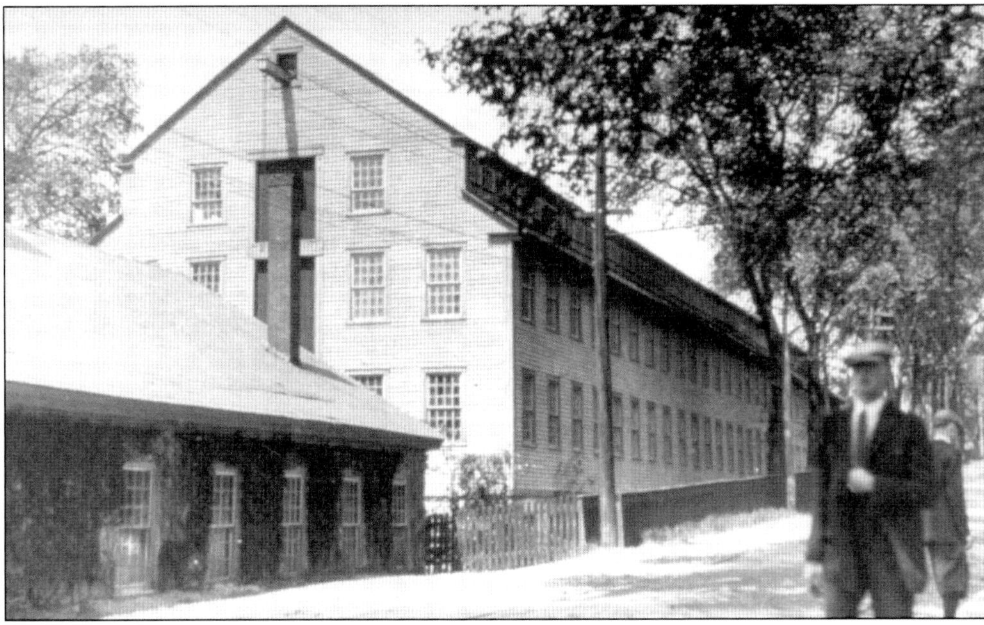

The back of the Lanphear Machine Shop is visible in this c. 1910 photograph. The building, constructed in 1847, was located on Main Street in Harris just west of the Harris Bridge. Nathan Bennett was hired to demolish it in 1930. In 1851, a new mill was erected on the opposite side of the street. This mill still stands today but has been abandoned. Pictured below is the weave shop of that mill in its heyday. A third mill was built in 1860 but has not survived.

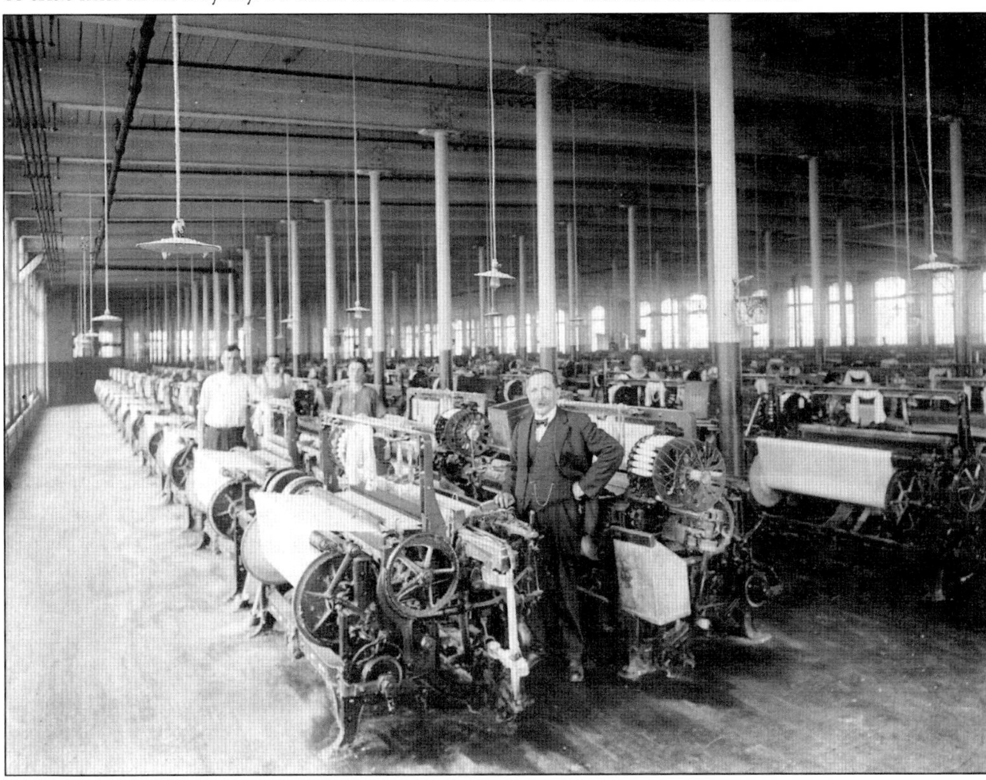

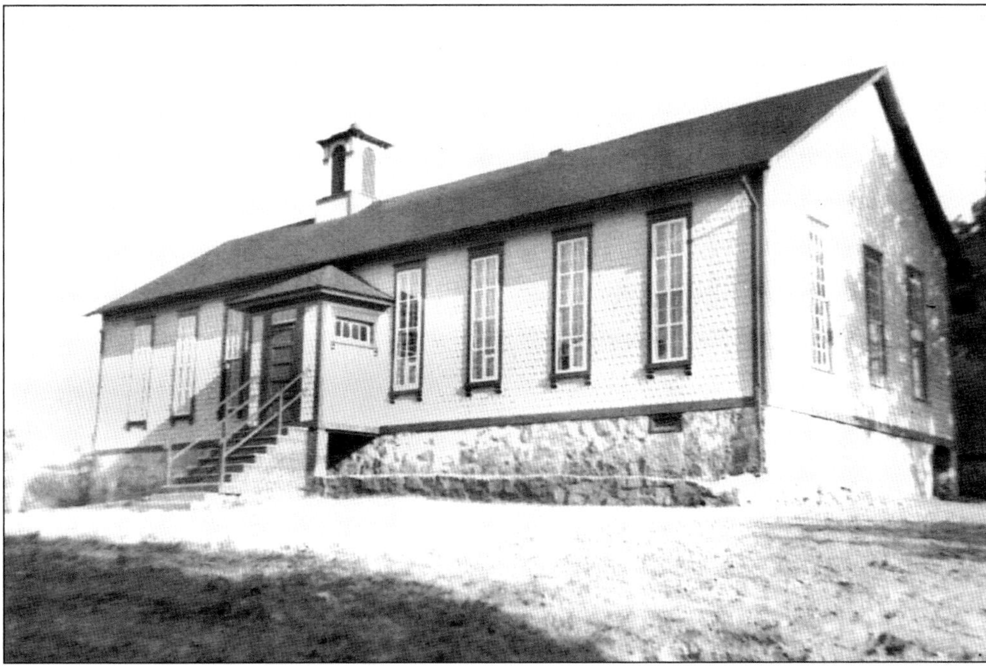

The Harris Heights Elementary School in Coventry is pictured here before it burned down on January 22, 1971. The 125-year-old, four-room school was totally destroyed and not rebuilt. The photograph below shows the Harris Heights School's first and second grade, 1958 and 1959 classes. Ada B. Sykes, a teacher here for 36 years and a substitute for 10 years, stands by the piano. Not pictured here is principal Elsie H. Cowen, who also taught here for 32 years. The poster on the door encourages the children to "Be Kind To Animals." (Both, courtesy of Gerard Tellier Jr.)

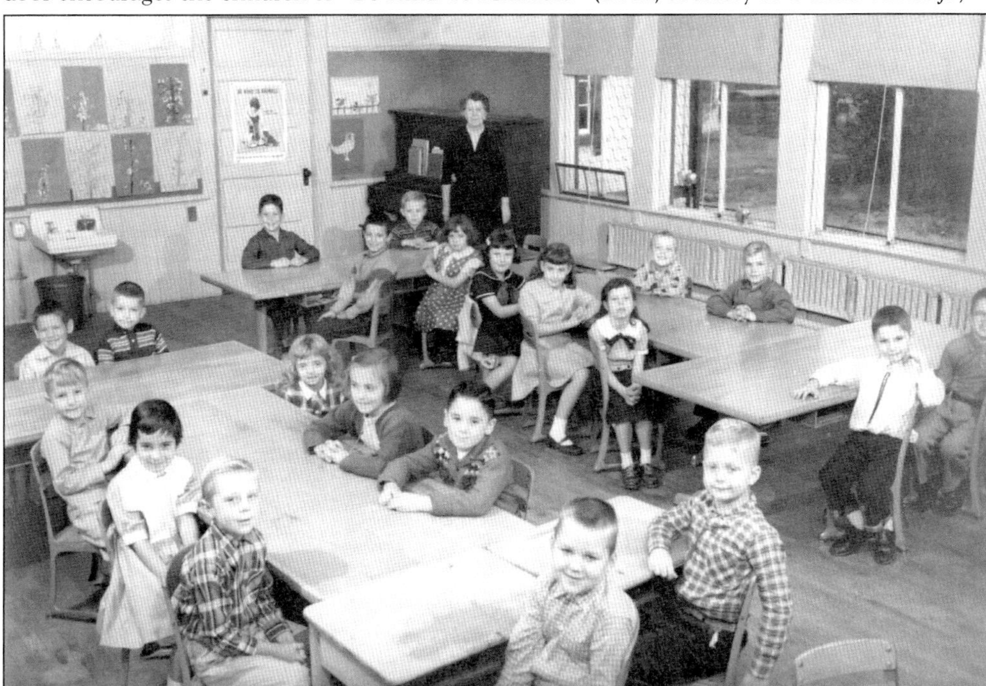

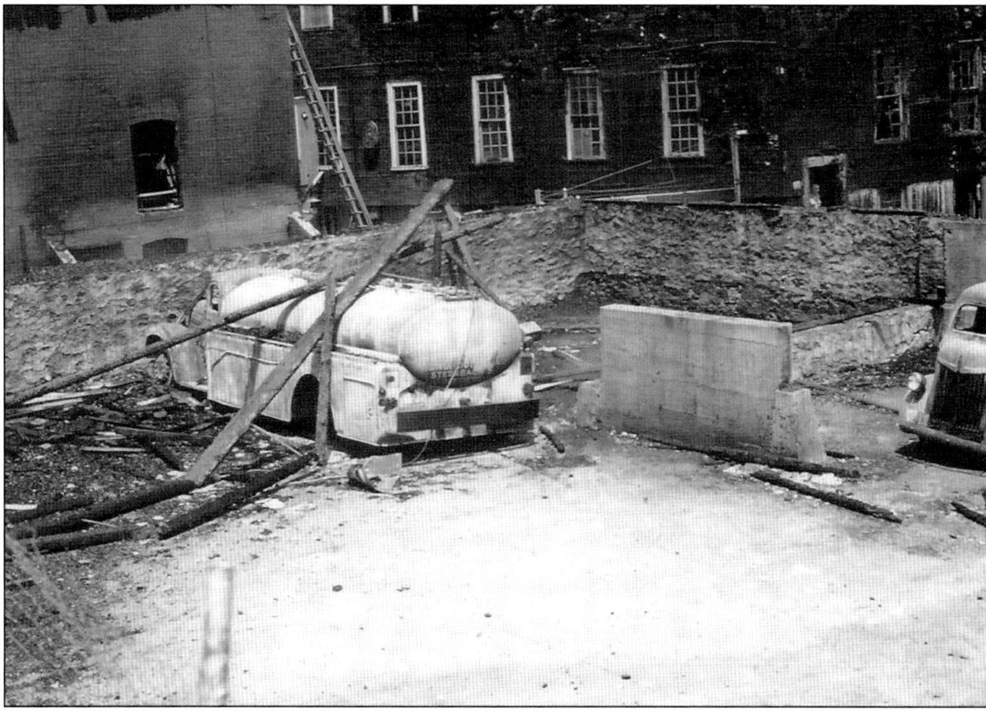

On the early morning of Sunday May 24, 1964, a fire broke out at a complex in Harris. Raymond and Morris Sternbach of Phenix owned the Campbell Grain Mill, shown on the facing page, which was totally destroyed. They also maintained a fuel oil storage depot nearby and lost two of their trucks, seen above. Below are the remains of the Pawtuxet Valley Dye Works. The total estimated damage was over $500,000. Manuel Simas, a night watchman, discovered the fire about 3:00 a.m. At one time, the family car was occasionally a nine-passenger station wagon, like the 1963 Chevrolet pictured below. (Both, courtesy of Gerard Tellier Jr.)

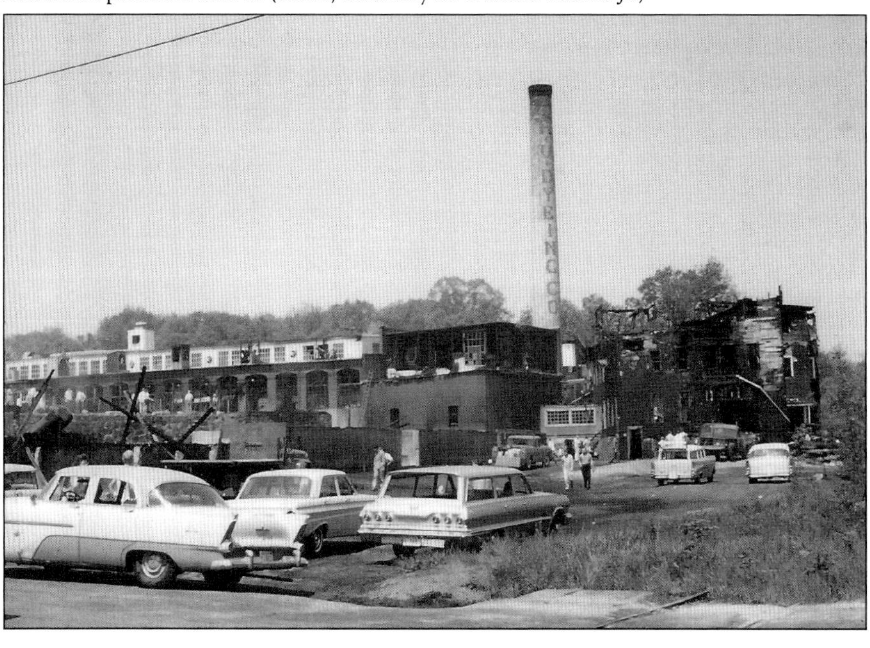

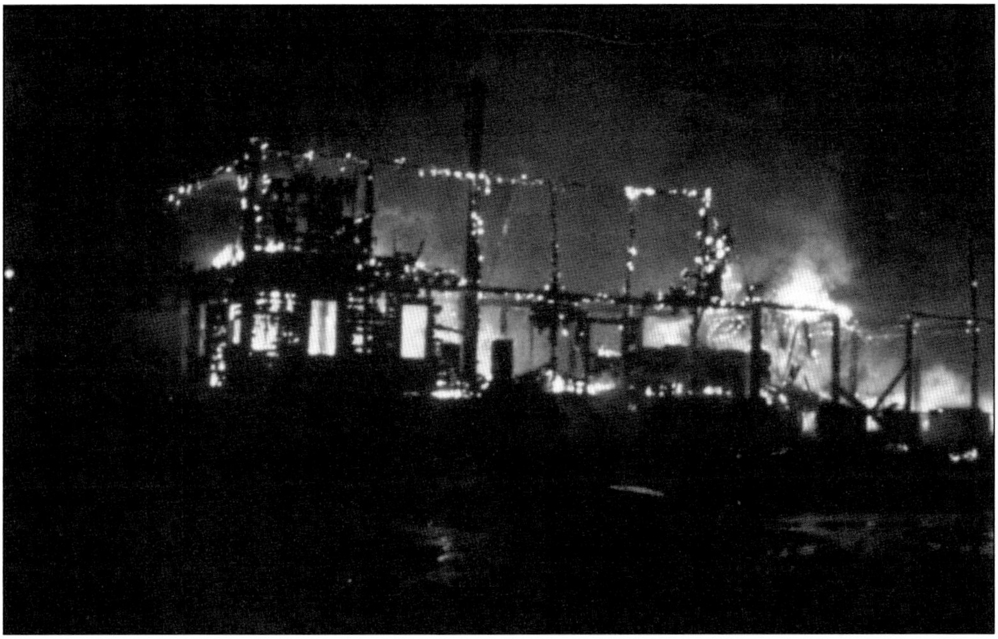

This photograph was taken just about the time that the fire was finally under control. The following eight fire companies, representing 200 fire fighters, fought the blaze for two hours: Harris, Anthony, Washington, and Hopkins Hill, all of Coventry; Lippitt and Arctic of West Warwick; Fiskeville of Cranston; and Hope-Jackson of Scituate. (Courtesy of Gerard Tellier Jr.)

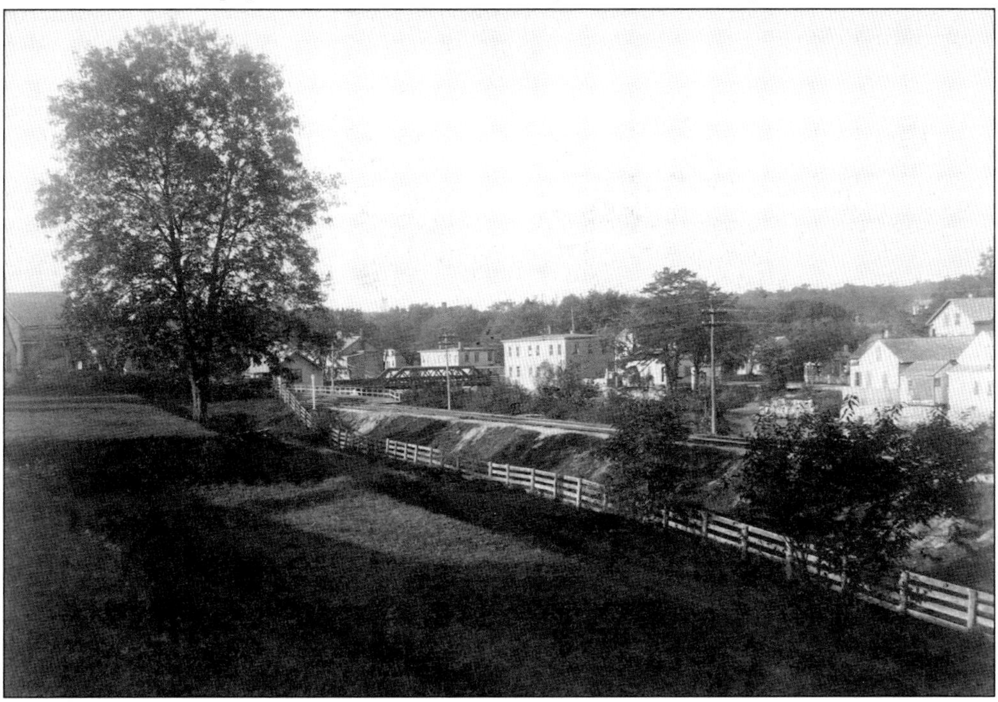

This 1880s photograph of Harris faces west from the south side of the railroad tracks. The Harris Bridge is seen in the distance, as well as on page 54. The grain mill and dye works were south over the bridge and just out of this view. (Courtesy of Donald Carpenter.)

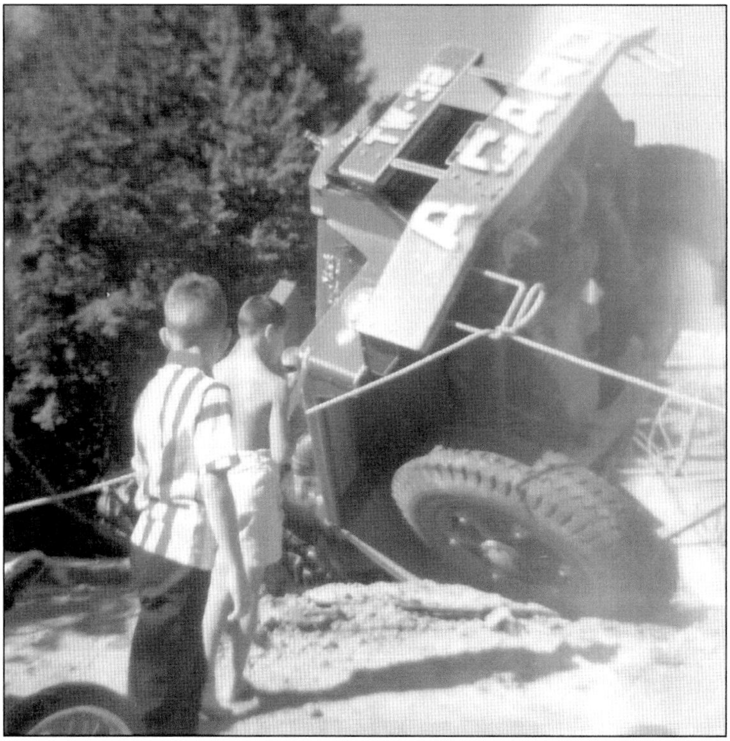

This Saturday morning in August 1966 started off like any other for Lawrence Scungio Jr. He was to deliver a load of gravel from A. Cardi Construction Company in Coventry to the Pawtuxet Valley Dye Company on the other side of Harris Bridge; however, part of the 100-year-old bridge collapsed into the Pawtuxet River. This is the scene that followed. The image at left shows the truck being pulled out of the river as children watch. (Courtesy of Gerard Tellier Jr.)

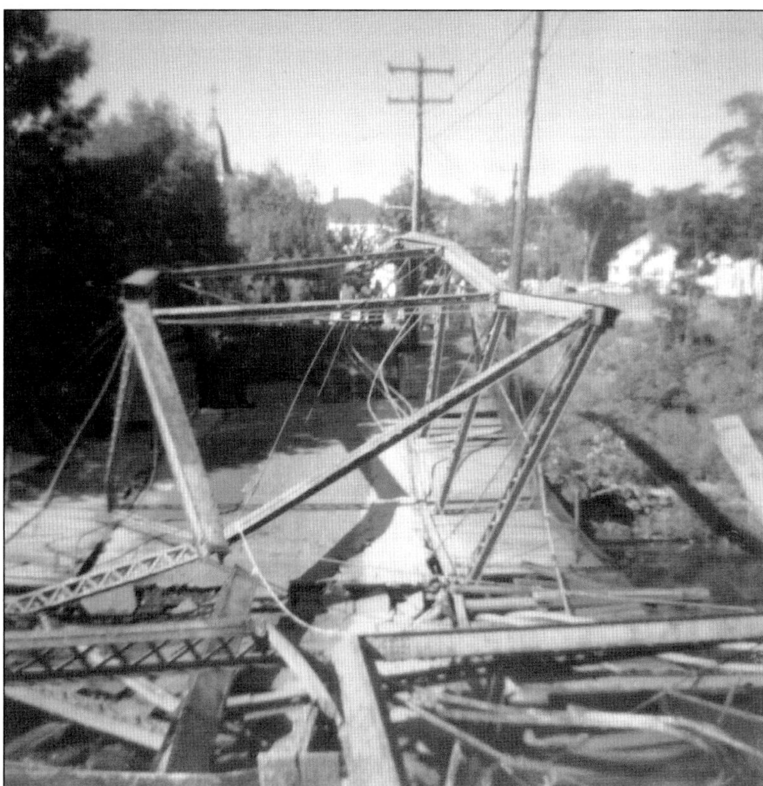

Scungio was lucky that he was not hurt. This photograph shows the tangled post-accident mess of steel and concrete. (Courtesy of Gerard Tellier Jr.)

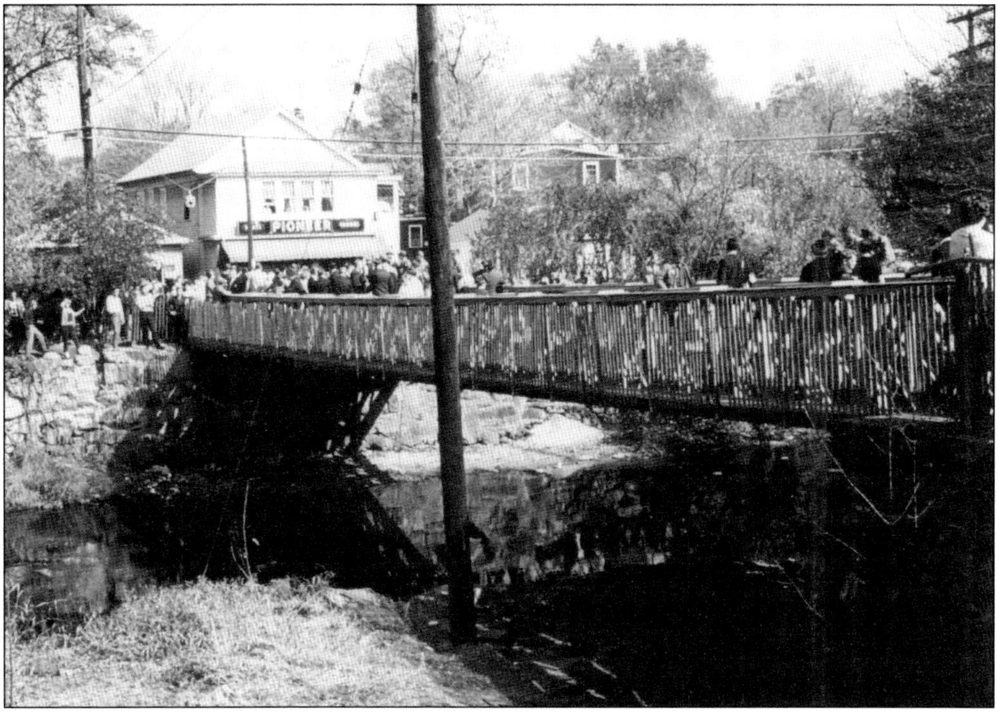

The first person to the scene of the accident was Rudolph Legault, an employee of the Pioneer grocery store seen above, situated opposite the bridge. This temporary bridge pictured was constructed after the entangled steel had been cleaned out of the river. The new bridge seen below was built in 1967. It was positioned opposite Broad Street to carry Lincoln Avenue traffic directly to the intersection. A three-story building of the Harris Mill Complex can be seen in the upper left, and the Pioneer grocery store can be seen on the right. (Both, courtesy of Gerard Tellier Jr.)

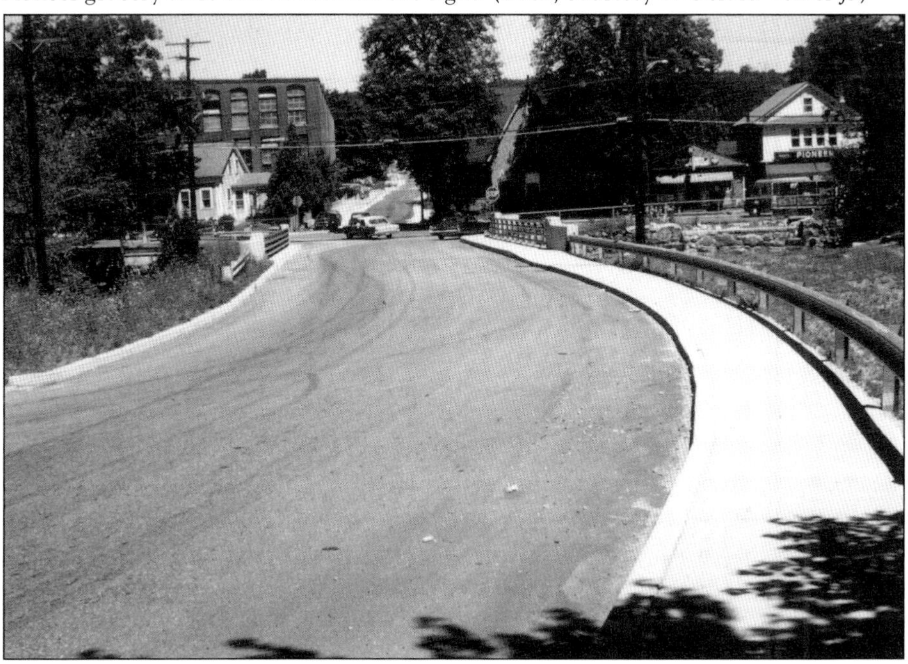

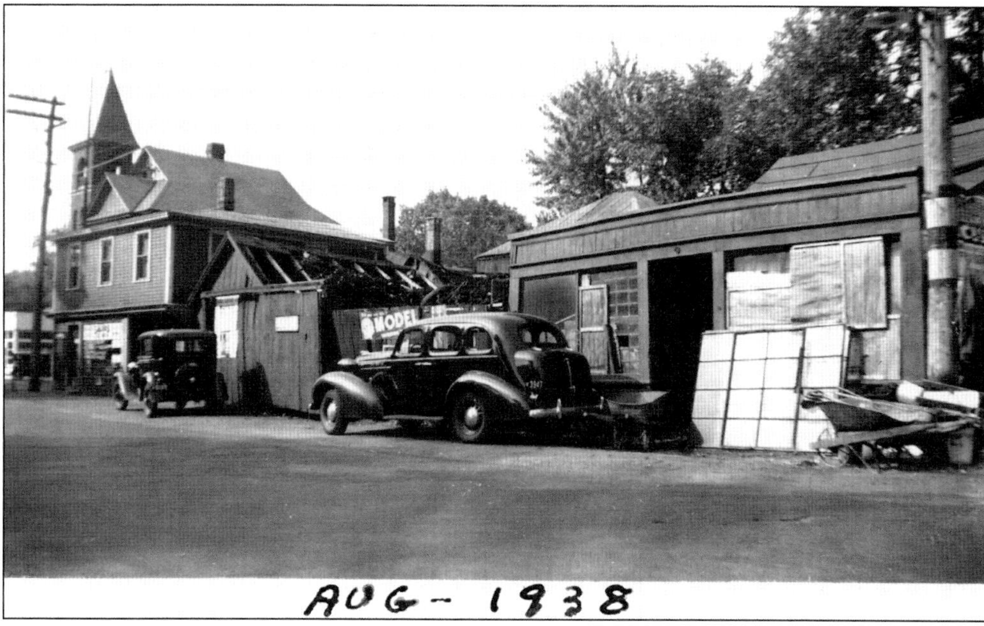

This photograph, taken in August 1938, a month before the famous 1938 hurricane, shows Main Street from the Richfield Station, facing east. The Phenix-Harris Fire Station steeple can be seen to the left and on page 107 of *West Warwick*. (Courtesy of Gerard Tellier Jr.)

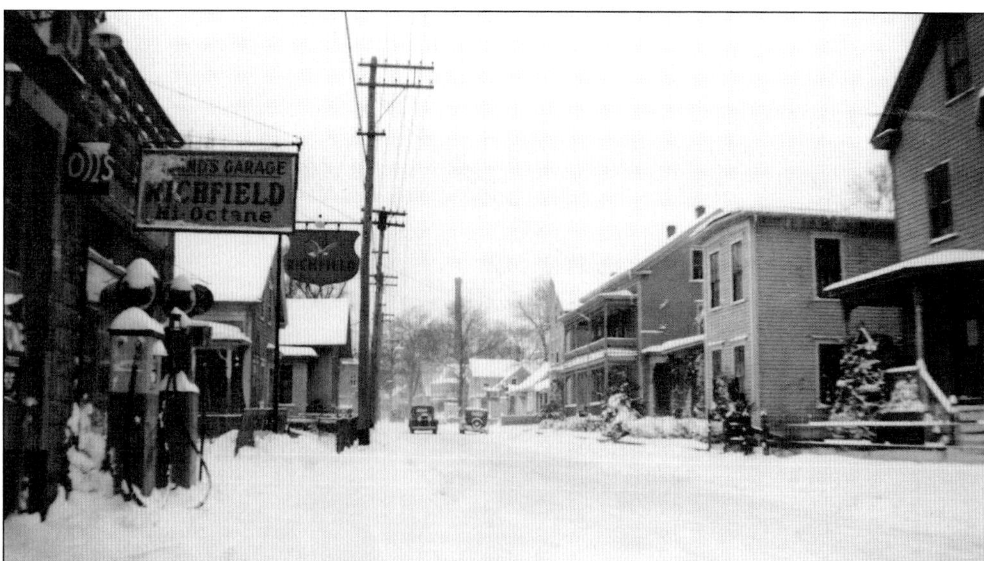

The garage on the left advertises Richfield Hi-Octane gasoline. Atlantic Refining was founded in 1866, while Richfield Petroleum was founded in 1905. In 1966, the two companies merged together to form Atlantic-Richfield with their new logo being Arco. The Harris Mill smokestack can be seen in the center above the tree line. (Courtesy of Gerard Tellier Jr.)

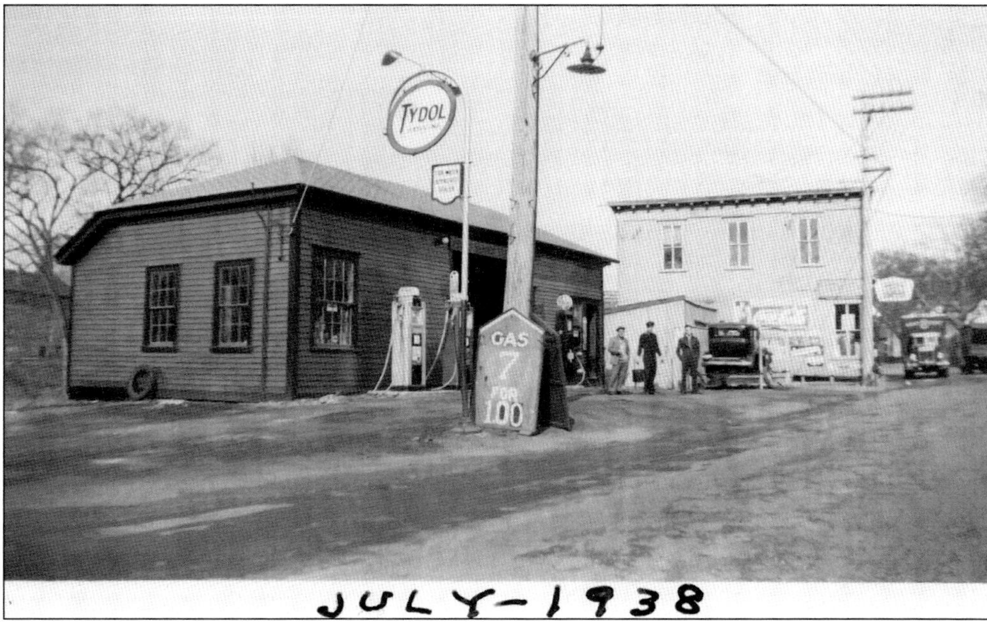

This Tydol service station was located between Main Street and the Pawtuxet River, just east of the Harris Bridge. Tydol Gasoline was a brand used by Tidewater Oil Company. The company was founded in 1887. In 1932, the company labeled their premium-grade gasoline Flying A. There is a sign on the corner of the building that advertised Norwalk tires and batteries. Below is a view of the rear of the same building extending over the Pawtuxet River. It is said that this was the customers' restroom area. That rumor could not be verified. (Both, courtesy of Gerard Tellier Jr.)

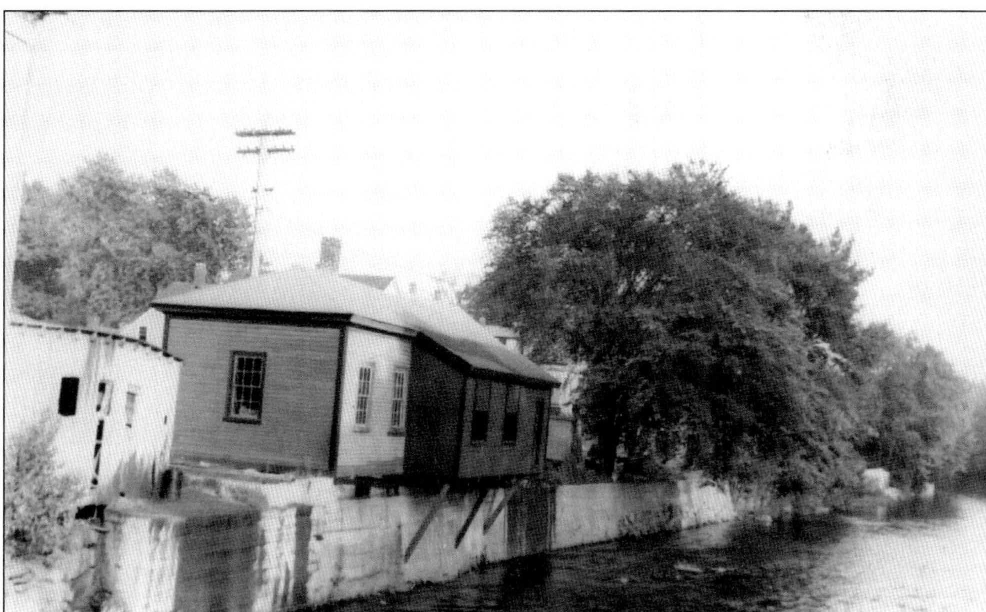

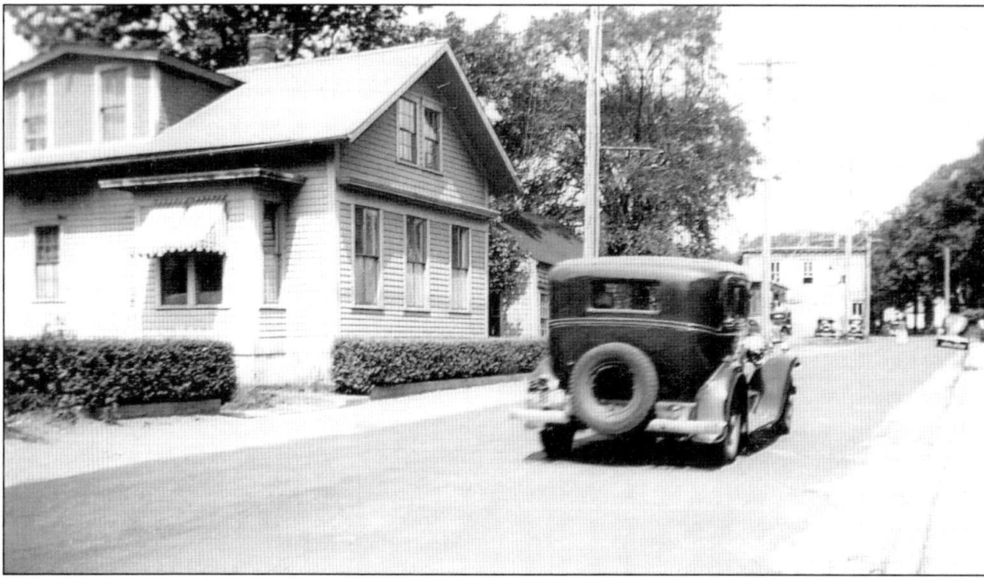

This house was fated for a new future when this photograph was taken; however, that did not mean it was going to be destroyed. Back in the day, instead of tearing it down, the owner would just up and move it, as seen below. In 1938, the moving company raised it off the foundation and moved it to Main Street on its way to 18 Broad Street, where it resides today. The following verse is from "The Homestead" by Helen O. Larson, written in 1999 at the age of 88: "Oh! That homestead, of so long ago / A place where happiness lived, God willed it to be so." (Both, courtesy of Gerard Tellier Jr.)

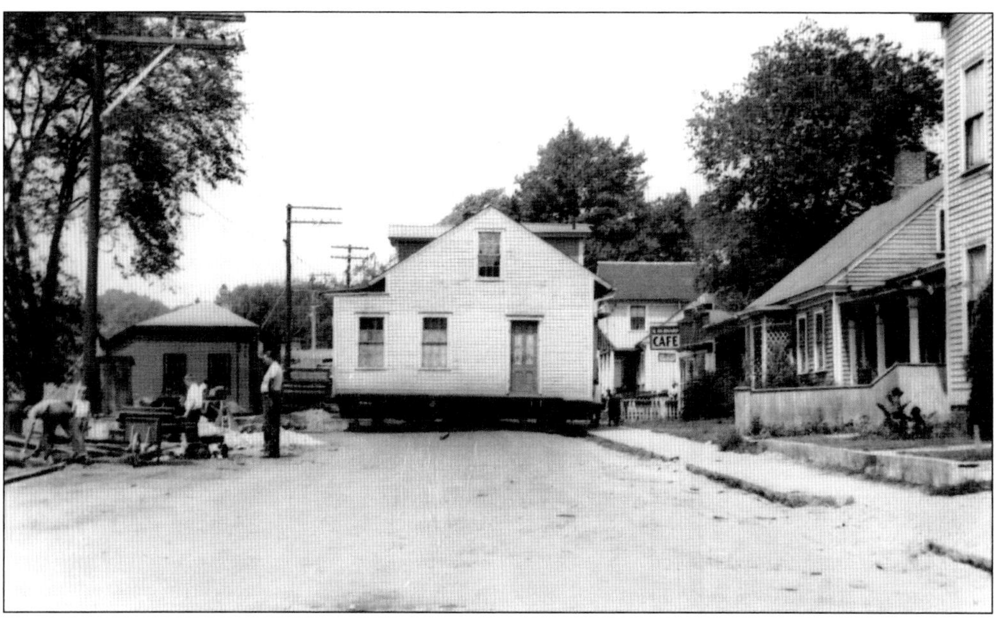

This June 27, 2011, photograph shows Roger Chabot, mascot for the Phenix Fire Company in 1928. He can also be seen in *West Warwick* on page 107 as a young boy, posing with all the firemen. (Courtesy of Gerard Tellier Jr.)

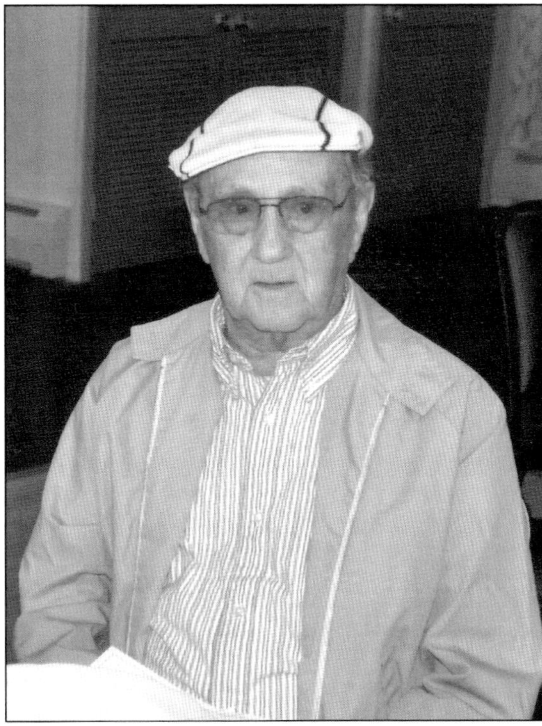

This group of retired firemen from the Harris Fire Company met at the station frequently to play cribbage. They are, from left to right, (first row) Joe Petrin, Tom Scally, and two unidentified; (second row) Fred Colvin, Ernest Heroux, Al Hudson, and Joe Salvas. This 1955 photograph was taken at Scally's house, when he could no longer walk to the station.

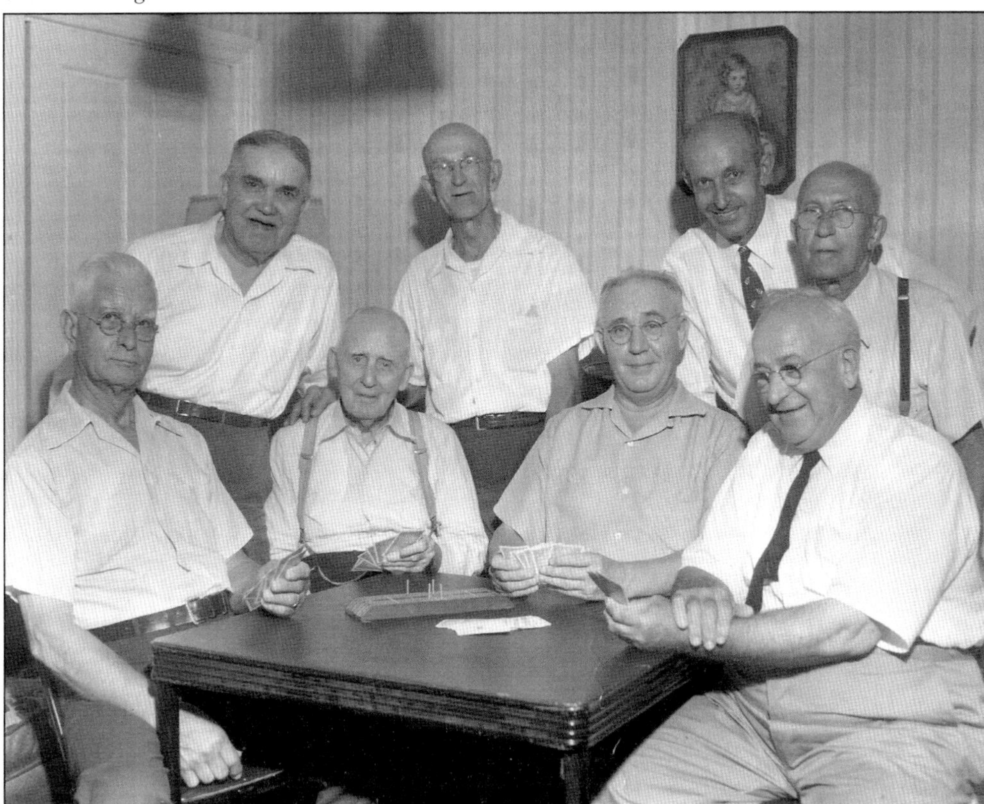

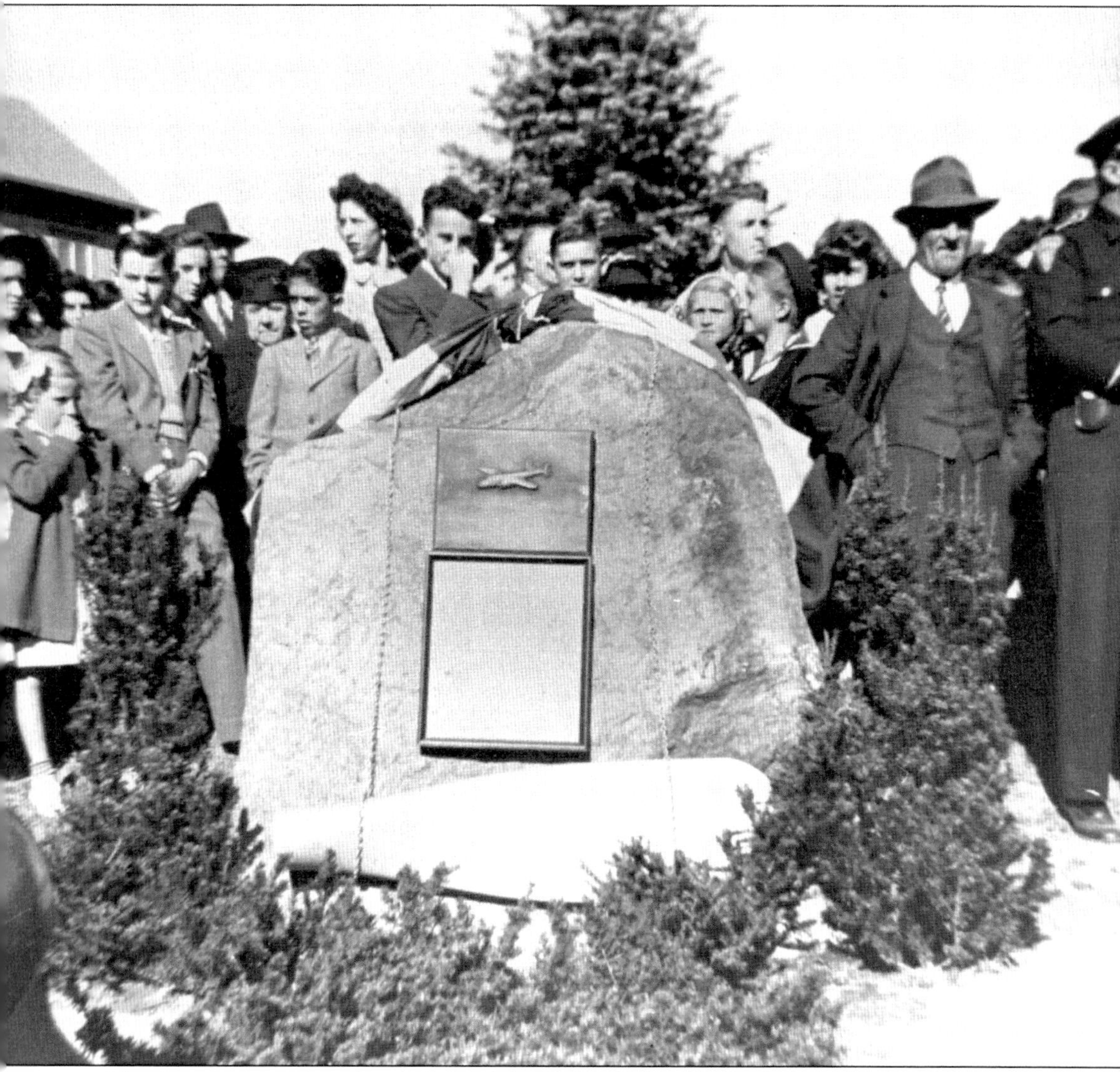

This large stone with a plaque, located in the northeast corner of the Phenix square commons, reads, "To Commemorate the Flight of Staff Sergeant Omer A. Duquette over Tokyo, Japan April 18, 1942." Duquette was born January 25, 1916, in West Warwick. The bottom plaque reads, "In honor of the men and women from Phenix who served in World War II and in memory of those who died." They are George L. Arcand, Alfred Belanger, Napoleon Benoit, John J. Bryant, Raymond L. Chamberland, James F. Dinsdale, William N. Forrest, Edward F. Kernan, Henry Leveillee, Aldrege A. Martin, Robert C. Mercier, Oscar Oakes Jr., Russell J. O'Rourke, Eugene Petrin, Richard W. Pierce, Marvin S. Sternback, and Henry D. Theroux. The only two identified in this photograph are Arthur Thibeault (third from the left), the boy with his hands crossed, and Carol Bouchard LeBeau, the blonde-haired girl peeking over the right side of the stone. The following verse is from "Old Glory" by Helen O. Larson: "I love that beautiful flag, it stands for freedom in the U.S.A. / So many young men died for it, in a country far away."

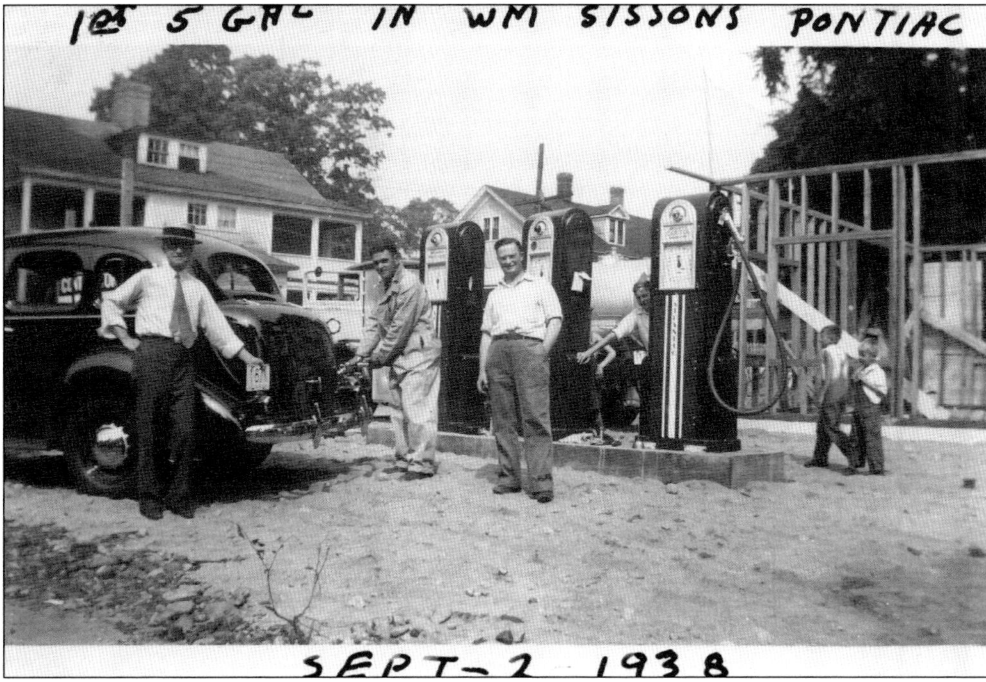

This September 2, 1938, photograph shows William Sisson receiving the first five gallons of gasoline sold. He pumps it into his Pontiac even before the building is completely constructed. The new station, still in existence, is located across from the monument on the facing page. It was an Atlantic gasoline station at the time. (Courtesy of Gerard Tellier Jr.)

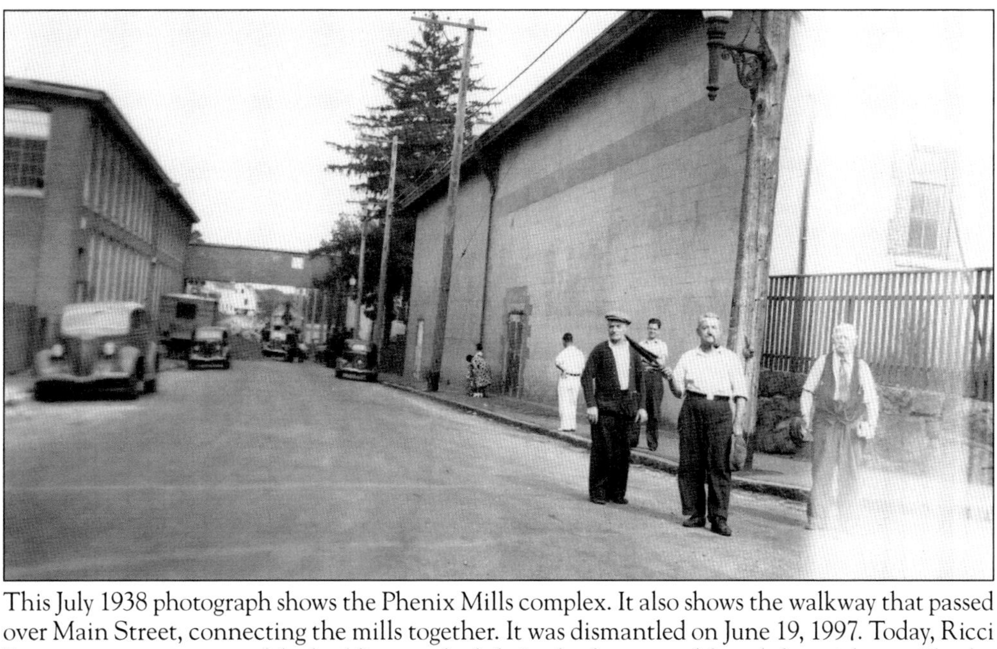

This July 1938 photograph shows the Phenix Mills complex. It also shows the walkway that passed over Main Street, connecting the mills together. It was dismantled on June 19, 1997. Today, Ricci Furniture occupies part of the building on the left. In the foreground from left to right are Charles Hopkins, Nick Pelky, and Walt Hopkins. The lady on the sidewalk is Harriet Smith with her son. (Courtesy of Gerard Tellier Jr.)

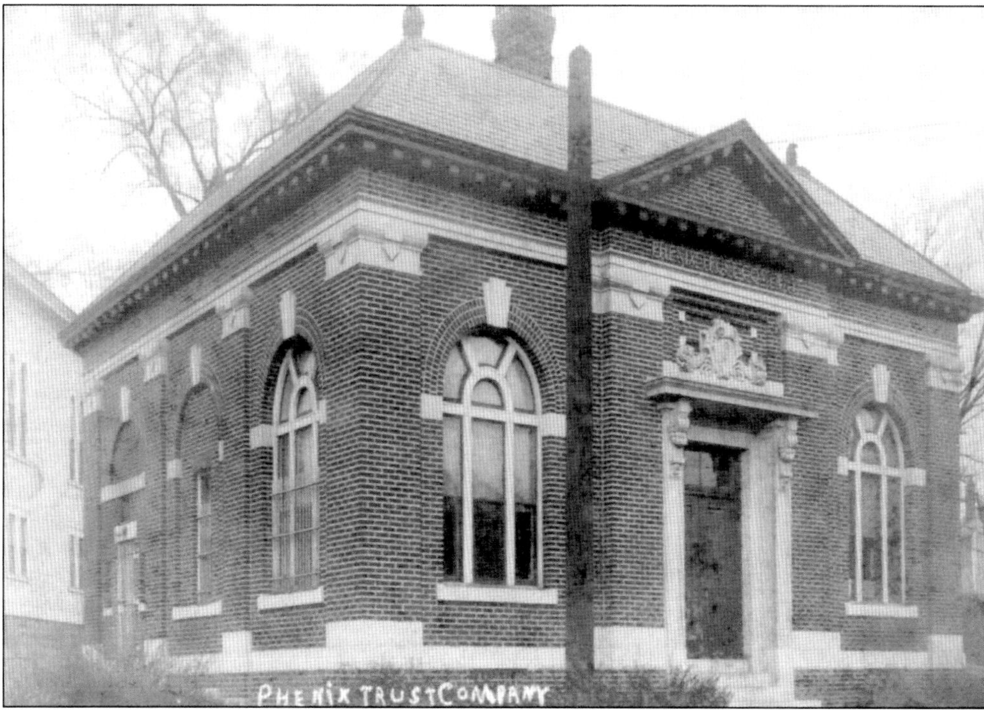

The Phenix Trust Company Bank, built in 1917, was the second bank in Phenix. To the left and in the rear is the Phenix Methodist Church, built in 1859. It was torn down in the 1970s to make room for a Cumberland Farms Convenience Store. The photograph below shows the Phenix Baptist Church (erected in 1869), the wooden bridge, (built in 1858), and James P. Arnold's Furniture and Coffin Warerooms building, where the McGregor post of the Grand Army of the Republic (GAR) occupied the top floor. (Both, courtesy of Donald Carpenter.)

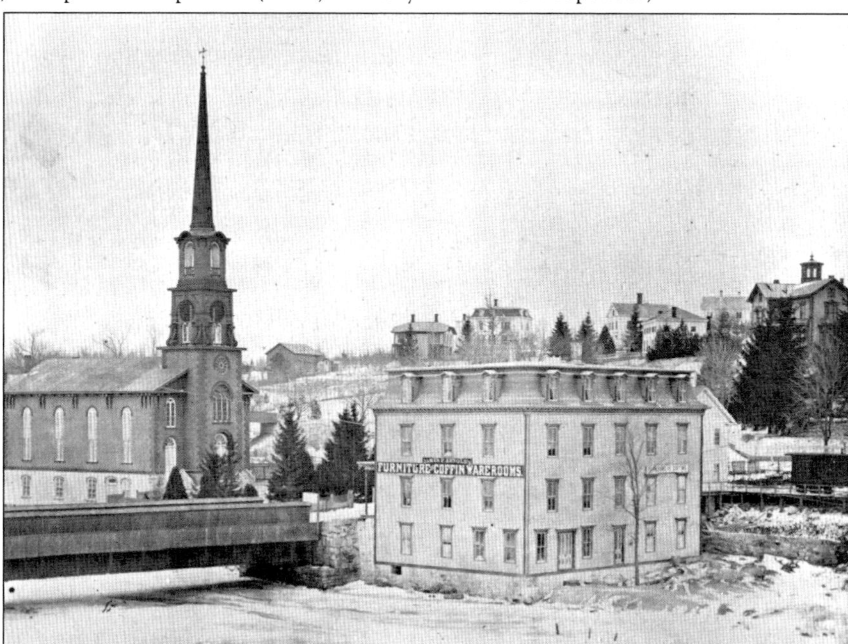

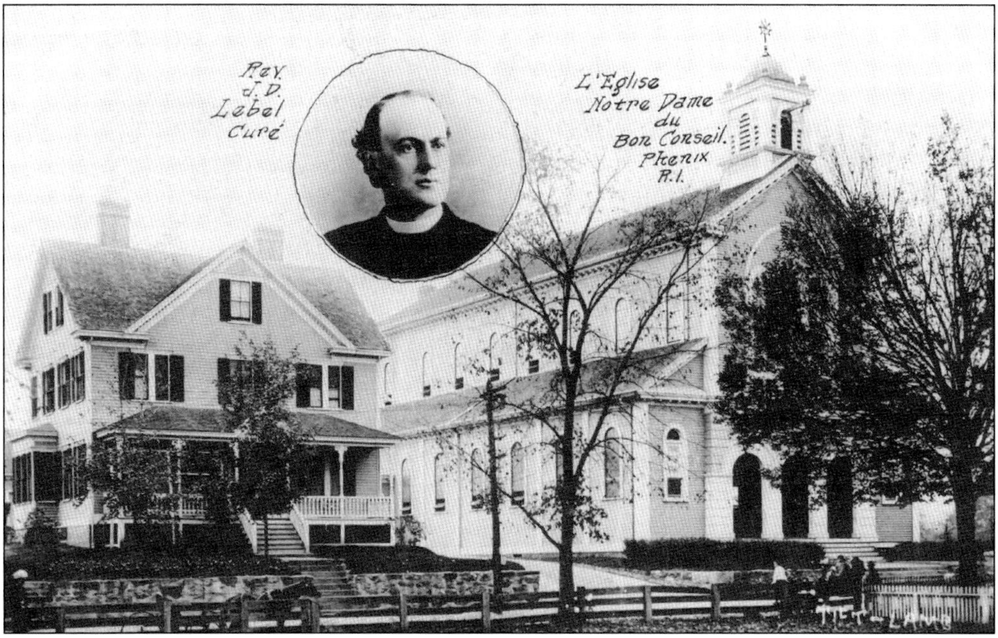

On September 17, 1897, the parish of Our Lady of Good Counsel was formed. It acquired property on the corner of Summit and Pleasant Streets and, in September 1903, completed the church seen above. The rectory to the left was erected in 1898. By 1916, two parcels of land were purchased across the street to eventually build a school. The school was completed in 1925 and named Our Lady of Good Council School. By 1970, with attendance down, the congregation joined the parish of SS. Peter and Paul to combine forces and form the Notre Dame Regional School. The photograph below shows the stunning interior of the church; however, it was too expensive to heat. Therefore, in 1979, the top 13 feet were removed, and a new roof was constructed. Rev. Jean D. Lebel, pictured in the inset above, was the first pastor. (Above, courtesy of Richard Siembab.)

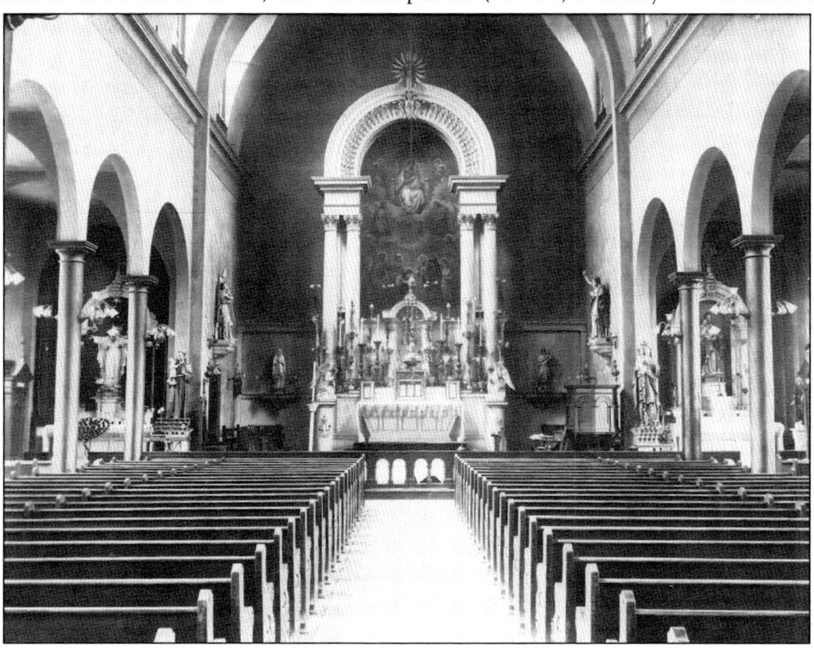

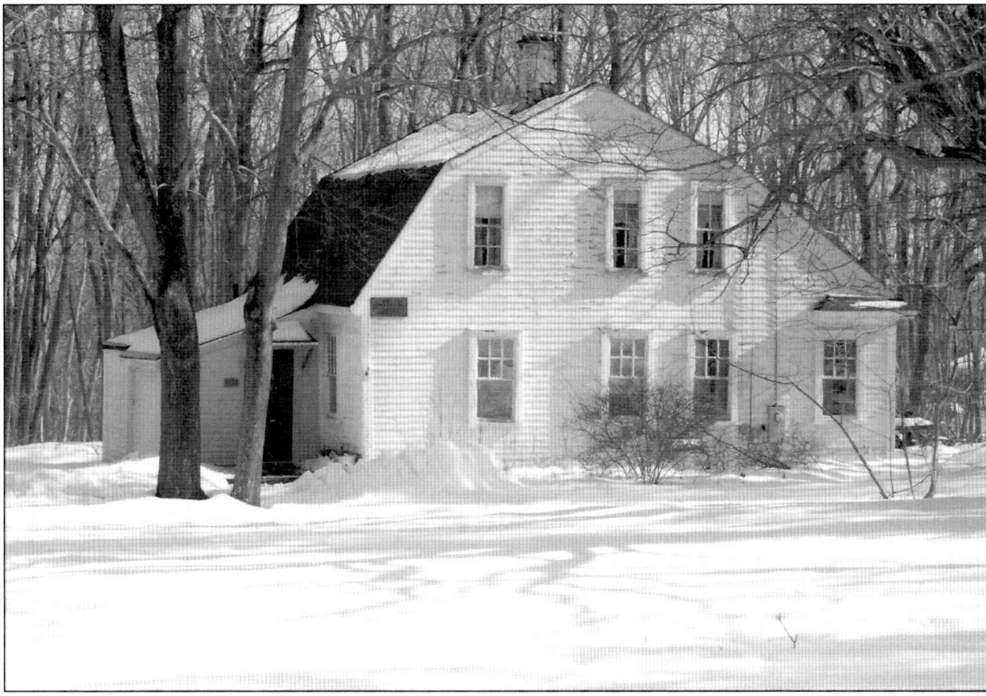

The Carr-LeValley homestead, named Mount Eagle, is located at 42 Fairview Avenue. It is the oldest house in West Warwick, built in 1722 by the Carr family. After Sarah Carr inherited the house, she married Rev. George Pigot. Later, he would trade houses with his friend Peter LeValley in Marblehead, Massachusetts. (Courtesy of Gerard Tellier Jr.)

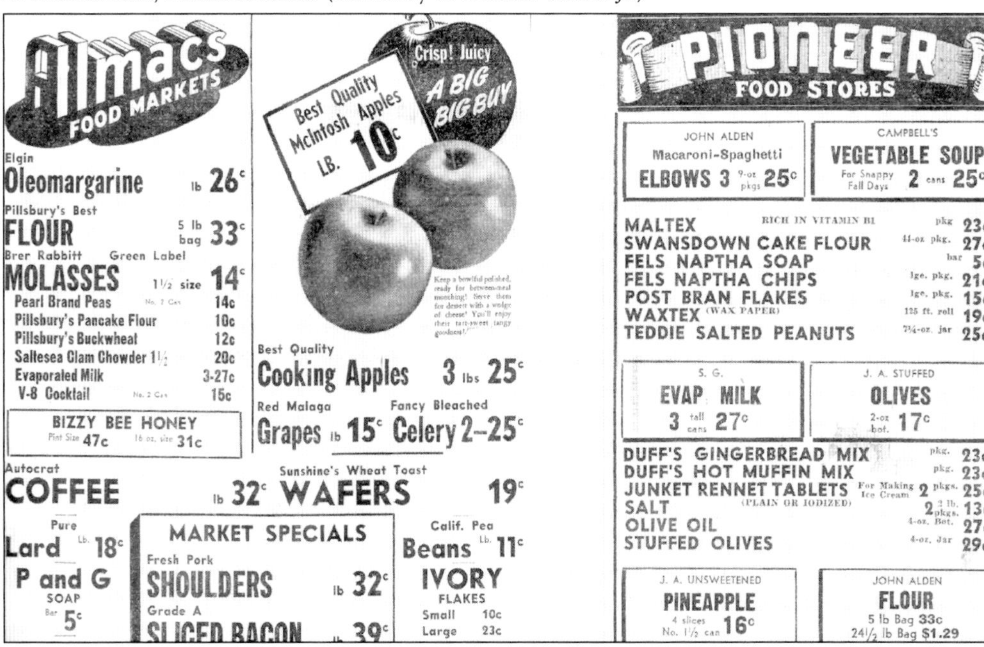

These advertisements are from the September 30, 1943, *Evening Bulletin*. There was a war going on, and many Americans had victory gardens. The government encouraged everyone to grow their own food because of the shortages as a supplement to food stamps. (Author's collection.)

Four

Lippitt and Clyde

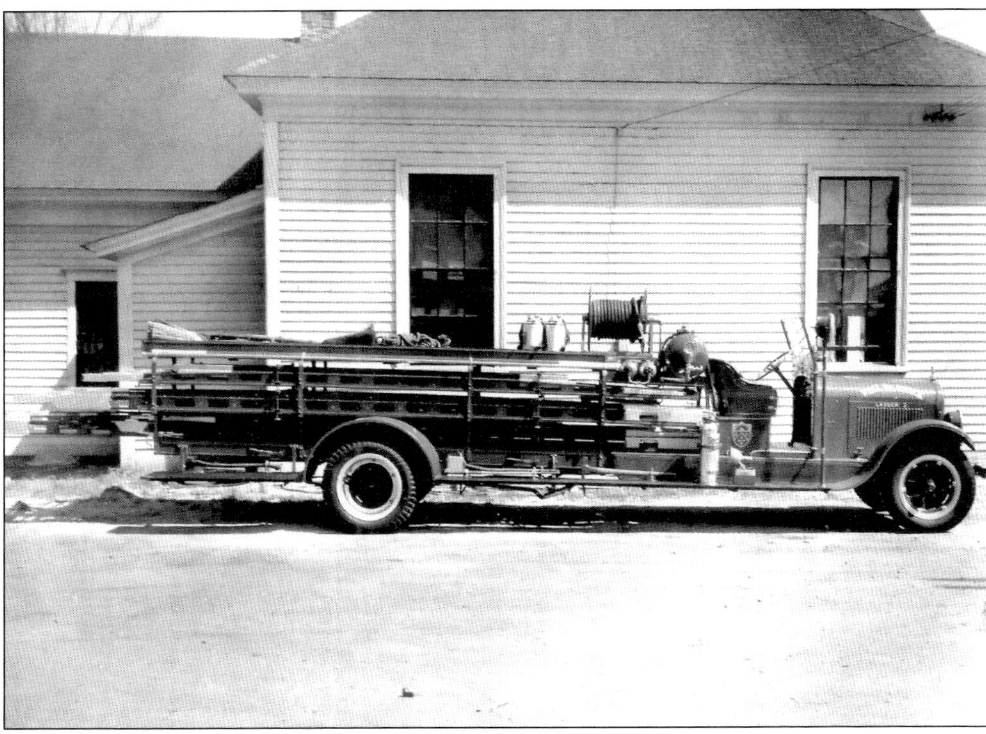

This 1929 Reo fire truck was originally assigned to the Phenix Fire Department. Later, it was transferred to Station No. 2 in Lippitt Village. The following verse is from "Dedicated to Firemen," written by Helen O. Larson at the age of 70: "When the siren starts screeching, they're once more on the go / They jump on the trucks, there's another fire we know." (Courtesy of Gerard Tellier Jr.)

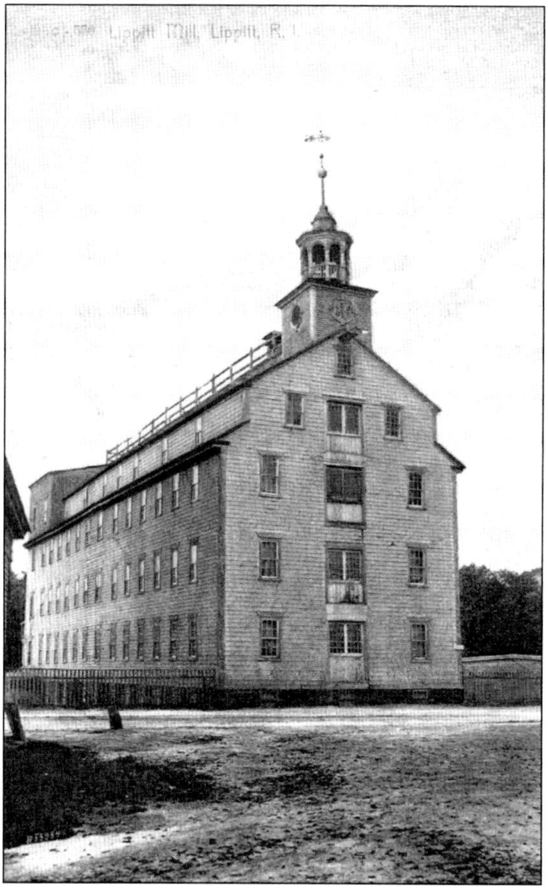

The Lippitt Mill was built in 1809. Today, it is in danger of being razed. The last company to occupy the building vacated it in 2012. The future does not look good for this 200-year-old landmark. (Courtesy of Lawrence G. Soucy.)

This 1985 photograph shows Lippitt Dam. SS Peter and Paul Church is visible on the hill on Highland Street. Just to the left, not visible in this photograph, was the Phenix Mill, destroyed by fire in 2005. (Courtesy of Lawrence G. Soucy.)

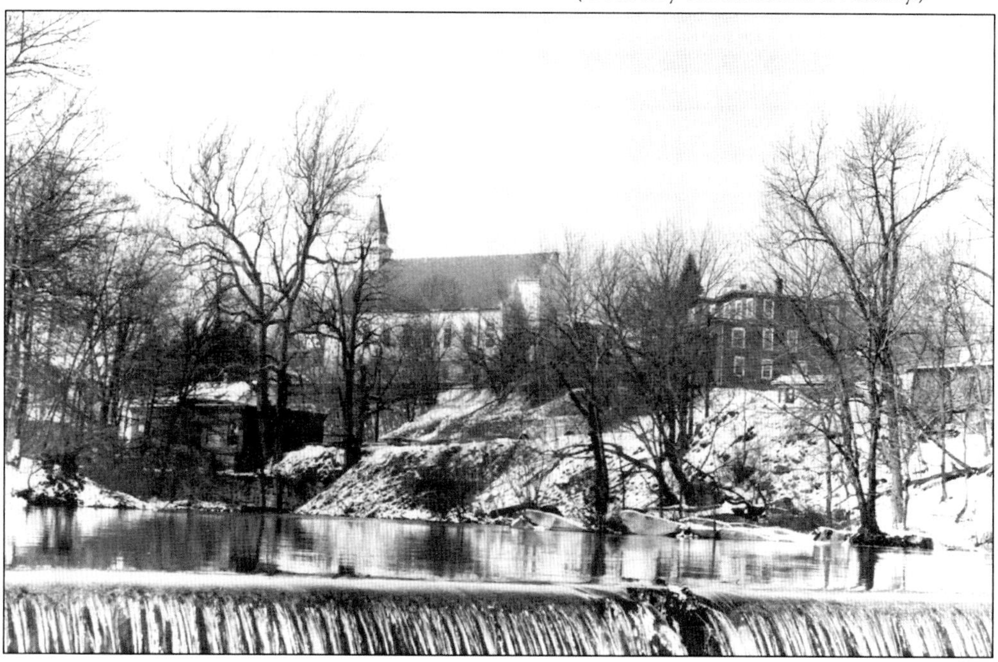

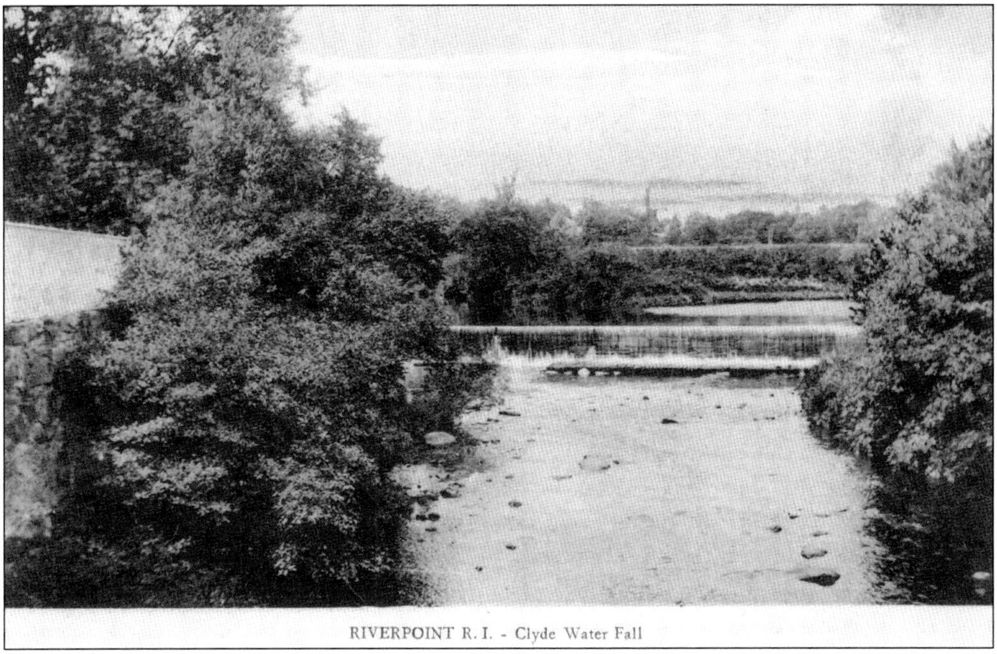

This postcard shows the Clyde Dam from the Clyde Bridge. It also shows the Pawtuxet Valley Railroad Bridge in the distance. Behind the bridge, the smokestack of the Phenix Mill is visible. At the time of this photograph, the area was known as River Point. The dam no longer exists.

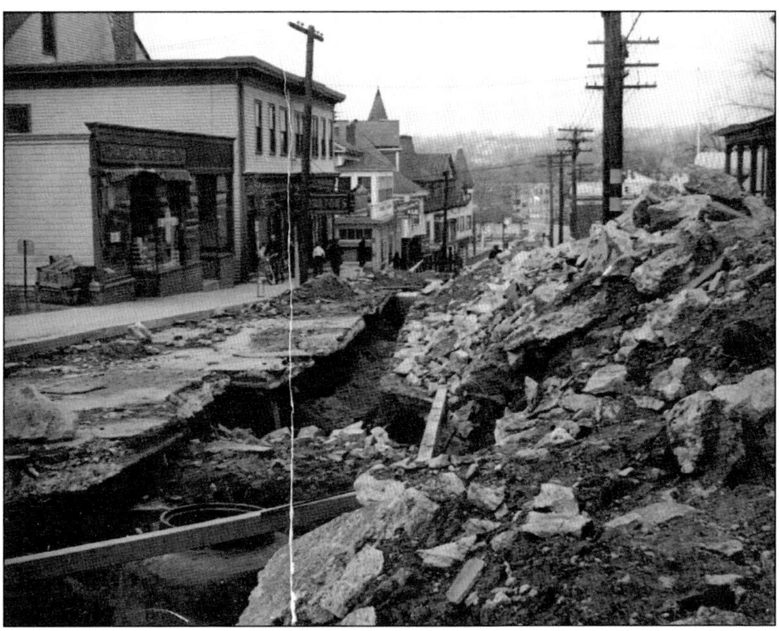

The sewer line was laid through Main Street in Clyde in the 1930s. Thornton's Theatre marquis can be seen on the left. Peeking above the rooflines is the steeple of the Clyde Hotel, also seen on the next page.

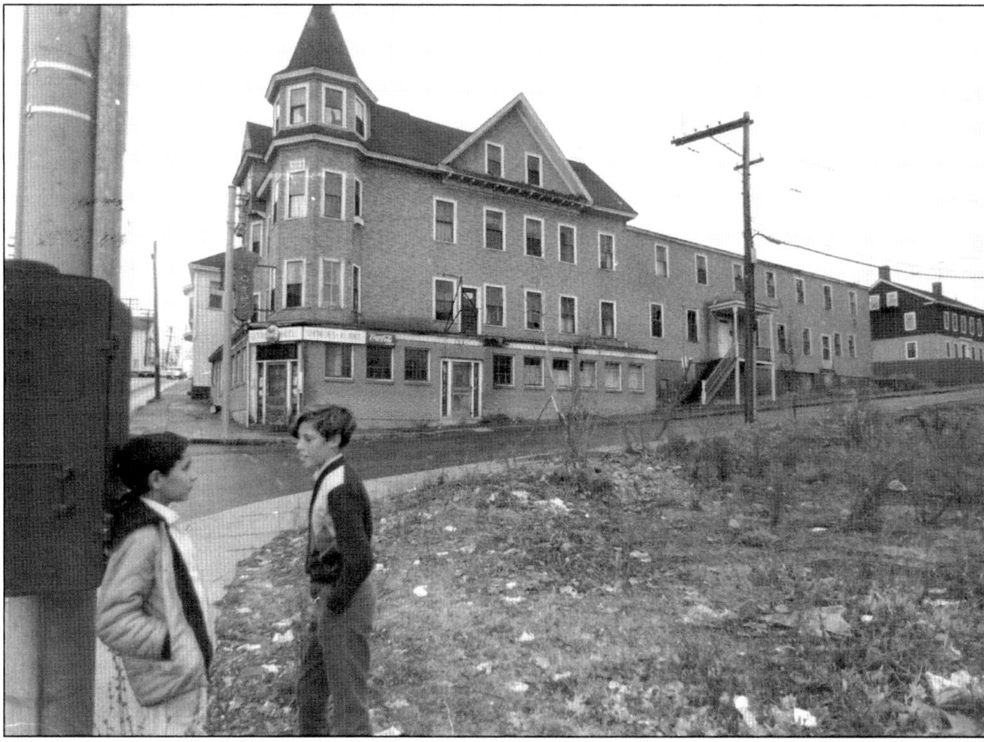

The Clyde Hotel, built in 1892, is still standing. However, the J. Flanagan Building to the right of the boys has been razed. The photograph below was taken before Allen Street was renamed Main Street, after the trolley came through (1894), and after Thornton's Theatre was rebuilt and opened in 1911. A fire had destroyed the Thornton's Opera House on Thanksgiving Day in 1910.

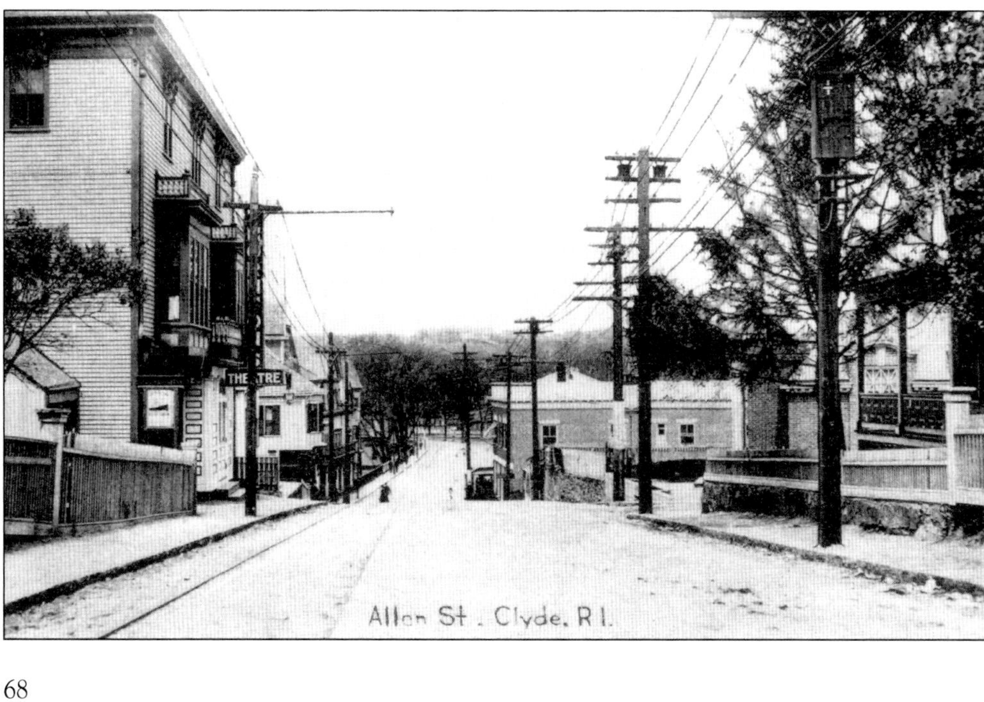

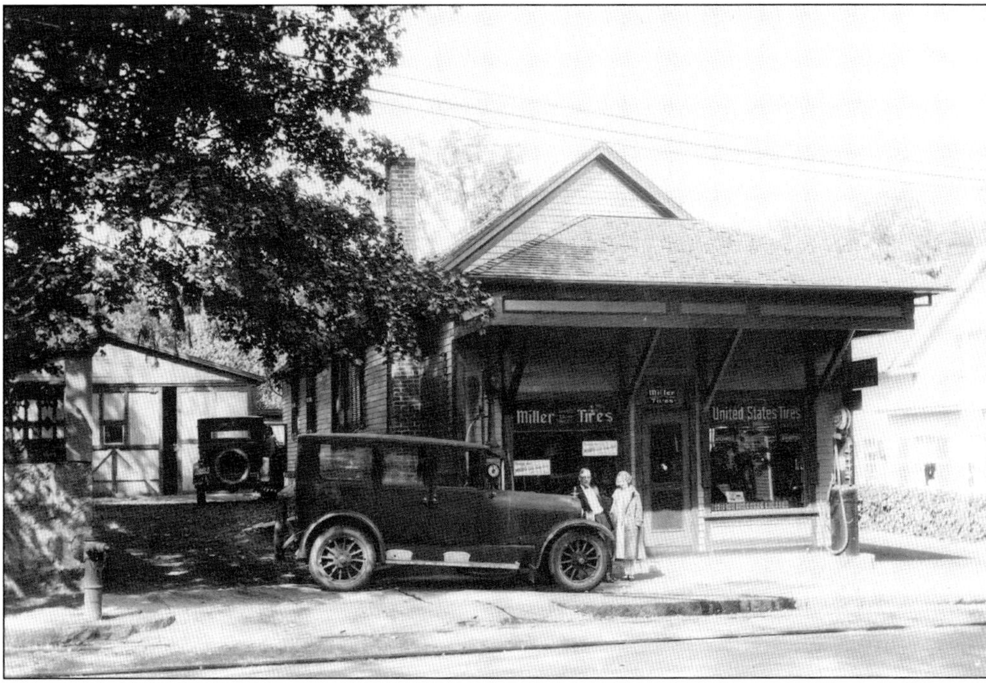

An 1889 map of Clyde locates the A.W. Knight Store on Allen Street (now Main Street) at the corner of Woodside Avenue, situated to the right. Both of these 1931 photographs show A.W. Knight's son Harold Knight with his wife, Olive. Above, the store advertises Miller Tires and United States Tires in its windows. Note the gas pump to the right. Below, the advertisement to the left suggests it offered Mobil Gasoline along with Mobiloil. Harold and Olive pose for a photograph in their office area. (Both, courtesy of Donald Carpenter.)

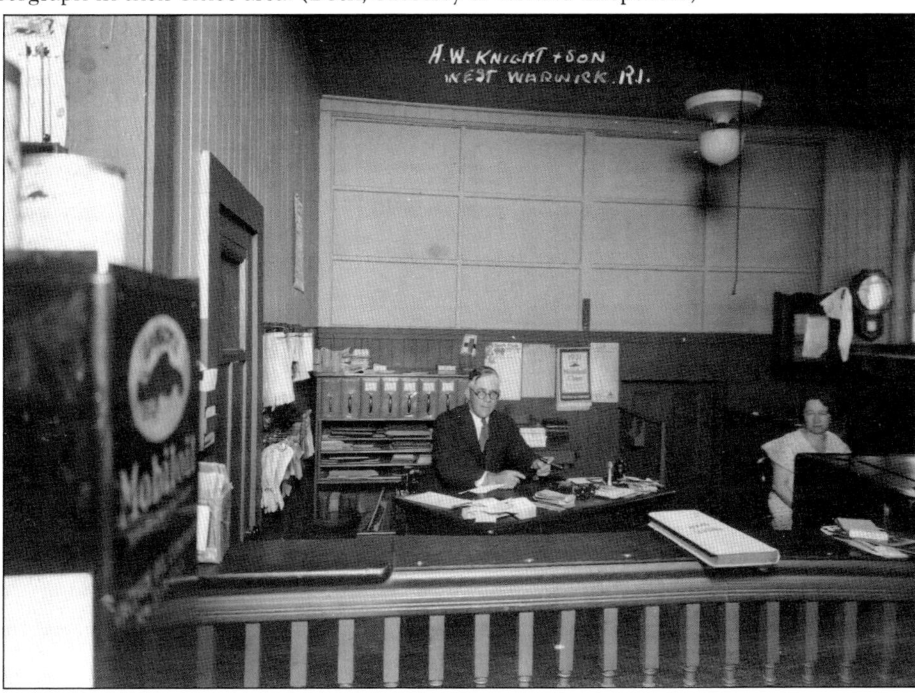

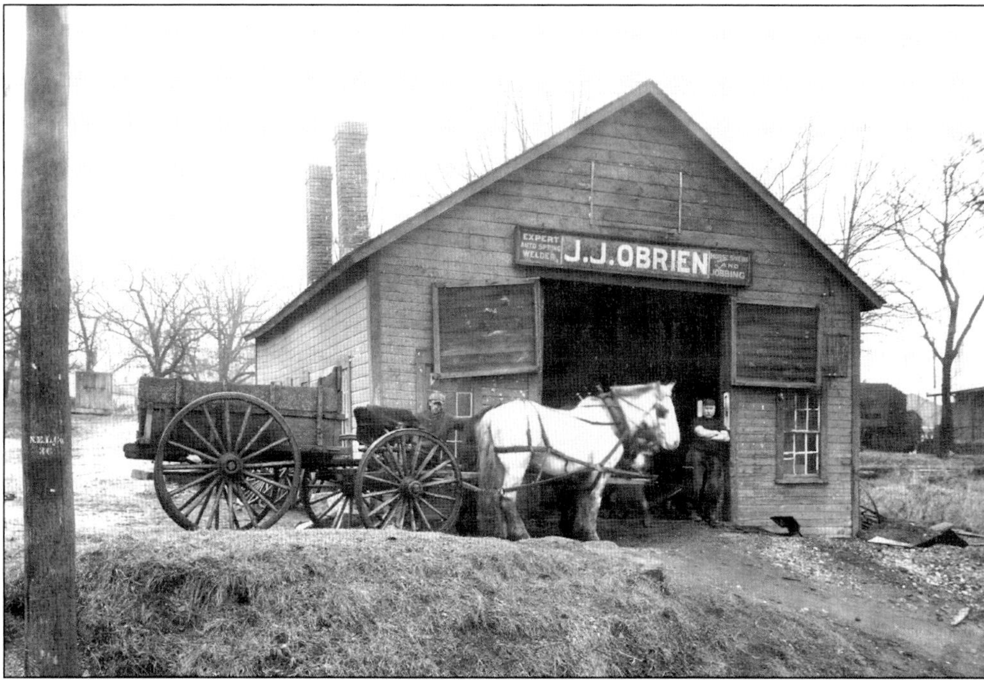

J.J. O'Brien's place of business was located somewhere in Clyde. The left side of the sign states, "Expert Auto Spring Welding," while the right says, "Horse Shoeing and Jobbing." O'Brien may be the man leaning in the doorway as a client watches from behind the horse. (Courtesy of Richard Siembab.)

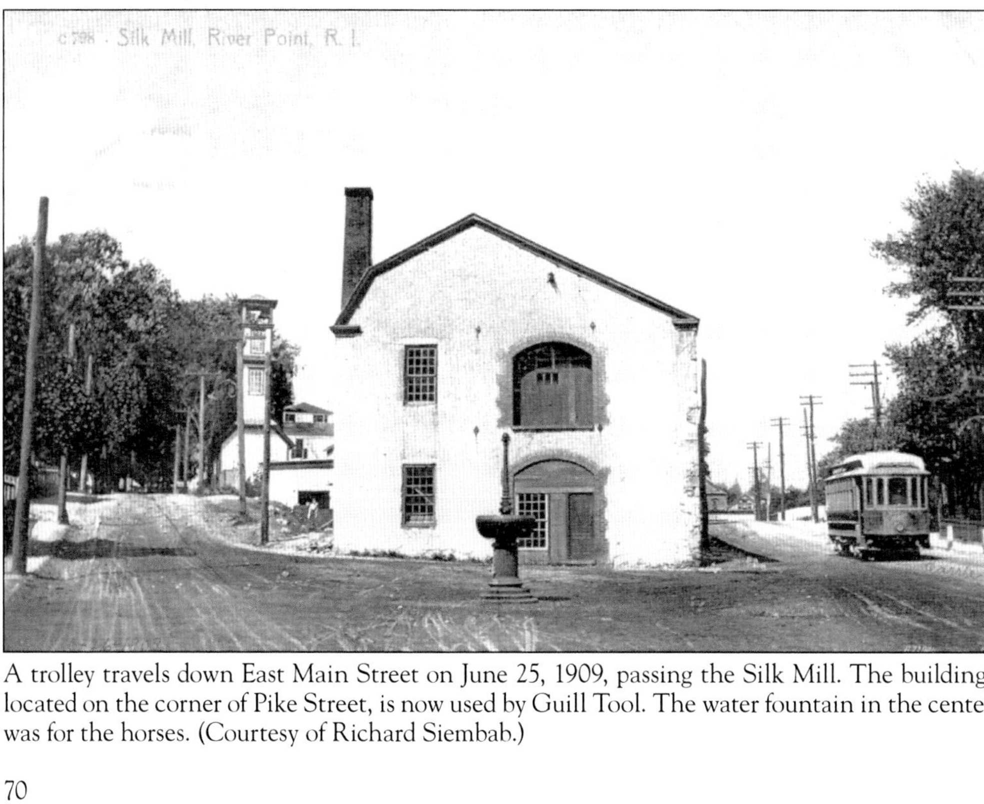

A trolley travels down East Main Street on June 25, 1909, passing the Silk Mill. The building, located on the corner of Pike Street, is now used by Guill Tool. The water fountain in the center was for the horses. (Courtesy of Richard Siembab.)

Five

RIVER POINT AND WESTCOTT

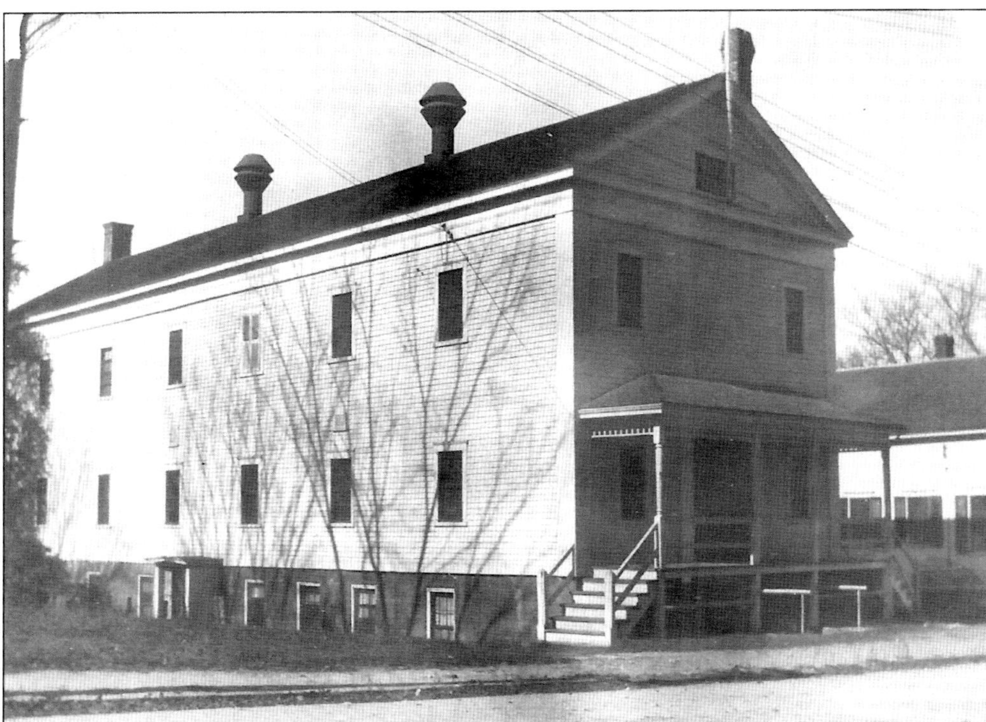

The home of the Independent Order of Odd Fellows (IOOF) was located in River Point. The command of the IOOF is to "visit the sick, relieve the distressed, bury the dead, and educate the orphan." The worldwide organization is still in existence today. (Courtesy of Donald Carpenter.)

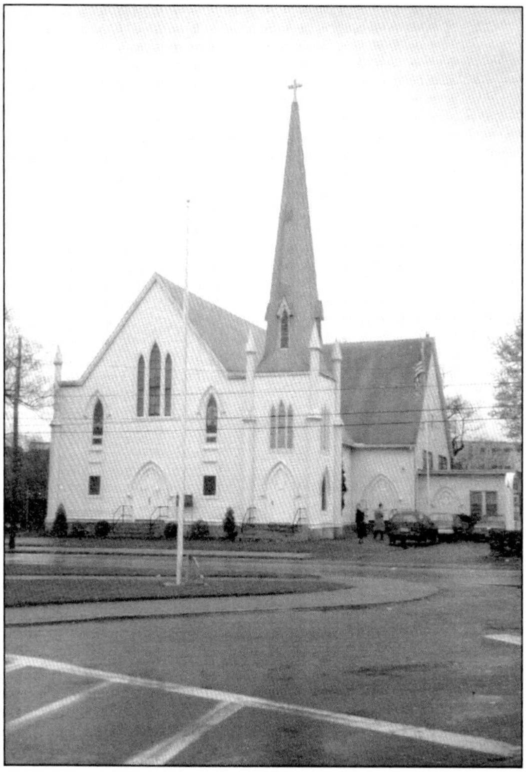

This 2012 photograph of the River Point Congregational Church, built in 1847, exhibits the Gothic Revival style and a very tall, flared spire. In 1849, a council met and organized the First Congregational Church of Warwick. (Author's collection.)

Below, seven women and seven men are lined up in front of the McCaughery Confectionary Company building, located on Allen Street, River Point (now Main Street, Clyde). (Courtesy of Richard Siembab.)

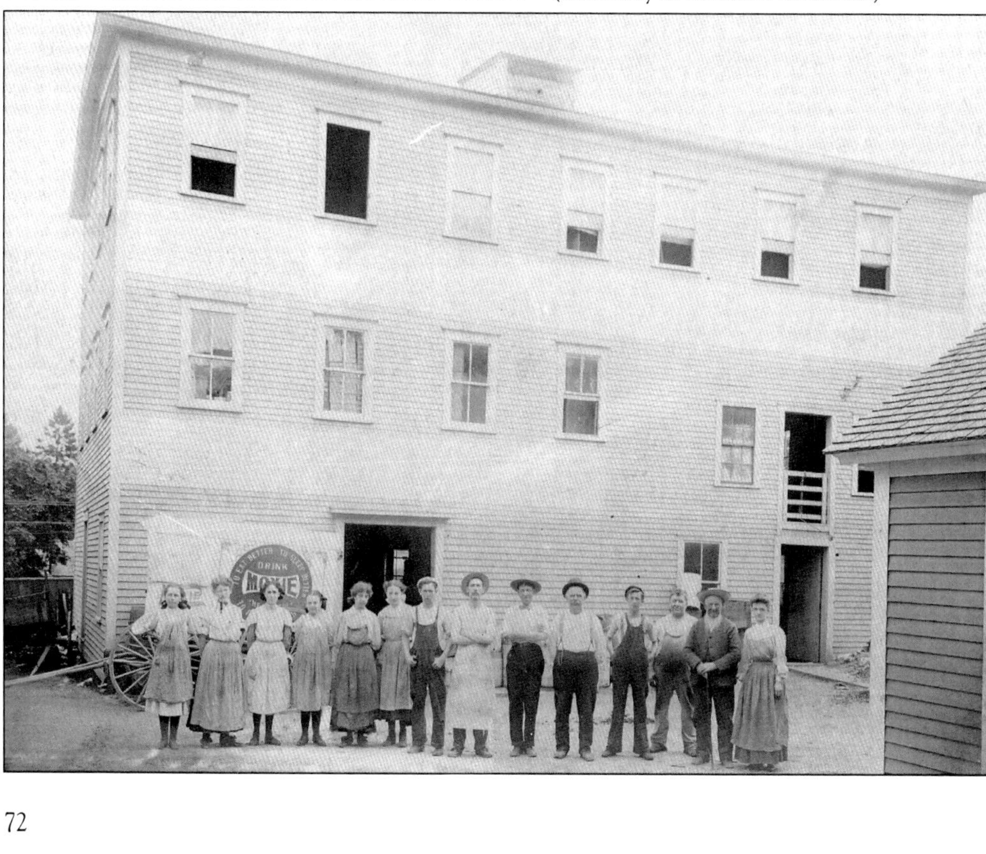

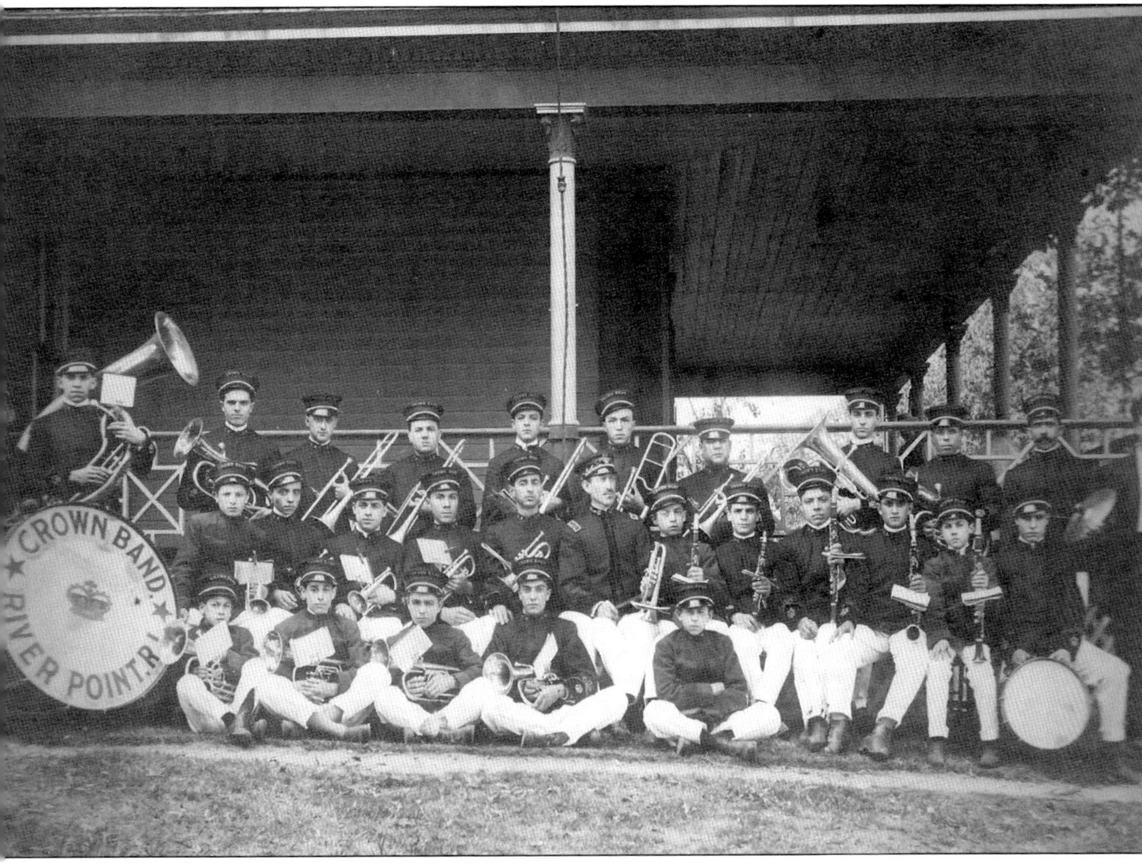

The Crown Band of River Point is gathered in front of the River Point Community House before 1928. The John F. Horgan Elementary School, built on this lot in 1928, can be seen in *West Warwick* on page 119. The marching band members are, from left to right, (first row) Manuel Mattias, Joseph Mello, Antonio Cambra, Manuel Fontes, and Manuel W. Simas; (second row) Anthony Mattias, Louis Brazil, Manuel Ray, Molly Couto, Anthony Mello, band conductor ? Gilbert, Manuel Silva, ? Cabral, Manuel Ferreira, unidentified, Joseph Ray, and unidentified; (third row) Manuel Amaral, ? Caplet, Joseph Miller, Frank Ray, Samuel Miller, Anthony Raposa, Antonio Couto, John Perry, Jesse Miller, Michael Mattias, Joaquin Mello, and Antonio Miller. The following verses are from "When the Parade Is Over" by Helen O. Larson at the age of 80: "They're waving American flags, they're shouting welcome home / But when the parade is over, will they be left alone. When the parade is over, don't put them out of your minds / Only by the grace of God, one of those soldiers could have been a son of mine."

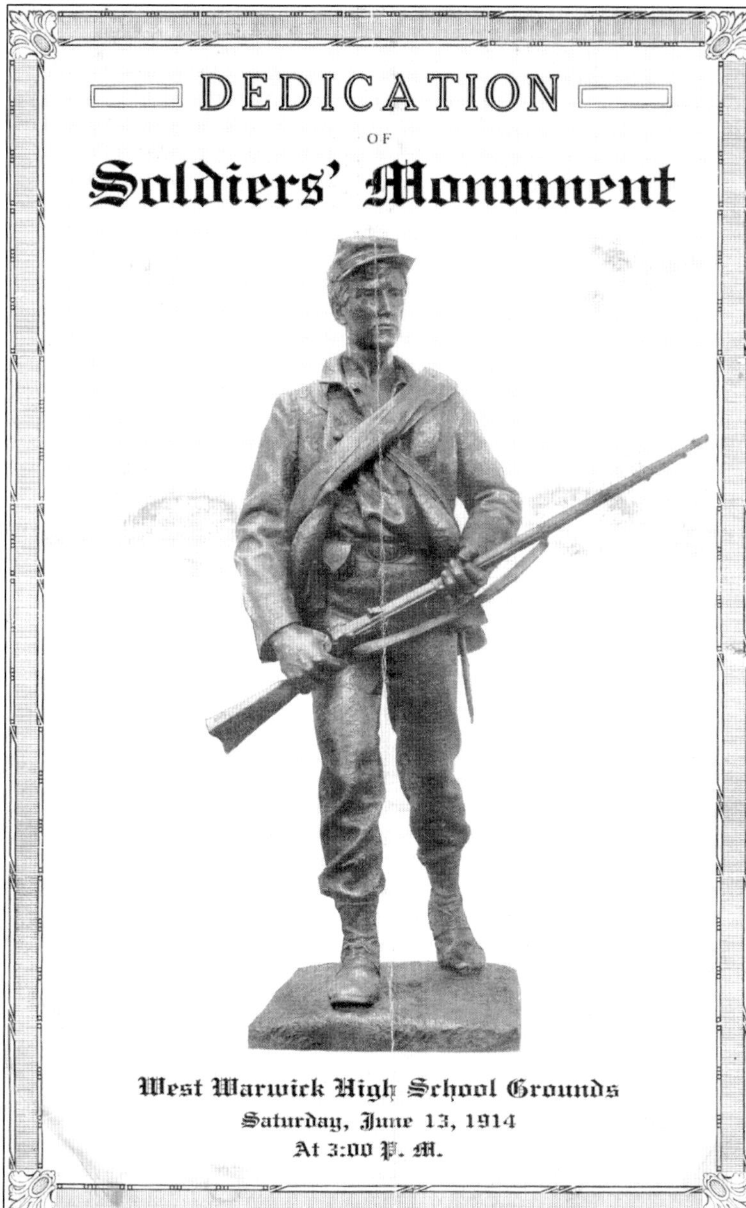

In 1904, Cmdr. Arthur W. Deane, McGregor Post No. 14, Grand Army of the Republic, had a dream to create a bronze monument of a Union soldier of the Civil War to honor the fallen soldiers of the Pawtuxet Valley. He was the first chairman of the monument committee, in charge of raising the funds needed to make his dream a reality. He passed away in 1909 before the committee had enough funds to place an order for the statue with the Gorham Company in Providence in 1913. This program was passed out at the dedication ceremonies of the unveiling of "Jerry" on June 13, 1914. The program ended with this: "With the placing of the statue in position on this giant boulder that seems to have been designed by nature for this purpose, the work of the Monument Committee is at an end. The figure of the soldier, virile in every line and feature, with feet firmly planted on the living rock, will stand for generations as the type of noble manhood consecrated to the highest ideals."

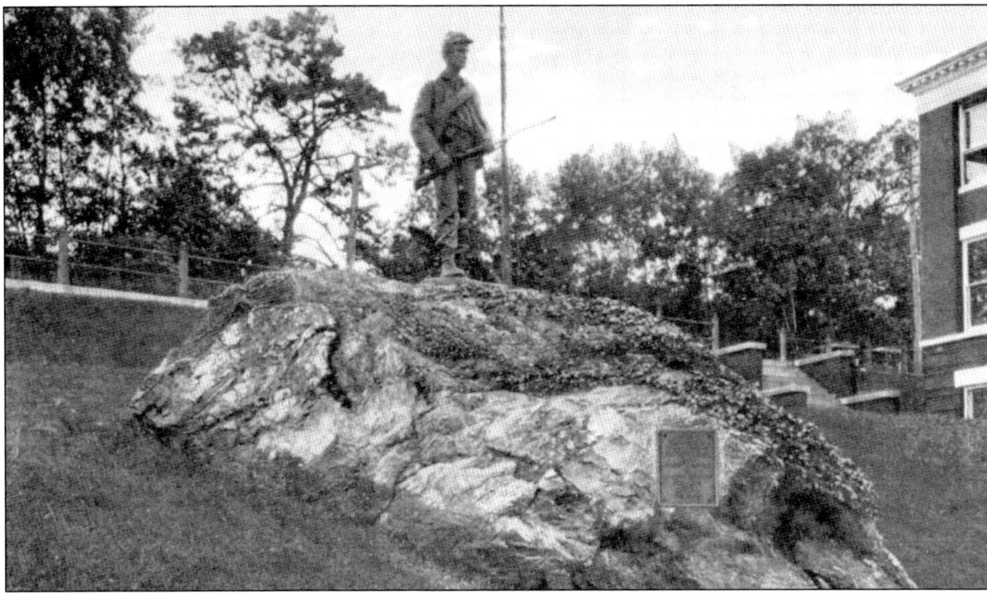

Jerry B. Foster headed the committee, which chose the Gorham Company to craft the statue. Theodora Alice Ruggles Kitson of the Gorham Company created it. The students from the high school used to eat their lunch on the lawn around the base of the boulder where he proudly stood. They soon began to affectionately call the statue "Jerry," and it has stuck. This postcard was mailed September 1920. This high school (visible in both photographs) was closed when a new one was built at the top of the hill on Factory Street. On June 13, 1967, Jerry was relocated there (see page 76). This was not good news for Jerry. At the new location, he was spray painted by vandals, then repaired. Within a year, he was tipped over, broken, and repaired again. Since an intensive publicity campaign, there has been little vandalism. (Above, courtesy of Richard Siembab.)

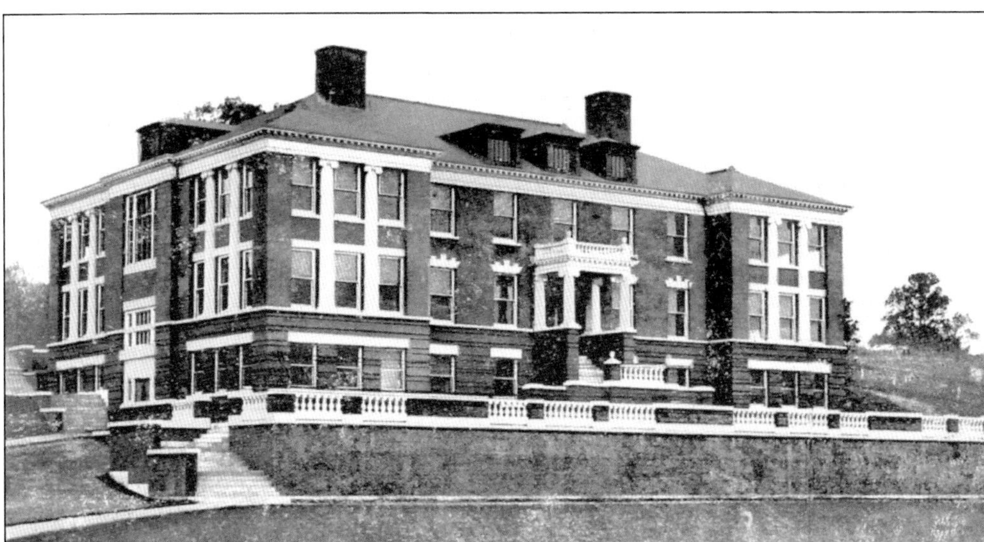

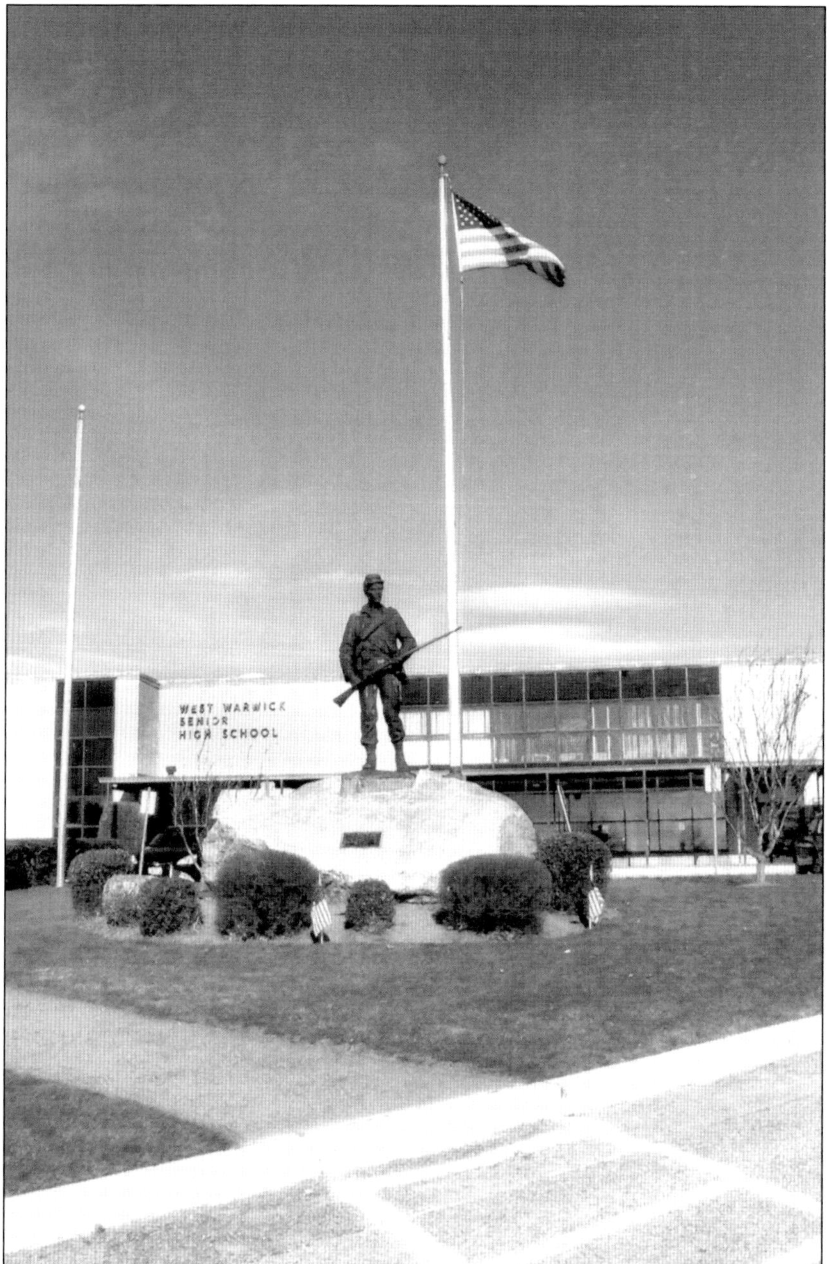

In 1989, Dick Hughes, a radio talk show host for WKRI, was disturbed and saddened with the deplorable appearance of Jerry, who was splattered with sun-baked paint. Dick contacted secretary-treasurer Amby Hughes of the West Warwick Veterans Council with his concerns. Hughes, in turn, viewed the statue and brought the matter before the town council. Mayor J. Michael Levesque declared that the town did not have the funds to take on this extensive project. Robert O. Pare, president of the Centreville National Bank, stepped forward and made a personal appeal to the board of directors. They, in turn, voted to guarantee the cost of refurbishing Jerry. The work was done at the Paul King Foundry in Johnston, Rhode Island. The rededication ceremony took place on April 7, 1990. This photograph was taken in 2011. (Author's collection.)

Six

Natick and Arctic

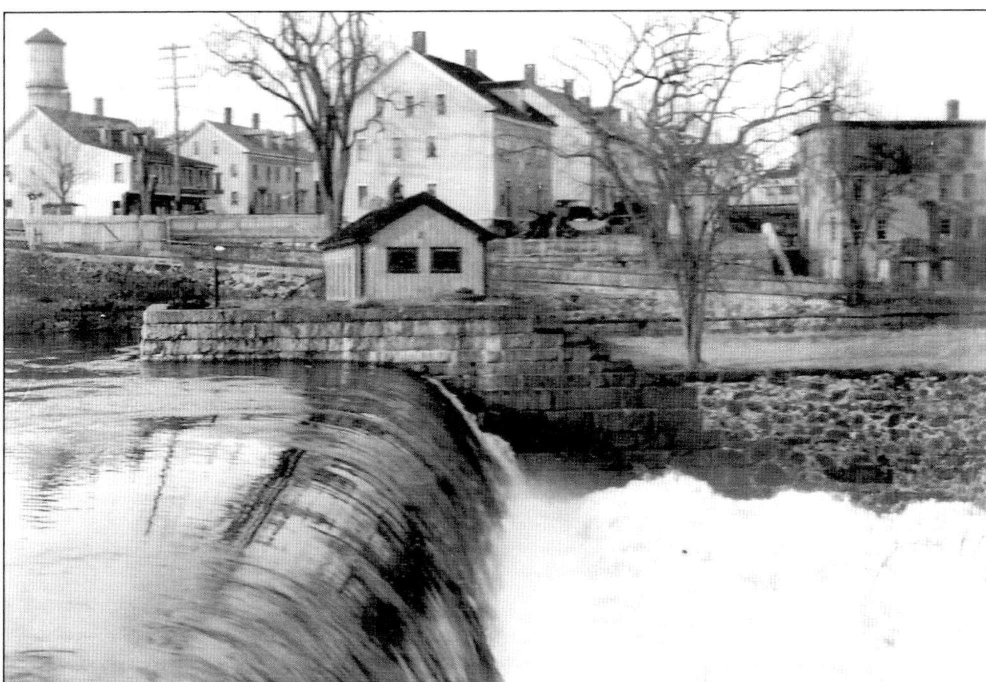

This photograph of Natick Dam was taken during the flood on March 19, 1936, at 4:05 p.m. Part of the Natick Mill Complex can be seen on the right. The water tower for the mill's sprinkler system is located at the top of Prospect Hill, seen to the left. (Courtesy of Providence Water.)

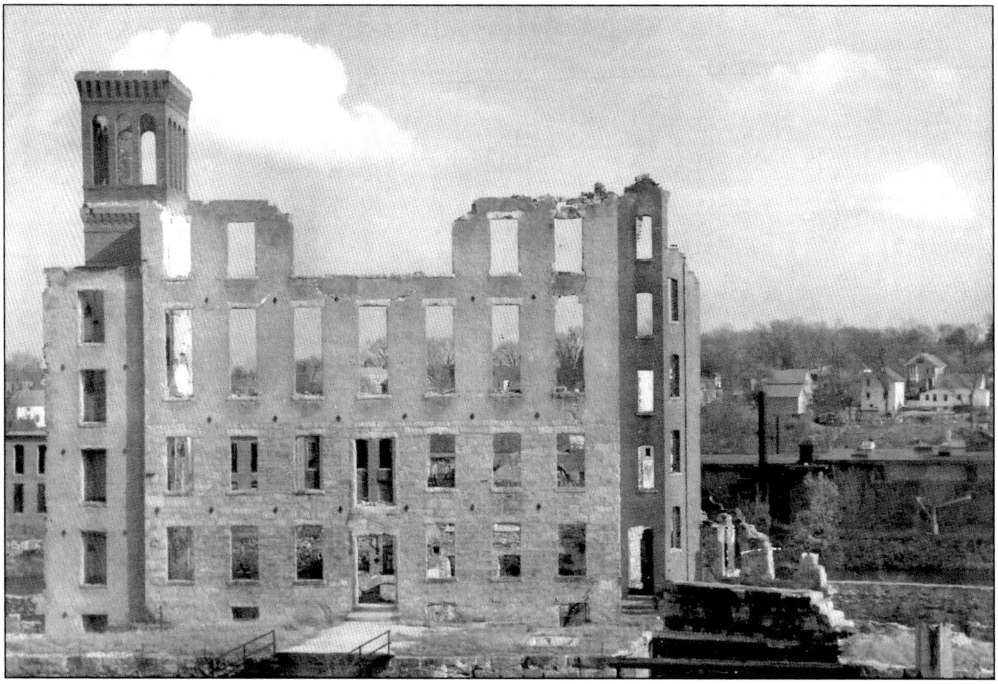

After the devastating fire on the evening of July 4, 1941, the Natick Mill Complex was an eerie sight; even this structure was later torn down. B.B. and R. Knight bought the mill from William Sprague in 1882 and owned it at the time of the fire. Below, the mill is visible from the Warwick side of the Pawtuxet River, looking at the back of the mill. The original mill was built in 1807 with more buildings added later. The mills ran continuously until they were sold at auction in 1935. In the foreground are the tracks of the Hartford, Providence & Fishkill Railroad.

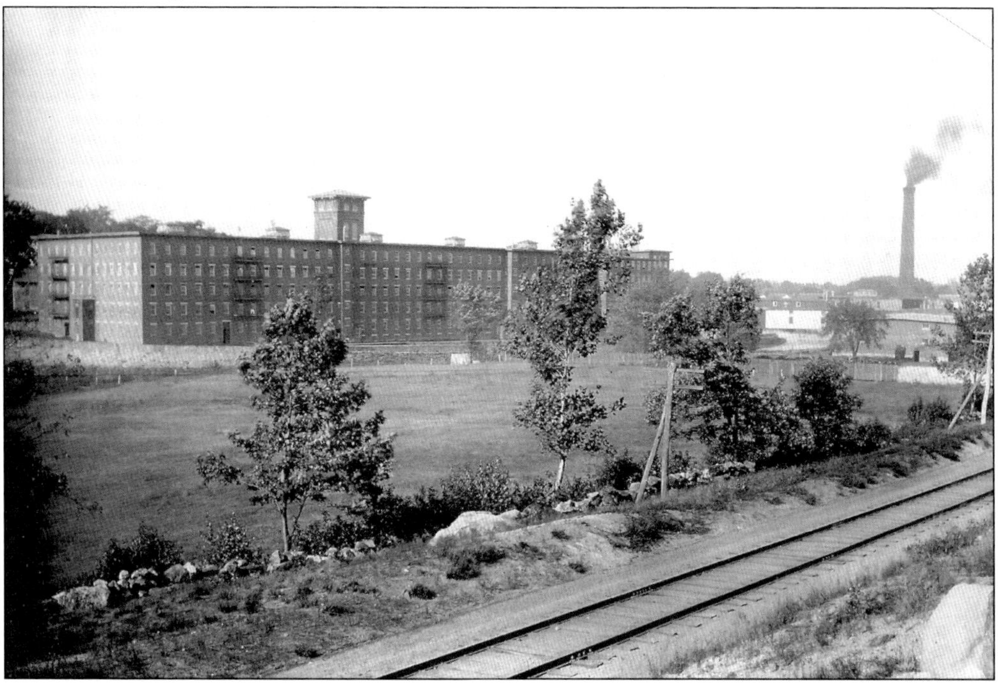

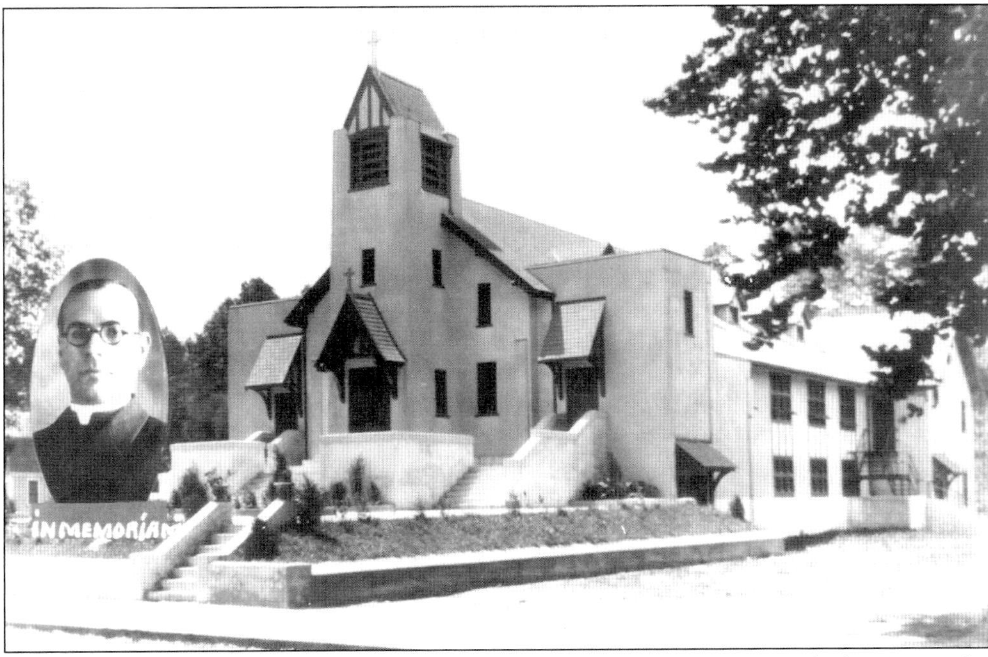

The dedication of Sacred Heart Church, designed in Spanish Mission style, took place September 2, 1929. Fr. Achille Tirocchi, pictured here, was the driving force behind the new church. He was appointed to be the first pastor and continued in the position until he passed away suddenly in 1935. (Courtesy of Lawrence G. Soucy.)

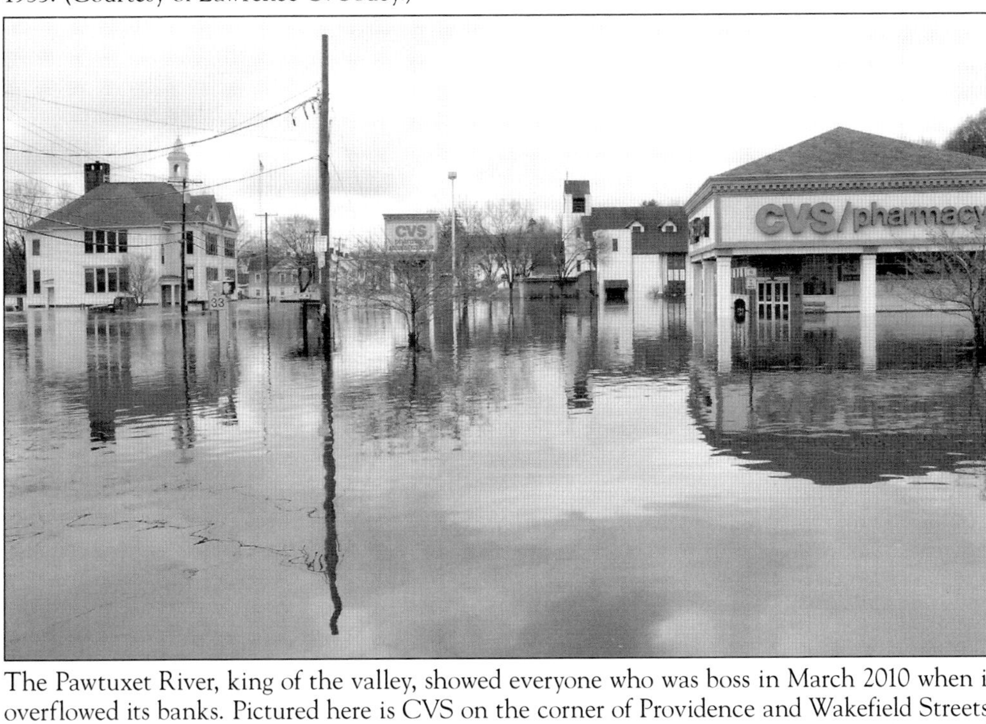

The Pawtuxet River, king of the valley, showed everyone who was boss in March 2010 when it overflowed its banks. Pictured here is CVS on the corner of Providence and Wakefield Streets. Behind CVS is Sacred Heart Church, which was also flooded. Across the street is the Natick School, built in the early 1900s. (Courtesy of Gerard Tellier Jr.)

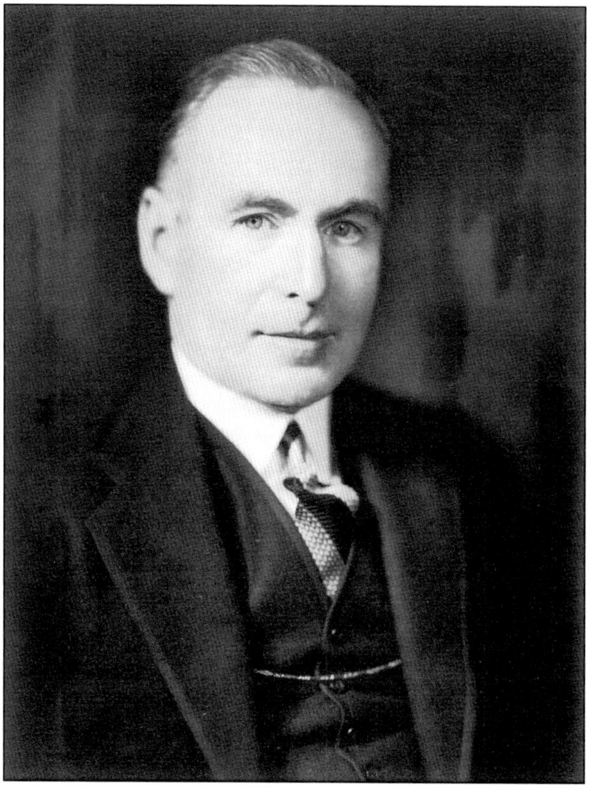

This 1937 photograph shows Gov. Robert E. Quinn, who held the office from 1937 to 1939. In 1941, he was appointed to a Superior Court judgeship. In 1951, he was named chief judge of a new US Court of Military Appeals. He retired from this position in 1975, the same year he passed away.

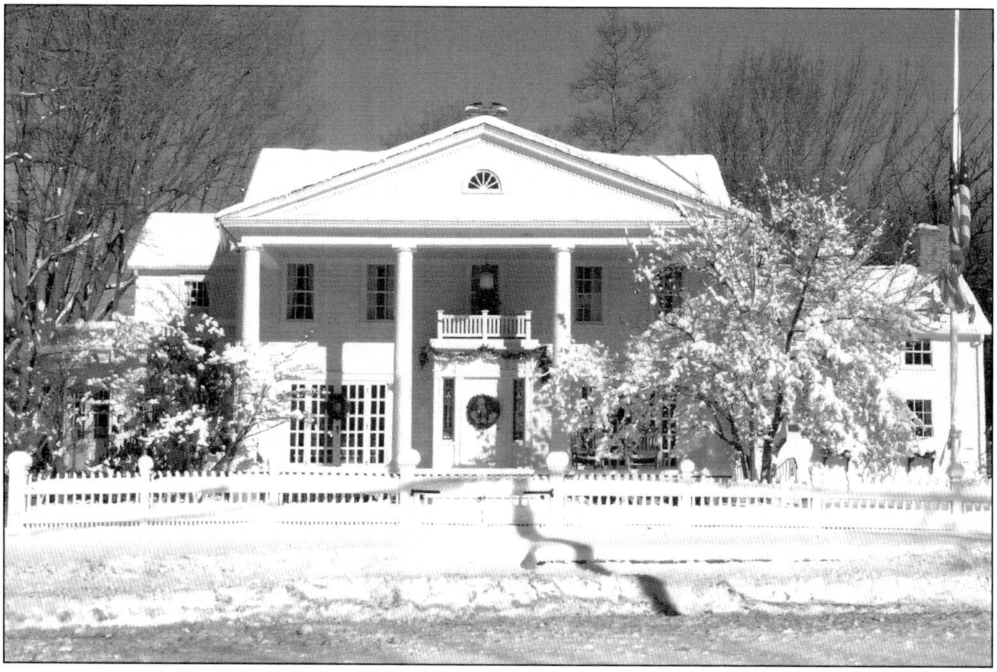

Governor Quinn's house, pictured in 2011, was built in 1740 and was originally part of the Burlingame Farm. Sitting on top of a hill, the Burlingames named it West Winds. Their family cemetery is across the road at 300 Wakefield Street. (Courtesy of Gerard Tellier Jr.)

This War Memorial was built by the Works Progress Administration between 1935 and 1937. It commemorates those who died in World War I. A bronze plaque was added later in memory of those who lost their lives in WWII. The following verses are from "The Unknown Soldier" by Helen O. Larson: "Maybe he was a father, of a beautiful baby boy / Broken hearted when he left him, he might have been his pride and joy. And when the war was ended, and the boys were coming home / He was lying in a grave, which was marked unknown. So let us bow our heads this day, and say a little pray / For the soldier who lies in a grave, for only God knows who's there." The back of the mill (sans the tower) is seen to the right of the monument, and pictured below is the front of Arctic Mill, built in 1852. (Right, author's collection; below, courtesy of Richard Siembab.)

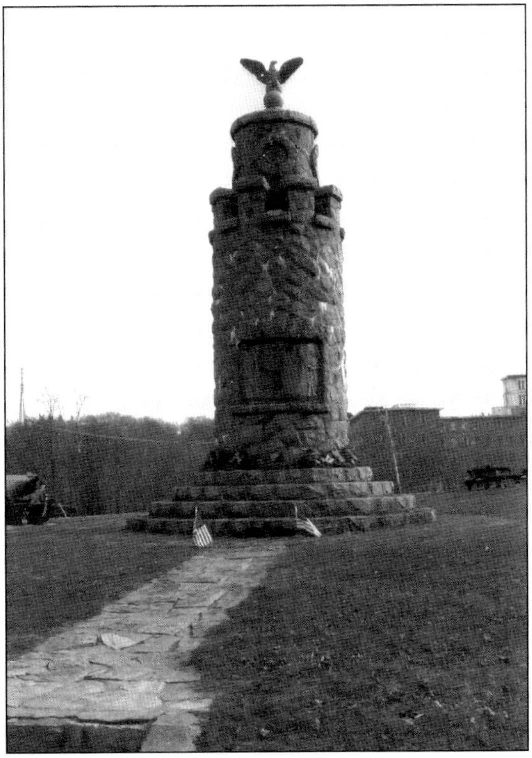

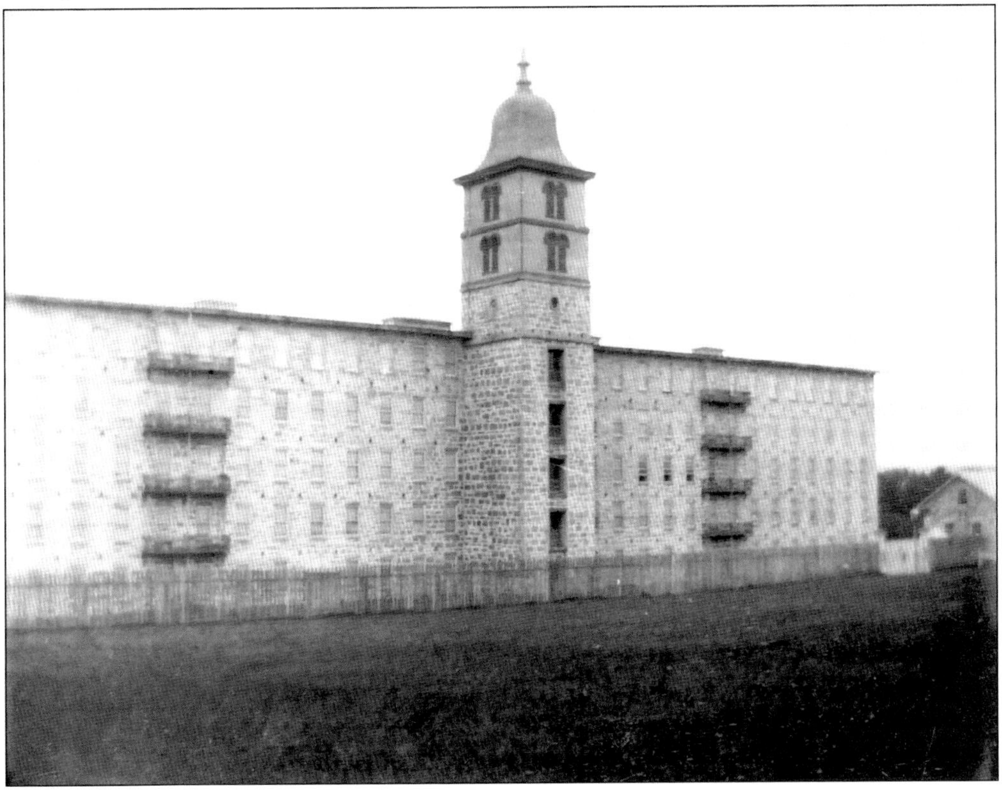

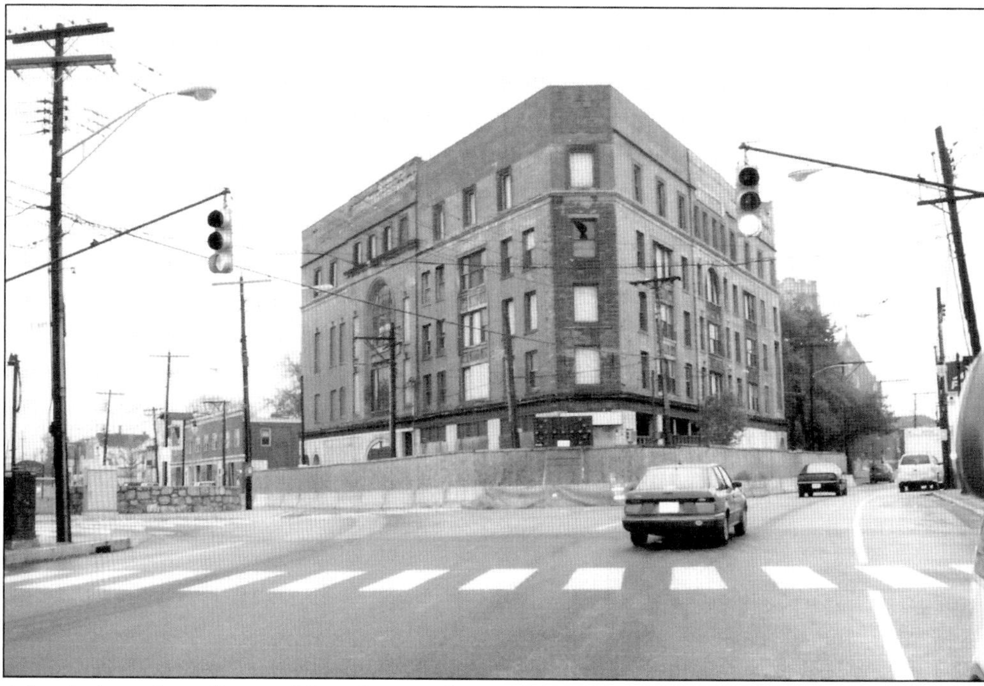

A book about the valley would not be complete without a two-page spread on the lonely Majestic Building. Joseph Archambault had it built in 1901, after a 1900 fire burned down his previous building. He had it built of brick, concrete, and steel so it would never burn down again. He was absolutely right in his thinking, and surely, he never expected anyone to knock it down, but here it sits, at the beginning of May 1999, waiting for the wrecking ball. On May 9, the demolition began; however, it was not as easy as anticipated. Archambault's building did not even shudder when the ball first hit. It stood there defiantly, as if saying, "I'm not giving up easily, and you're going to have to work to get me down." The stunning artwork on the ceiling of the Majestic Theatre is shown below. (Both, courtesy of Gerard Tellier Jr.)

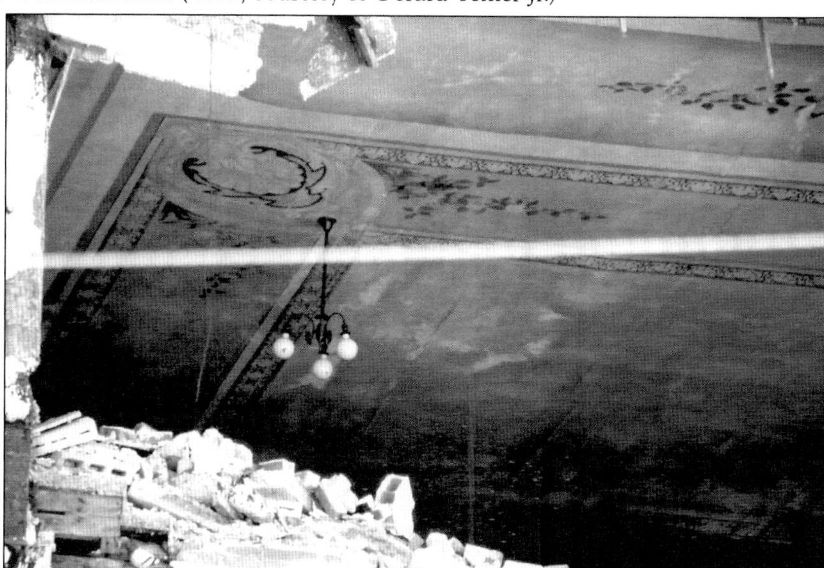

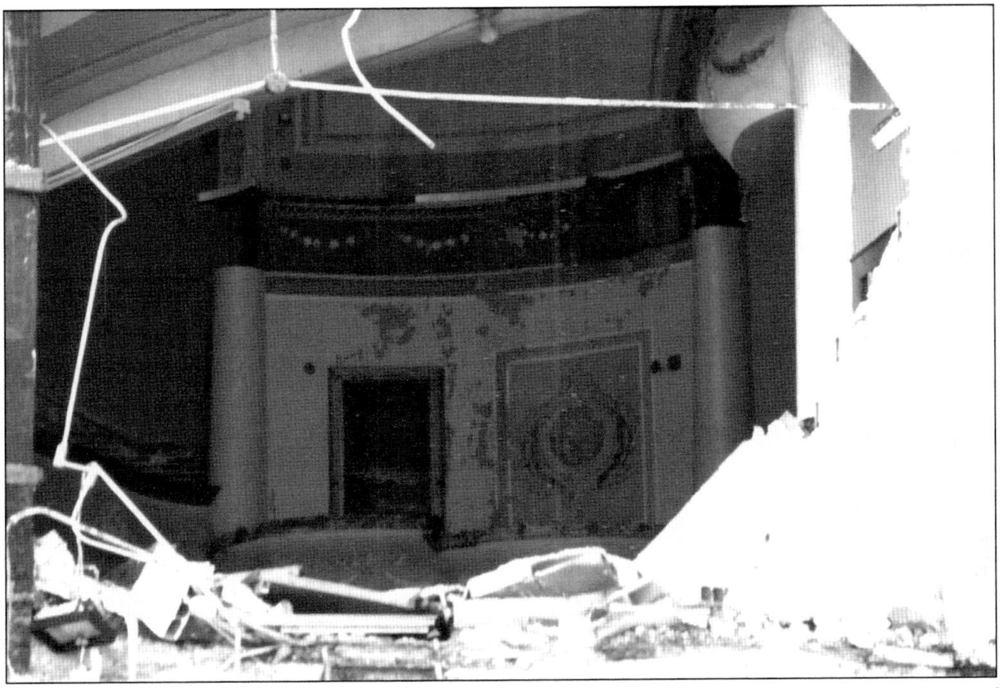

The photograph above shows one of the theater's private seating areas. Below, an open view of the theater screen and stage area is visible. The Majestic has been replaced by a gazebo and a bench that used to rest beside it. The following verses are from "The Man on the Bench" by Helen O. Larson: "I was walking along the street, I saw a man sitting on a bench one day / He had his head in his hands, as though he had bowed to pray. I said, may I sit down here, then we talked as I sat next to him / He told me he was depressed, and he couldn't take it in. He said the girl he was to marry, was killed by an auto one night / Now he would never see his sweetheart, dressed in bridal white." (Both, courtesy of Gerard Tellier Jr.)

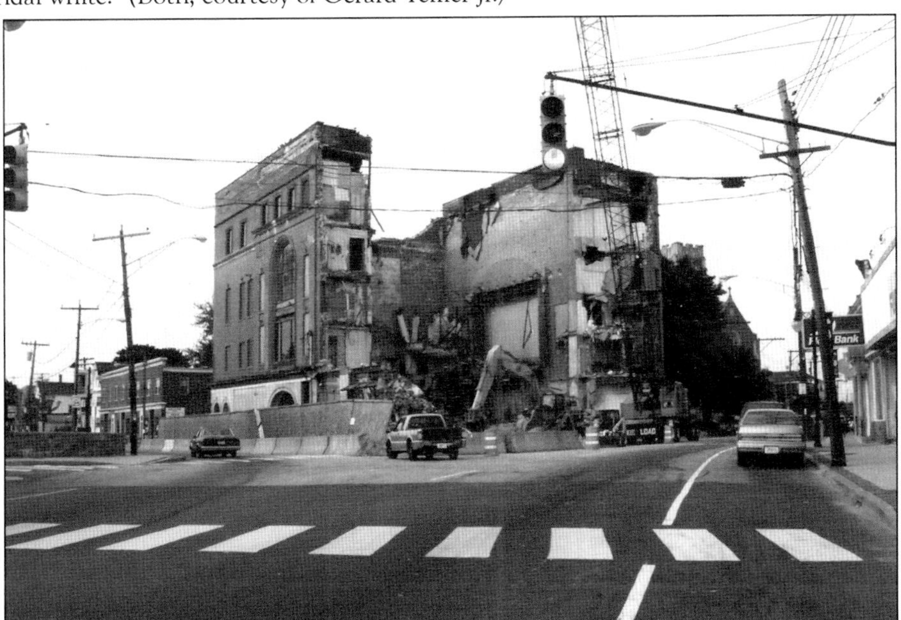

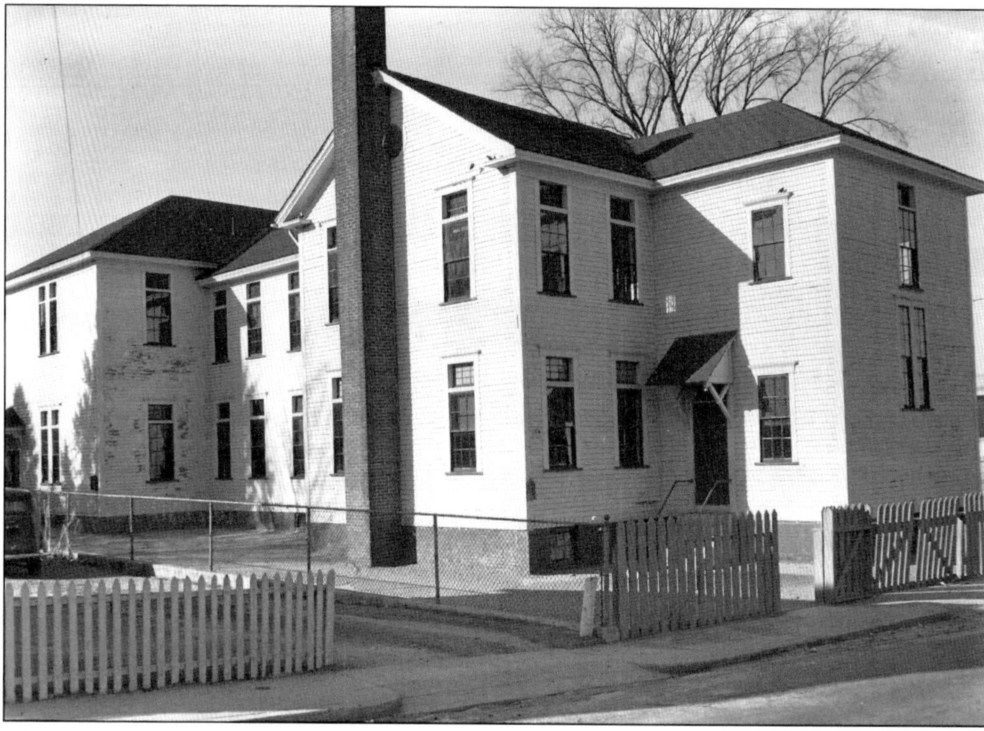

This 1936 photograph shows the Arctic Grammar School, located on Main Street next to Centreville Bank. It is now part of the bank's parking lot. This view is on Legion Way. This is the school Leo St. Onge Sr., pictured on the next page, graduated from on June 29, 1906.

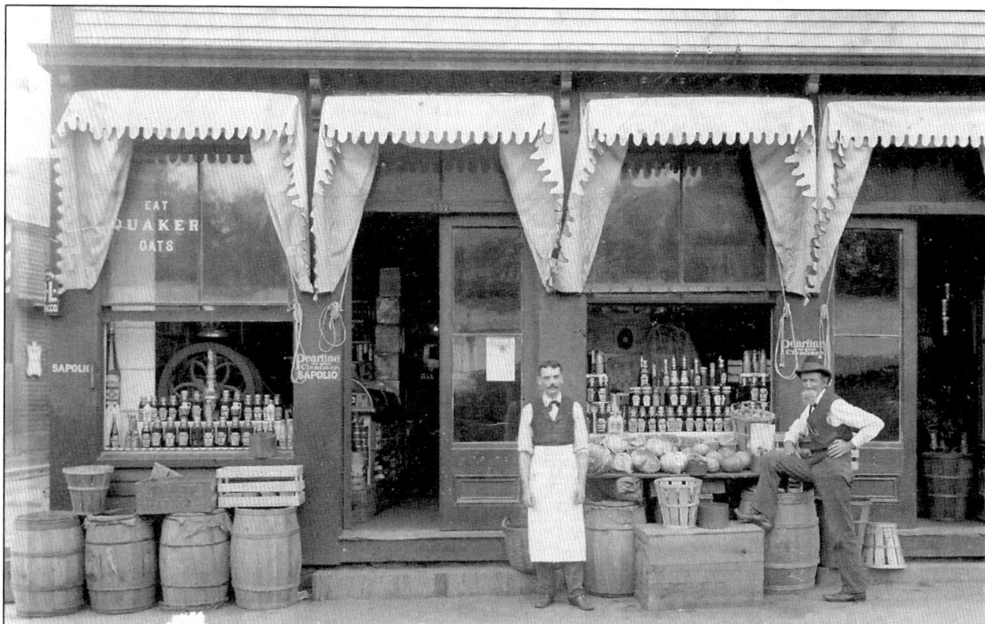

The Arctic Store's location is unknown. Note that no. 137 is visible over the left door, and over the right door is no. 155. The letters to the left of each doorway reads, "Pearline, the great cleanser, Sapolio."

Hormisdas J. Cartier constructed this building in 1890 for his jeweler, watchmaker, and optometrist business. He quickly built another building at 129–135 Washington Street and moved his business there. Dr. Charles E. Chagnon took over the building and began practicing medicine and filling prescriptions. He opened Chagnon's Family Drug Store and resided upstairs. When it closed in 1968, it was managed by Gerald Chagnon and Henry Lemoine. (Courtesy of Gary St. Onge.)

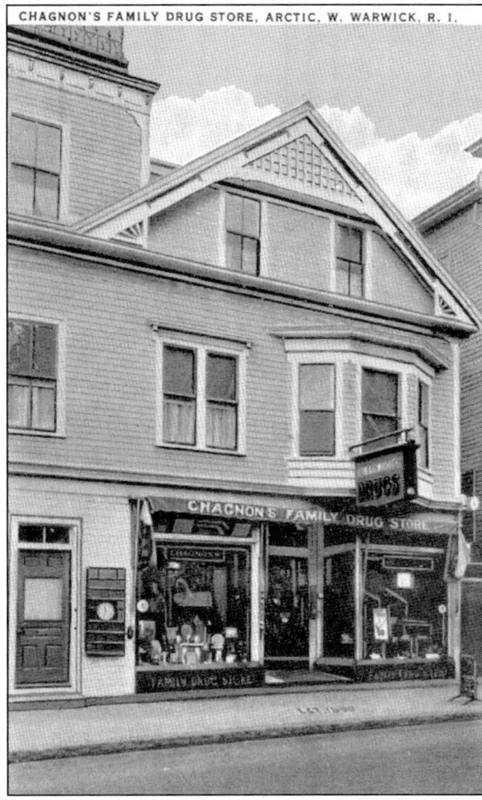

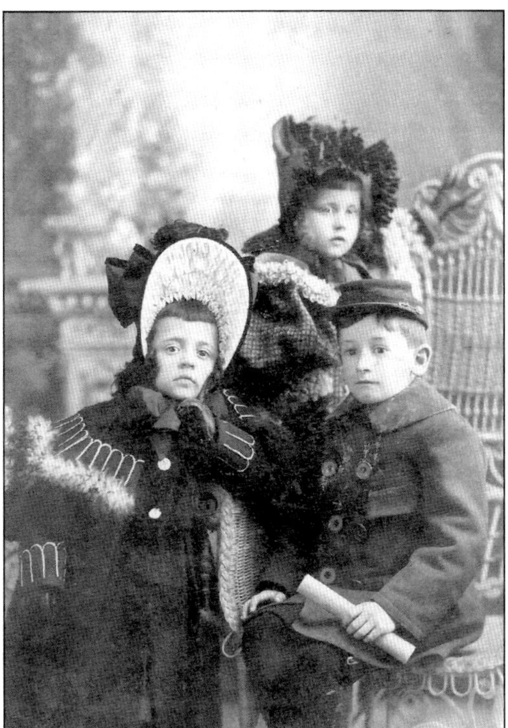

These children pose for the camera in 1896. The two girls are Doctor Chagnon's daughters Estelle (left) and Colombe, with Leo St. Onge Sr. He would later run the family business his father, Stanislas, established in 1894: the Star Clothing Store. It would later become St. Onge's. (Courtesy of Leo St. Onge Jr.)

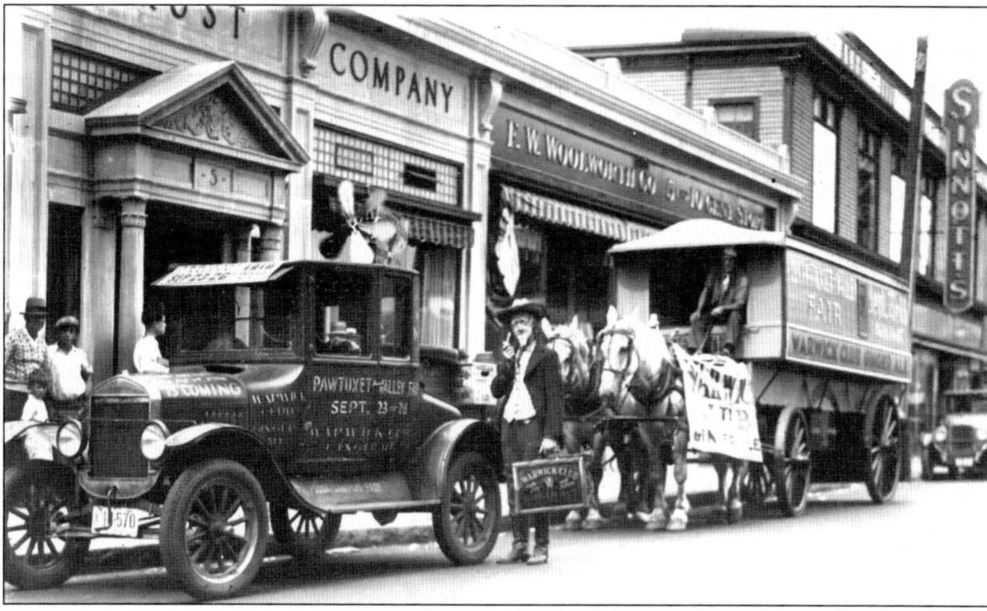

The Union Trust Company, F.W. Woolworth five-and-dime store, and the Sinnott's building (constructed in 1889) are visible in this photograph. Note that the automobile advertises the Pawtuxet Valley Fair. The gentleman with the beard and pipe promotes Warwick Club Ginger Ale on his suitcase. The horses and wagon endorse both. (Courtesy of Richard Siembab.)

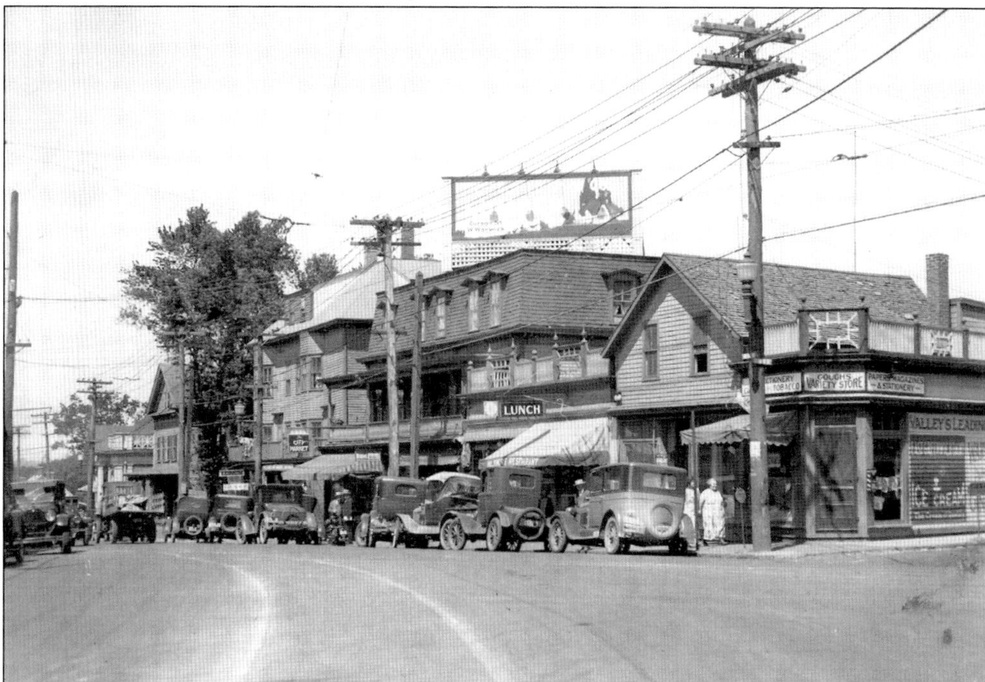

This is an easterly view of Arctic Square in 1927. The sign over the corner door on the right reads, "Gough's Variety Store." They advertise papers, magazines, and stationary. The next building is a restaurant. Before the City Market, a sign advertises rooms for rent, and then there is another lunch spot. A number of automobiles have wooden spoke wheels.

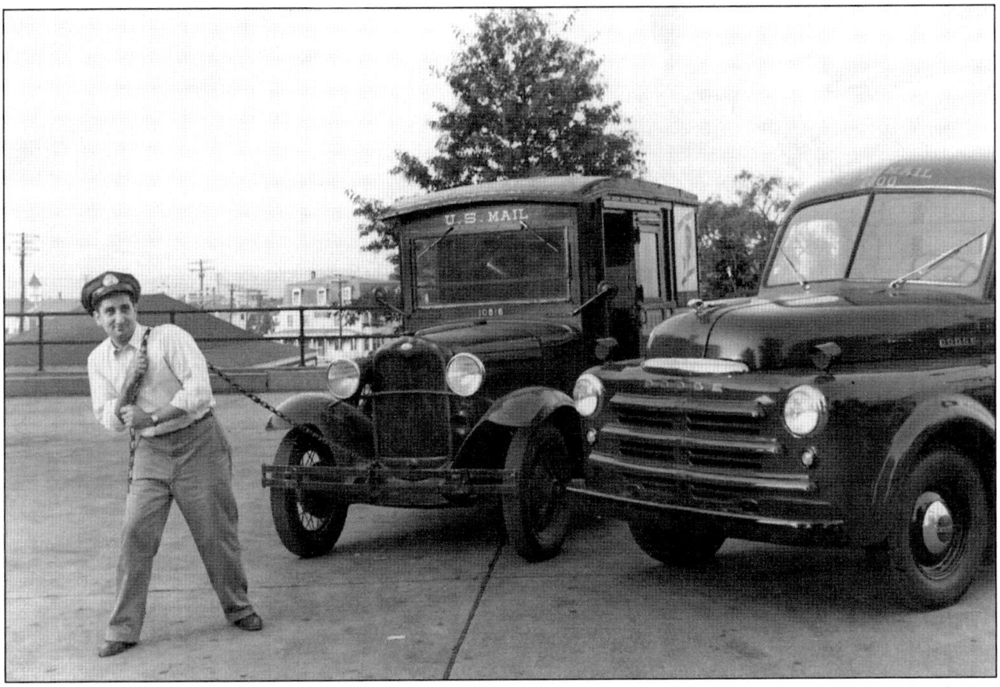

This 1950s photograph shows the new Dodge panel truck the US Postal Service had just purchased. Yvon Roy pretends he is hauling the 1930 Ford Model A to the junkyard. (Courtesy of Richard Hughes.)

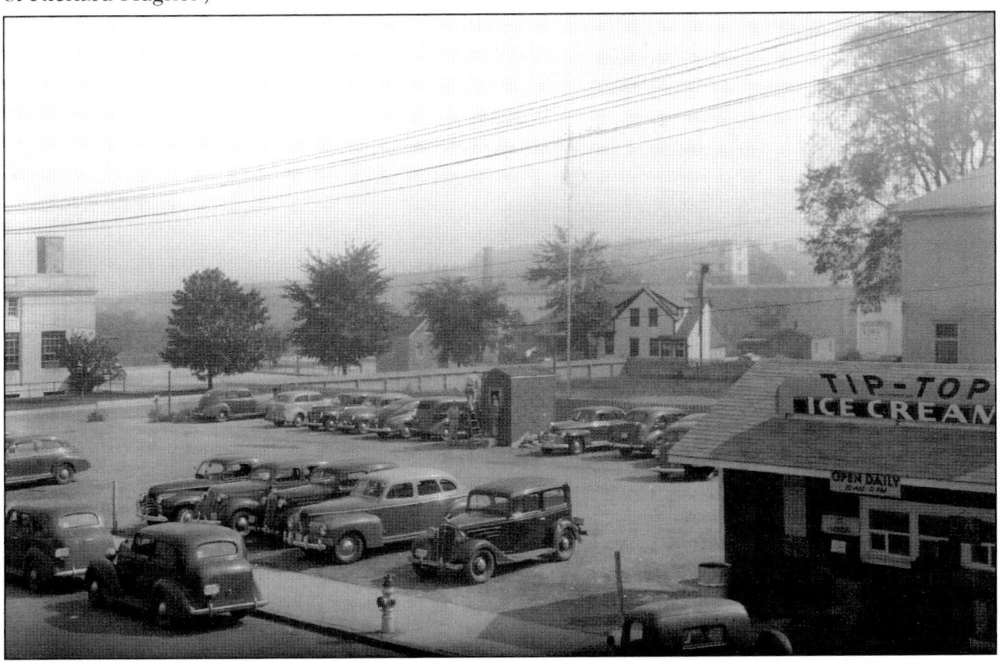

Pictured here in the 1950s, the building on the left is the West Warwick branch of the US Postal Service. The smoke stack of the Arctic Mill can be seen rising above the trees in the center. The Tip-Top ice cream business occupies the building that was the police station at one time. (Courtesy of Richard Hughes.)

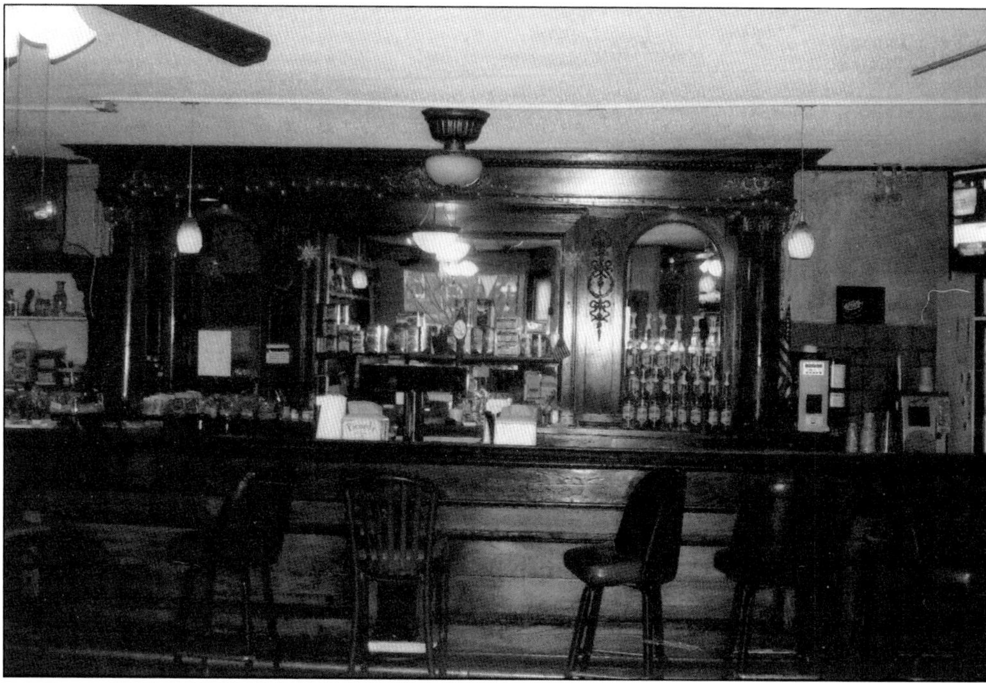

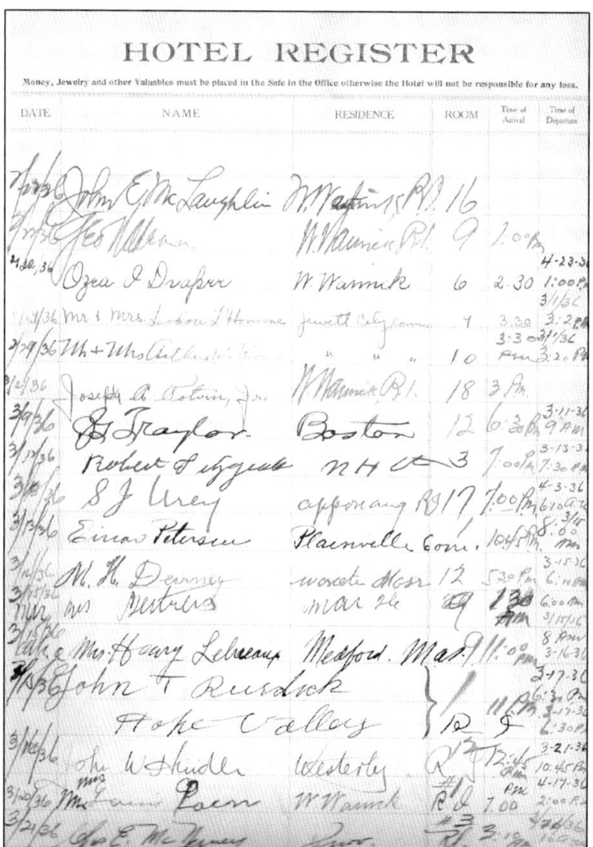

HOTEL REGISTER

Money, Jewelry and other Valuables must be placed in the Safe in the Office otherwise the Hotel will not be responsible for any loss.

DATE	NAME	RESIDENCE	ROOM	Time of Arrival	Time of Departure

The 2012 photograph above shows the beautifully crafted bar that adorned the lounge of the Winsor Hotel and Café, dating back to 1904. Proprietor Joseph Gendron, advertised it as "The Best Equipped and Most Centrally Located Hotel in the Pawtuxet Valley." It was on the electric car line, and rates were $1.50 per day or three days for $1 a day. The hotel was also equipped for automobile parties. A page from the hotel register, pictured left, documents guests from Connecticut, Boston, and Worcester, Massachusetts. Today, Dennis Picard runs Picard's Ice Cream & Coffee House in the very same Winsor Café space on the corner of Washington Street and Brookside Avenue. There, one can sit at his 100-year-old bar (or at a table) and sip a cup of coffee while eating a sandwich or enjoying an ice-cream sundae. (Above, author's collection; left, courtesy of Dennis Picard.)

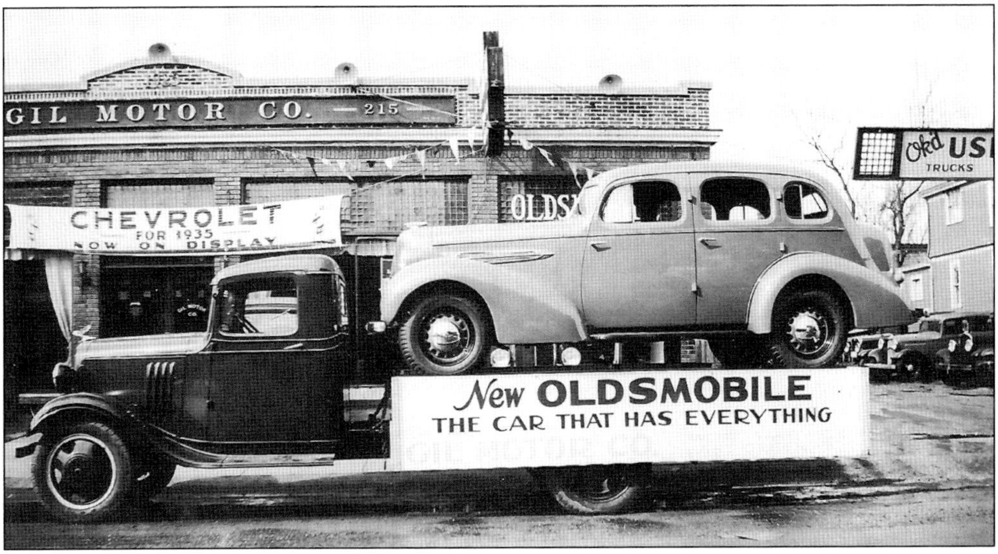

Gil Motor Company at 215 Washington Street proudly displays the new 1935 Oldsmobile. Note that the front and rear doors, also later known as suicide doors, open backwards. The photograph below was taken at an employee's outing in 1941. The name of the dealership had changed to Gil Chevrolet Inc. Pictured from left to right are (first row) sales manager Armand Soucy (first), George Sweet (second), ? Blais (third), Frank Kole (sixth), and Elphage Robert (eighth); (second row) Pete Russo (first), Frank King (third), and Tom Durand (fifth); (third row) Joe Richards (third) and Alex Malcolm (twelfth). (Both, courtesy of Lawrence G. Soucy.)

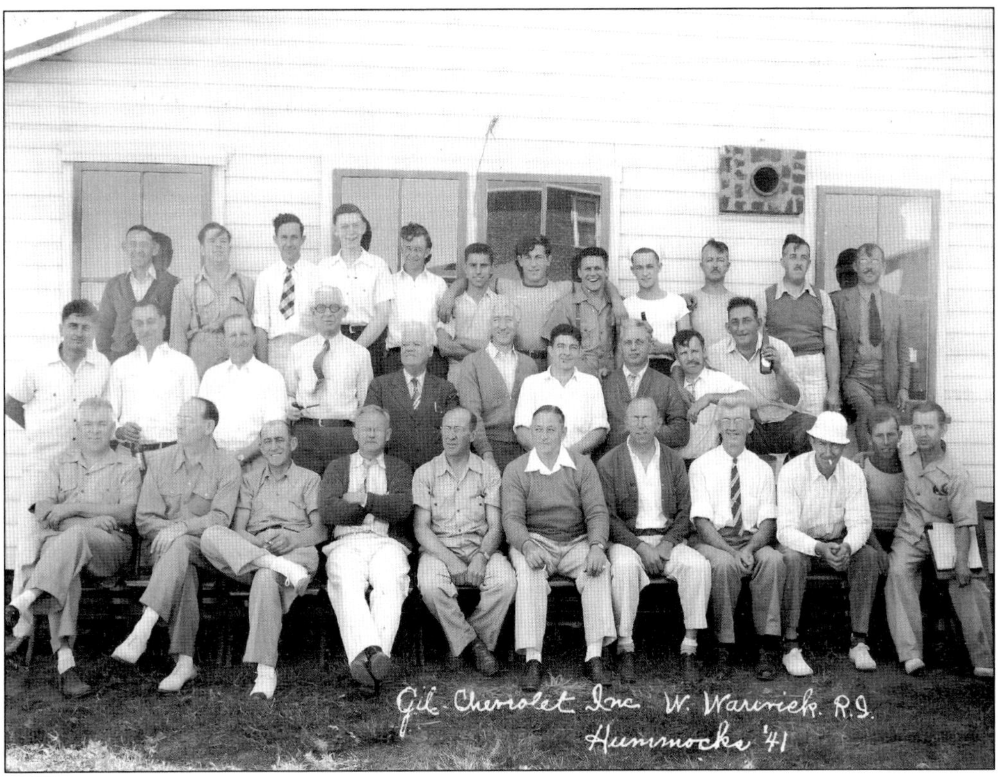

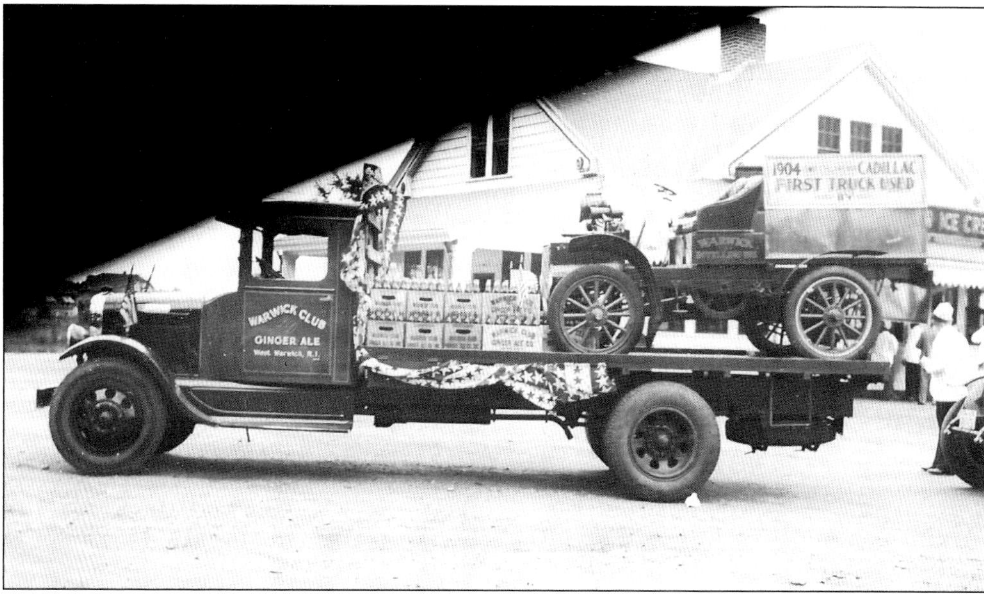

This Warwick Club Ginger Ale delivery truck carries another delivery truck. The sign states, "1904 one cylinder Cadillac—First truck used by Warwick Bottling Works." The company's plant was at 108 Pond Street in Arctic, seen in *West Warwick* on page 26. (Courtesy of Richard Siembab.)

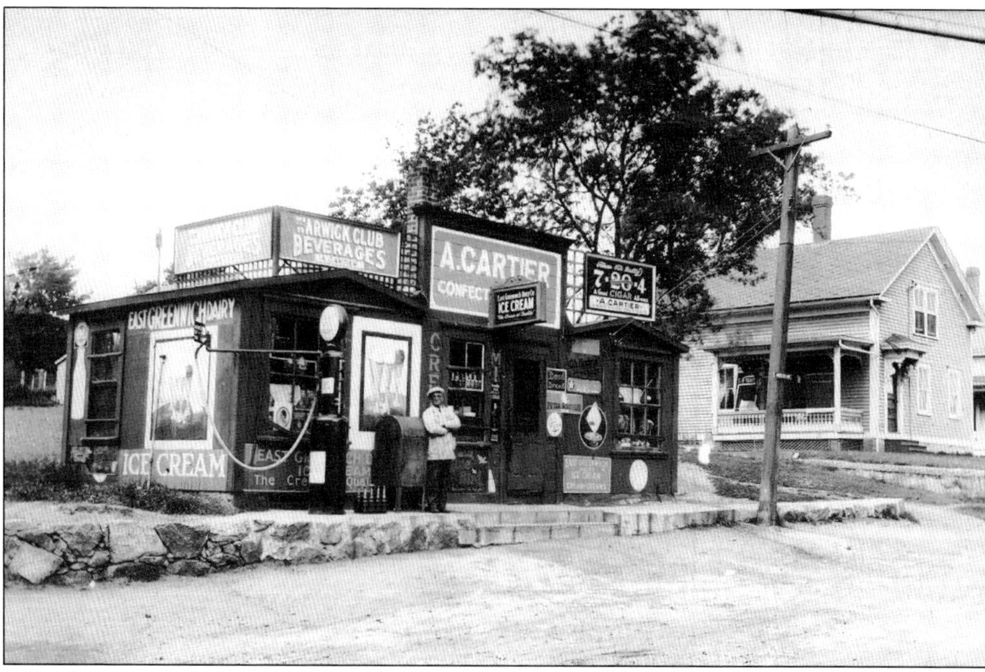

Alfred Cartier stands in front of his variety store. Above the door beside his name is a sign advertising "East Greenwich Dairy Co., Ice Cream, The Cream of Quality." To the left: "Warwick Club Beverages." To the right: "Famous for Quality, 7-20-4 Cigars, A Good Cigar Always." He also offers Bond Bread and Coke. Beside the gas pump is a case of one-quart jars of oil. His store, located at 2 Andrews Avenue, is now occupied by Pare's Garage. Cartier resided in the house to the right at 4 Andrews Avenue. (Courtesy of Richard Siembab.)

Seven

Centreville and Crompton

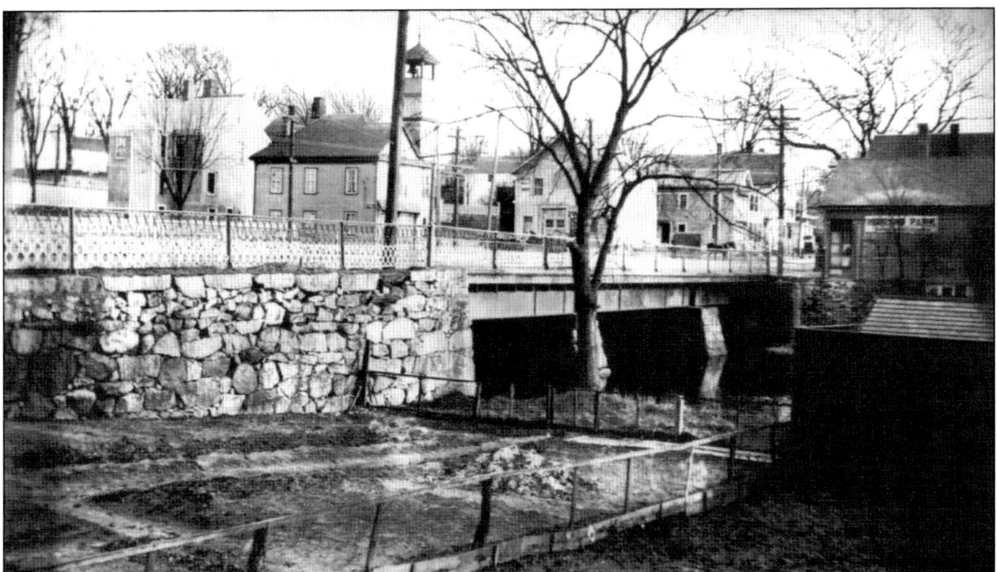

This December 1919 photograph shows the Centreville Bridge crossing the South Branch of the Pawtuxet River. There is a horse and buggy at the far end of the 110-foot bridge. The old Centreville Fire Station at the corner of Bridal Avenue is visible behind the telephone pole.

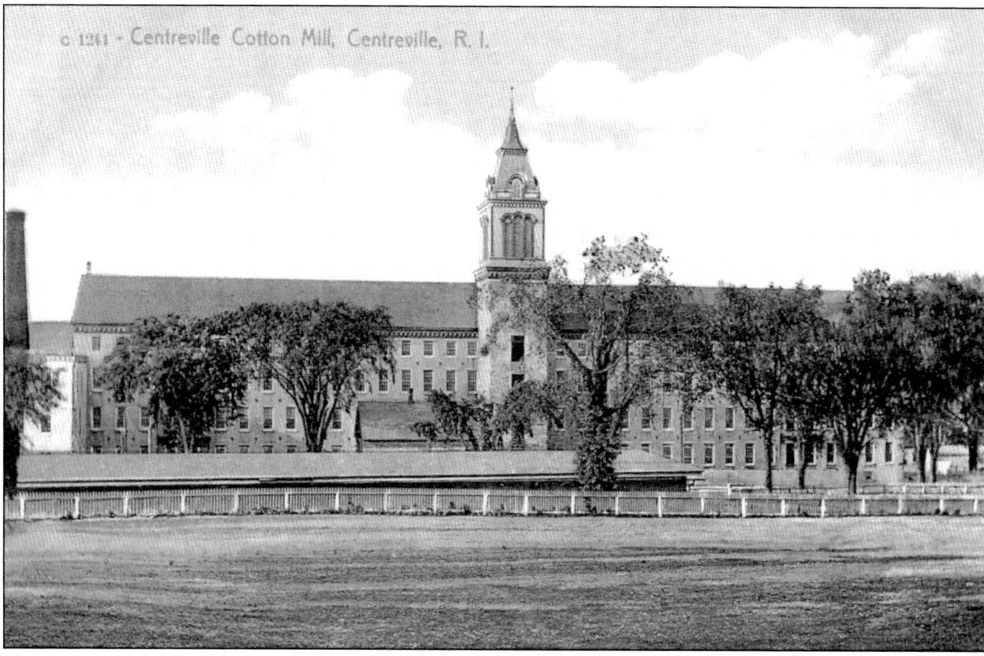

The Centreville Mill on Bridal Avenue was built on the east bank of the Pawtuxet River in 1873. It is a four-story building, 70 feet by 303 feet, with a center stairway. Part of the Centreville Mill Complex was the Waterhouse Mill No. 1. It was built on the west bank in 1807. One dam, built between the two mills, supplied power to both. (Courtesy of Richard Siembab.)

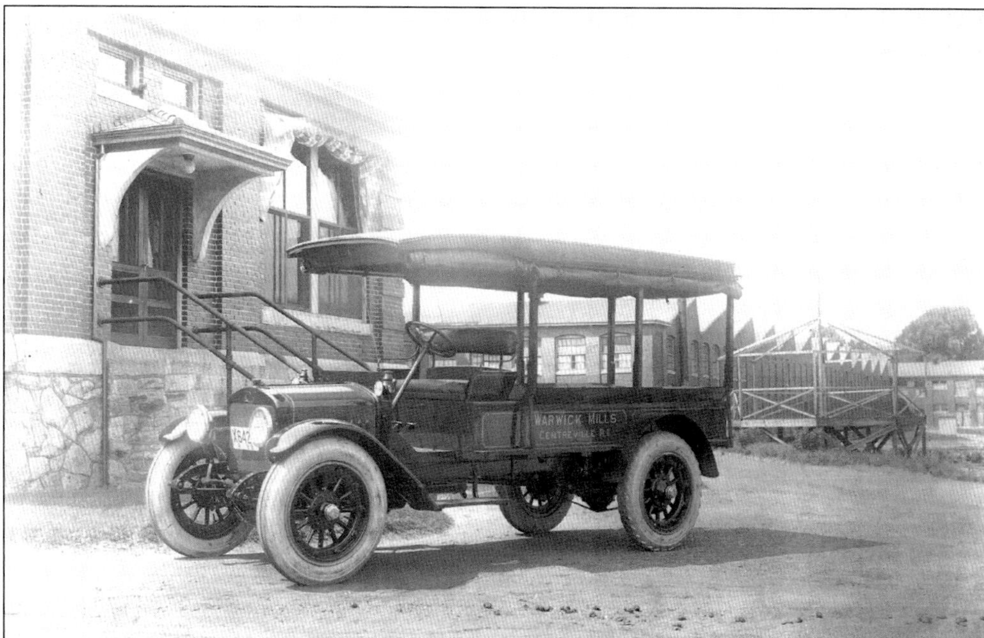

A Warwick Mills delivery truck is parked in front of the office. The saw-toothed roof of the weave shed, built in 1907, can be seen at the rear of the truck. The original mill, built in 1896 on Brookside Avenue, is 110 feet by 600 feet. (Courtesy of Richard Siembab.)

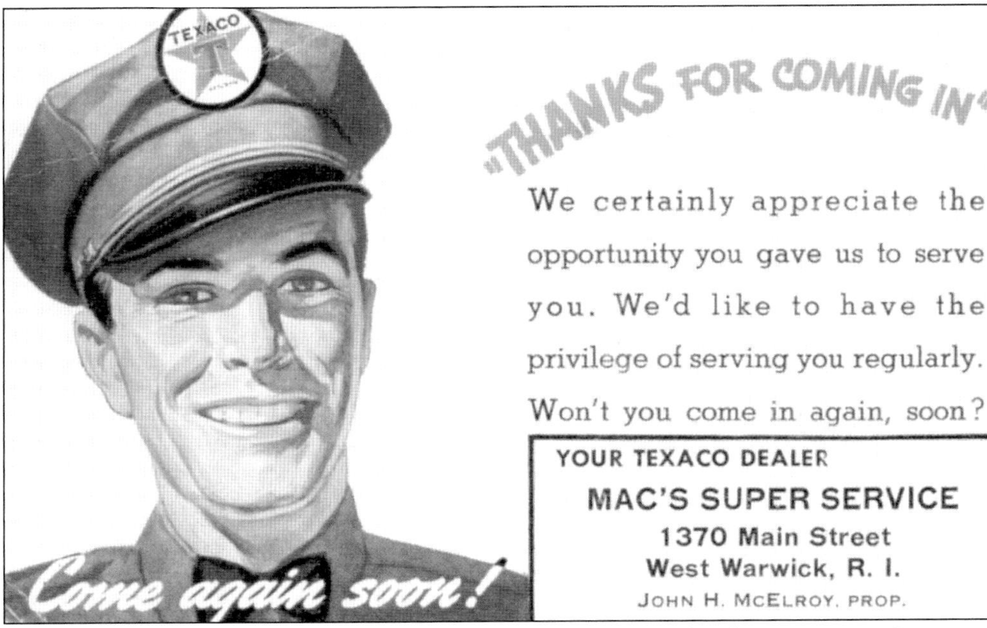

In the early 1900s, the filling station was a gas pump outside one's local grocery store. Customers could pump their own gas and then pay inside. Later, gas stations were built solely to sell gas. Then service stations emerged, where attendants wore uniforms, cleaned the windshield, and checked the oil and air in the tires as they filled customers' gas tanks. Today, it has come full circle to self-service filling stations, with a choice of paying inside or at the pump. (Courtesy of Richard Siembab.)

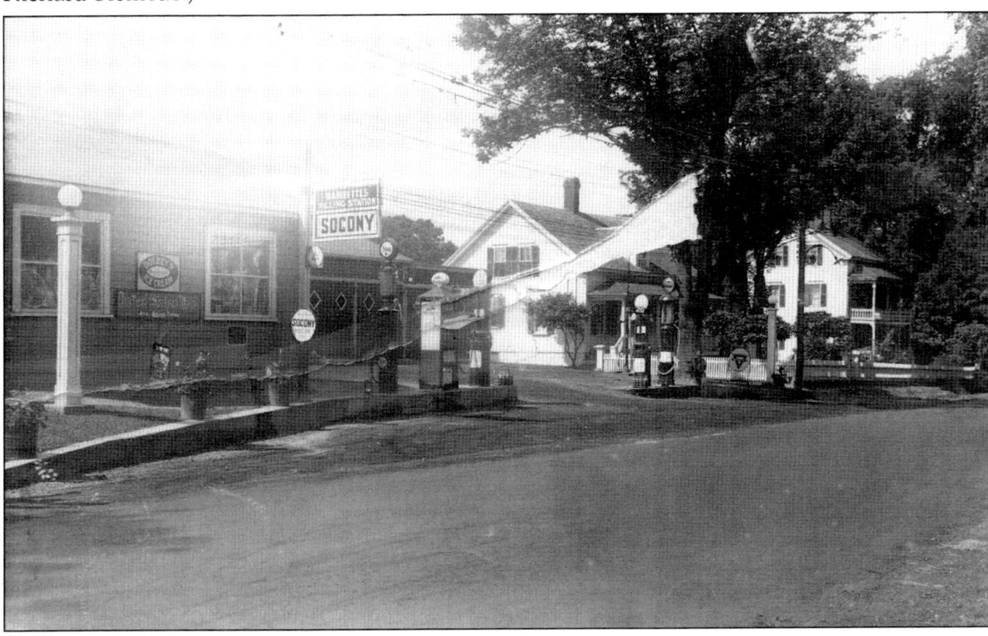

The original Barrette's Filling Station was located on the corner of New London Turnpike and Legris Avenue in Centreville. Only five pumps are visible; however, when Barrette built his new station, he had ten available for his customers. The variety of gasoline included Esso, Socony, Mobil, and Texaco, among others.

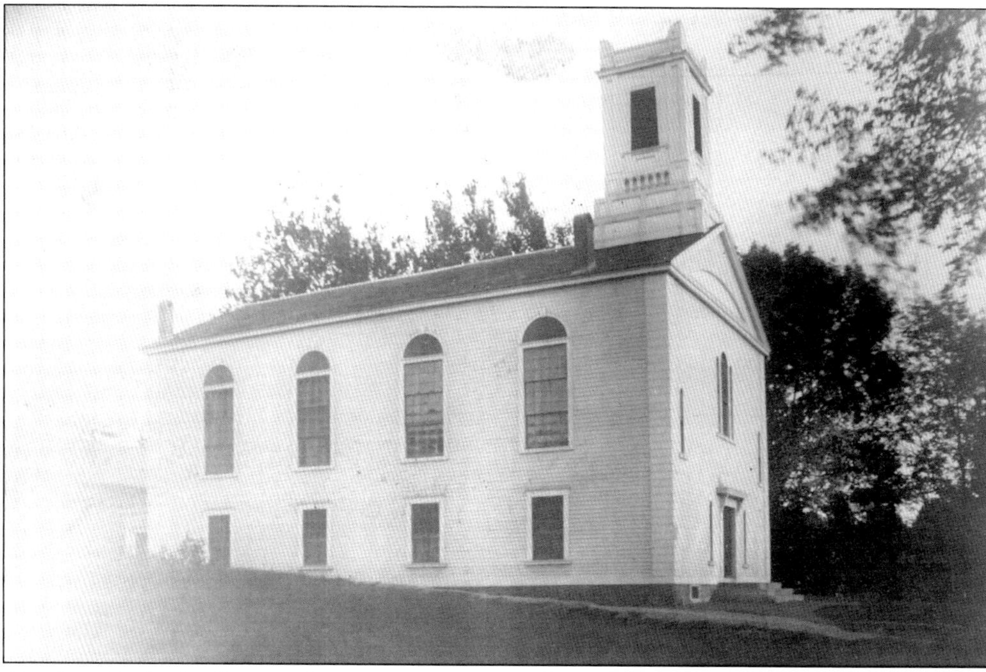

The first Methodist Episcopal services in Centreville were held by a circuit minister. In 1831, this building, pictured above and below, was erected on land donated by Joseph Greene. It was named the Methodist Episcopal Church and Proprietors Meeting House of Centreville. The interior of the church was very plain but functional. It was destroyed by a fire on February 9, 1902. Plans were immediately put in motion to build a new church. The new church structure, named Centreville United Methodist Church, was dedicated on June 6, 1903. It is a shingled building with a three-story tower entrance. (Both, courtesy of Donald Carpenter.)

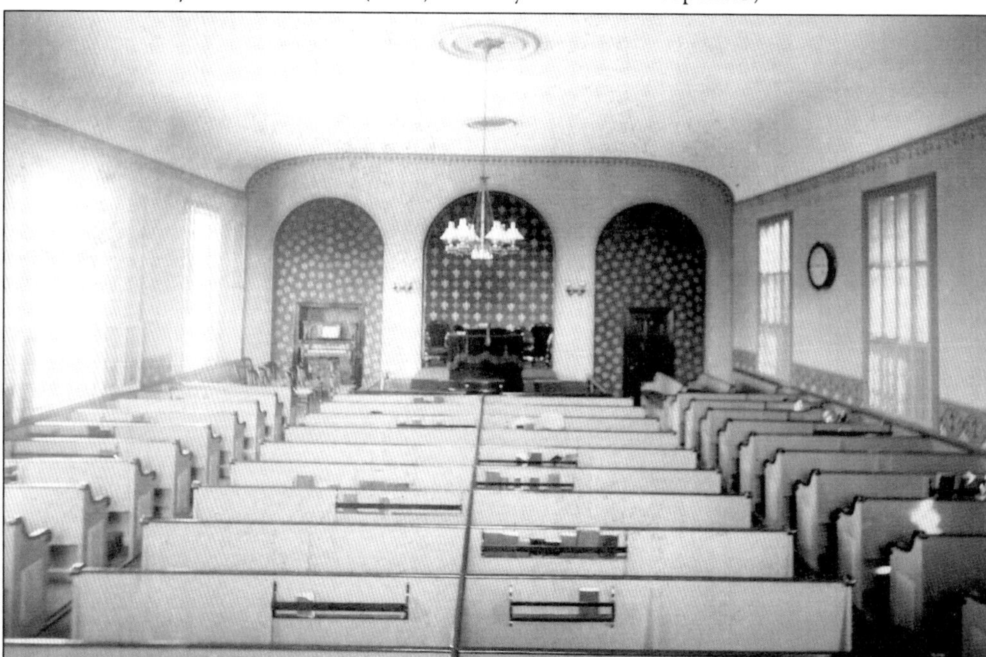

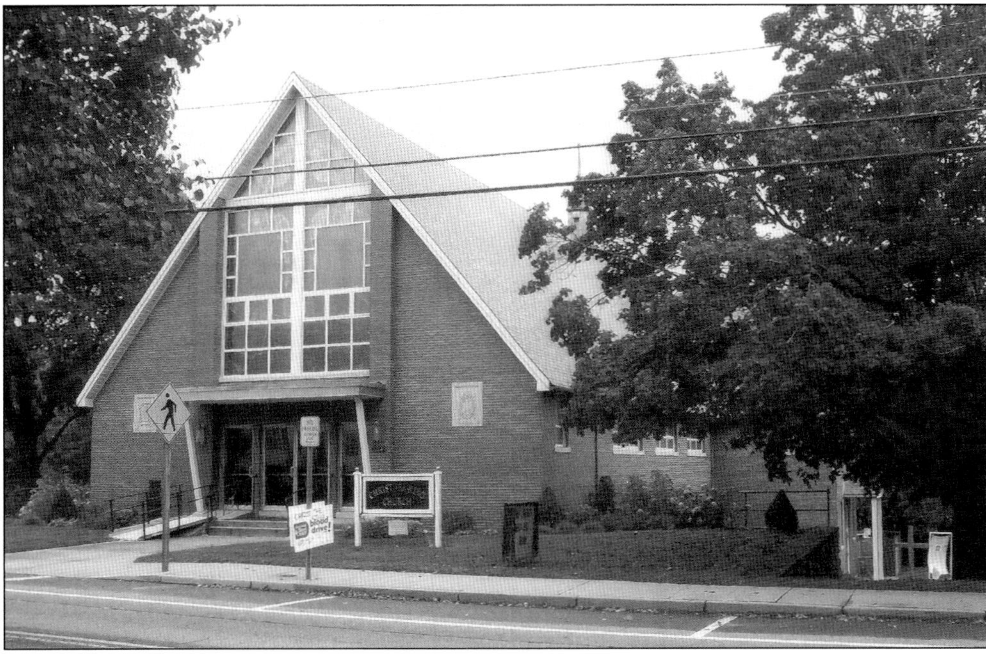

This 2010 photograph shows the Christ the King Church. When this property was purchased in 1931, it contained a large barn and a four-story building. By 1932, it was converted into a 450-person capacity church. The year 1933 saw the realization of Christ the King School, which eventually closed in 1975. On December 3, 1954, a fire gutted the original barn/church. The church pictured here was dedicated on September 22, 1957. (Author's collection.)

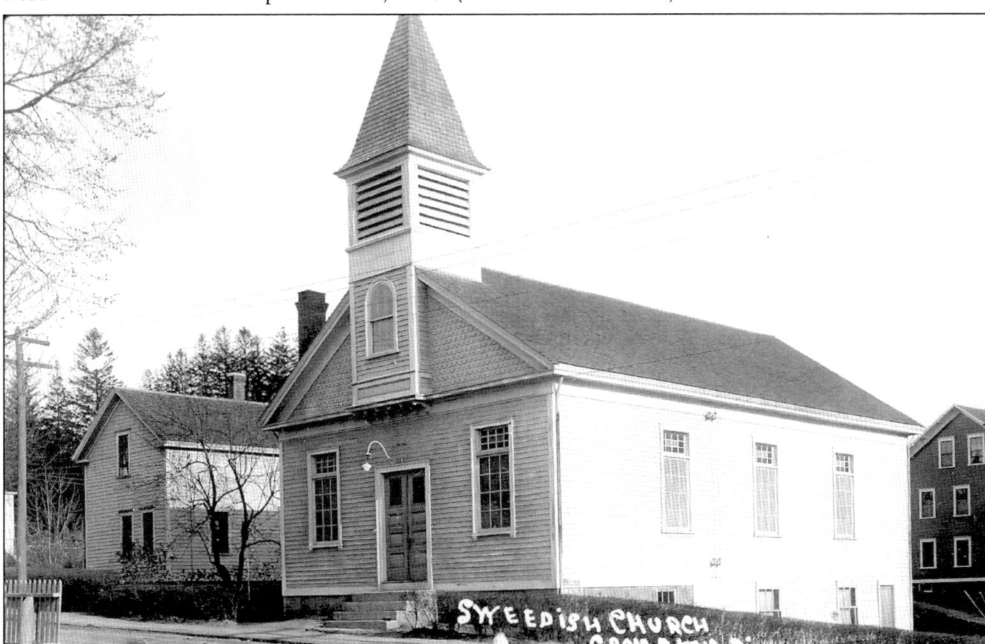

This early-1900s postcard shows the Swedish Lutheran Church in Crompton. It was built on a very small lot on the corner of Nestor Street and dedicated on November 10, 1893. (Courtesy of Richard Siembab.)

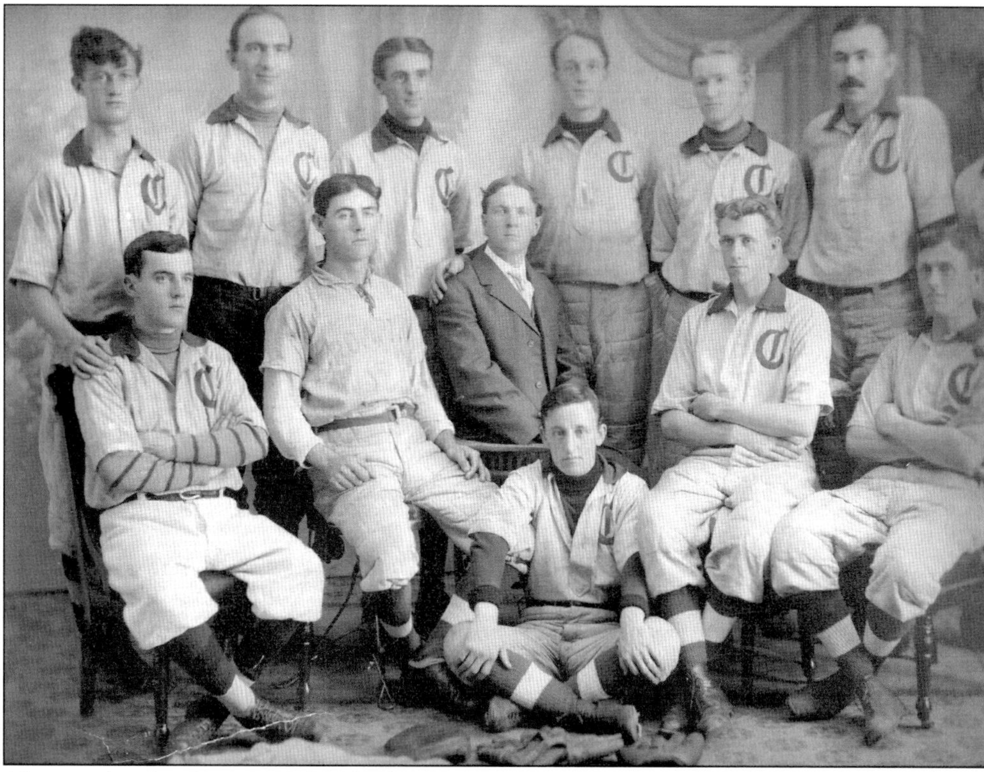

Above is the "Big Crompton" baseball team of 1908. Pictured from left to right are (first row) Jim Cummisky, Jim Daley, manager Bob Davis, Ted Nestor (on floor), Vic Loven, and Gus Bergstein; (second row) ? Johnson, Swan Swanson, P. Anderson, Jake Loven, Charles Carlson, Hunter White, and J. Murray (partly hidden). Below, a group of boys gather for a game in 1936. They are, from left to right, (first row) Maurice Russi, N. Russi, unidentified, and Joe Moniz; (second row) Alfred Papa, Leo Fleury, Manny Arruda, Albert Papa, Pasco Gallucci, Joe Pacheco, and Tony Pacheco.

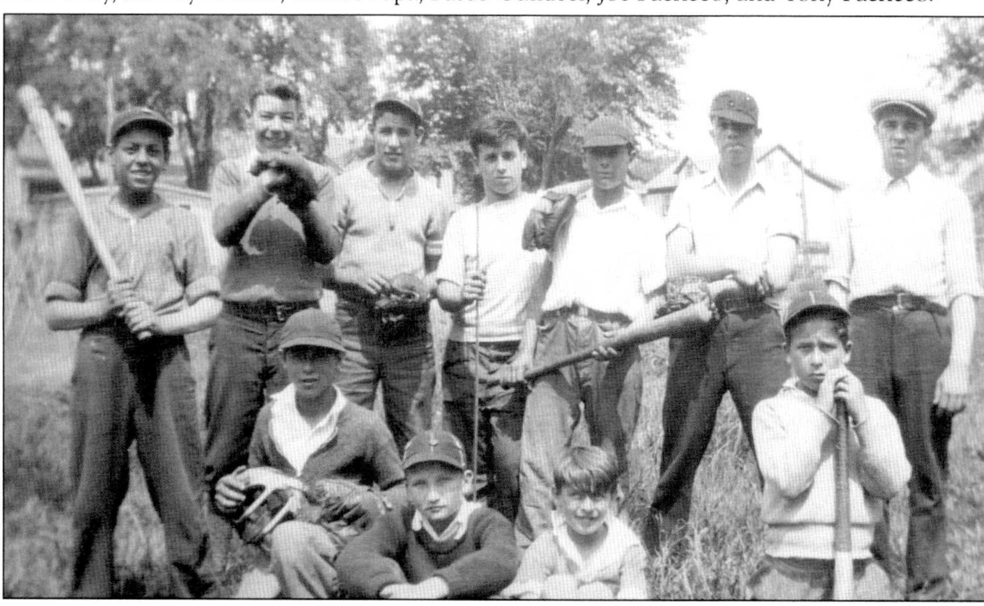

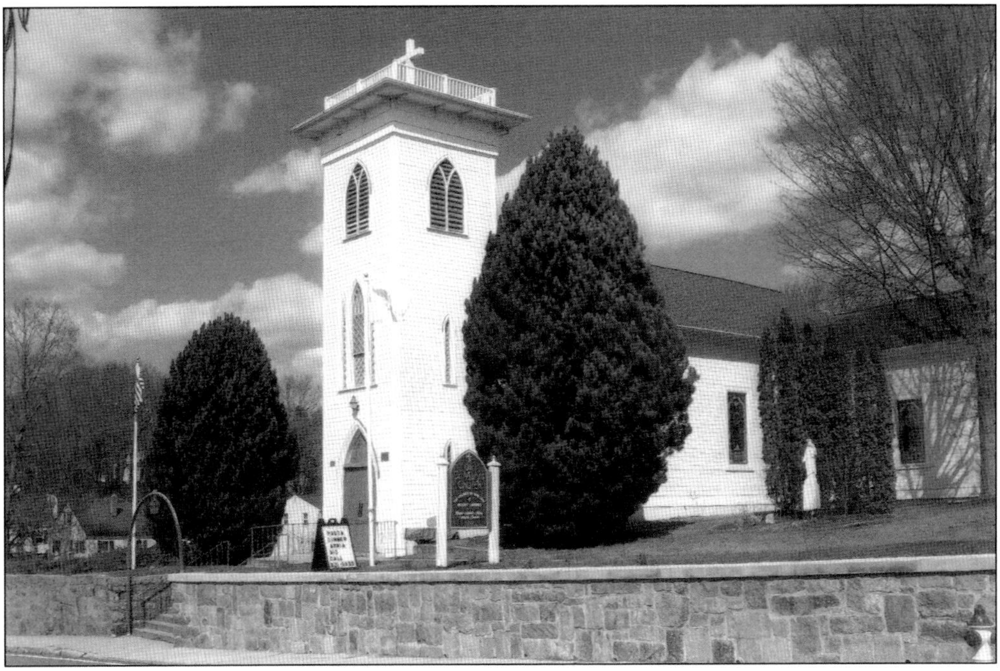

St. Mary's Church was built in 1844 and was the first Roman Catholic church building in the valley. It earned the title "Mother Church of the Valley." The central fore tower, containing the entrance and standing 45 feet tall, was added in 1859. The cemetery behind the church was established in 1849. St. Mary's Church is the oldest Catholic church building in the state still existing. (Author's collection.)

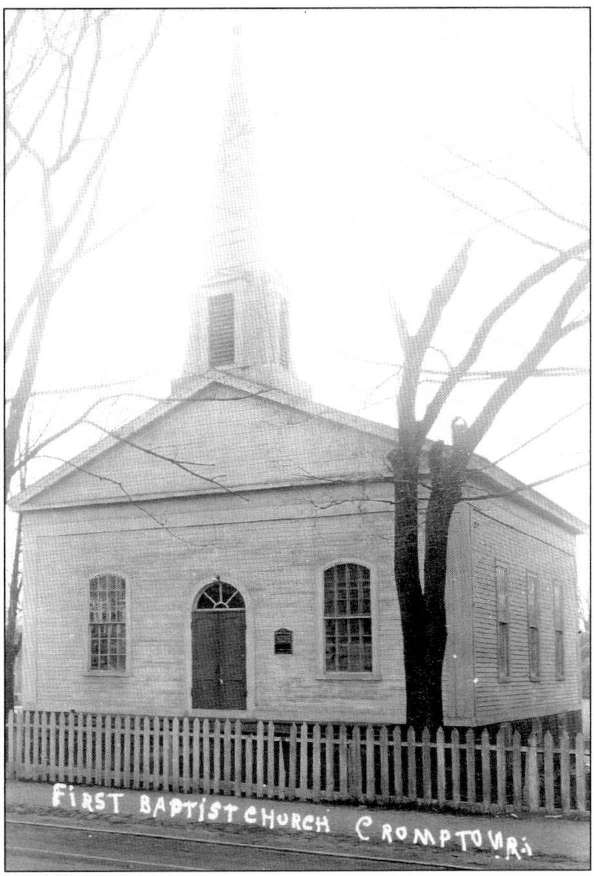

The First Baptist Church was built in Crompton in 1843. The congregation was organized in 1805, and services were conducted in various halls and houses in Crompton. The church changed its name to the First Baptist Church of Crompton in 1879. (Courtesy of Richard Siembab.)

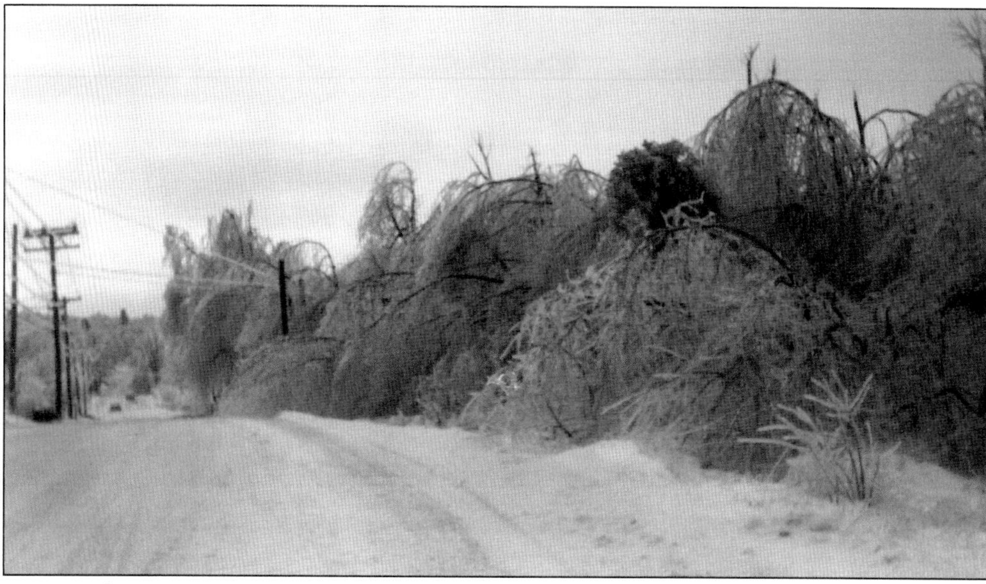

New London Avenue is visible during the ice storm of 1978, which blanketed Rhode Island on January 13, leaving more than 120,000 homes without electricity. Thousands of people spent several days in shelters. Then, on February 6 and 7, the famous blizzard of 1978 buried Rhode Island under more than four feet of snow. Below is New London Turnpike in front of the Crompton Library on the left. Richard Hughes's 1972 Buick is shown snowbound in the lower left corner. The following verses are from "The Blizzard of '78" by Helen O. Larson: "The blizzard came on February 6th, in every county and town / It didn't seem so bad, when the snow first came down. Then it snowed faster, and the wind blew / We had a state of disaster, to us it was something new." (Both, courtesy of Richard Hughes.)

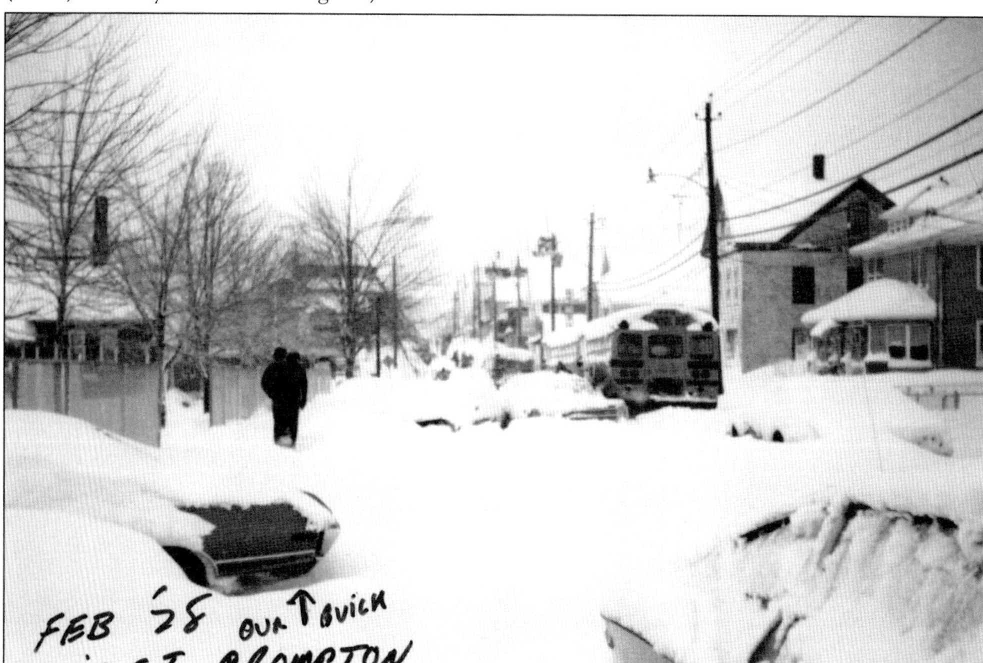

Eight

Quidnick and Anthony

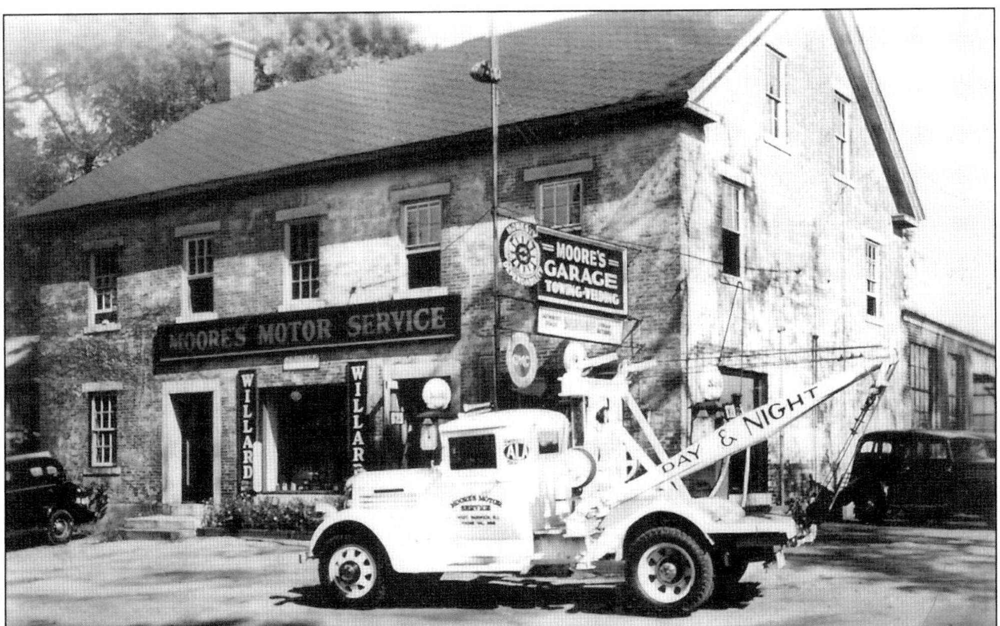

Stephen Taft operated a print works in this section of town, and the area became known as Taftville. Amasa and William Sprague bought the mill, and the village was named Quidnick. This postcard shows the old Sprague Store, built in 1849. Moore's Garage moved into the building in 1927 and still occupies it today. The Automobile Legal Association (ALA) advertises on the side of the tow truck. The association is no longer in existence. (Courtesy of Lawrence G. Soucy.)

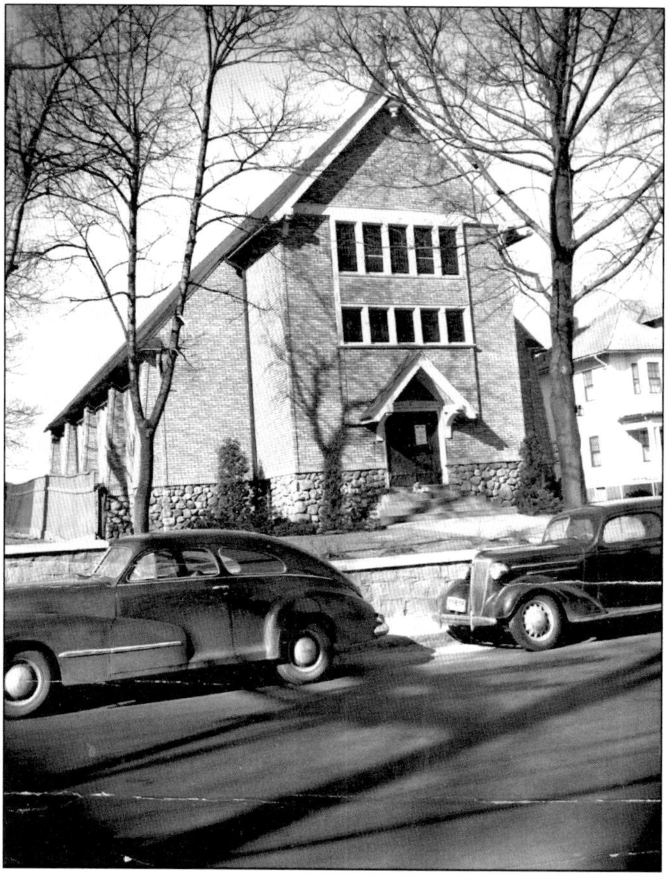

Our Lady of Czenstochowa Church is pictured above in 1948. In 1901, there were about 50 Polish families residing in the Pawtuxet Valley. The church was created in 1905, and the Rev. Francis Kluger was assigned as the first pastor. On February 12, 1906, the church bought one acre of land from Quidnick Manufacturing Company. On April 21, 1907, the congregation attended the dedication of the new church. In 1915, a rectory was built, and in 1934, a parish school was completed and dedicated. The photograph below highlights the detailed and intricate work of the interior.

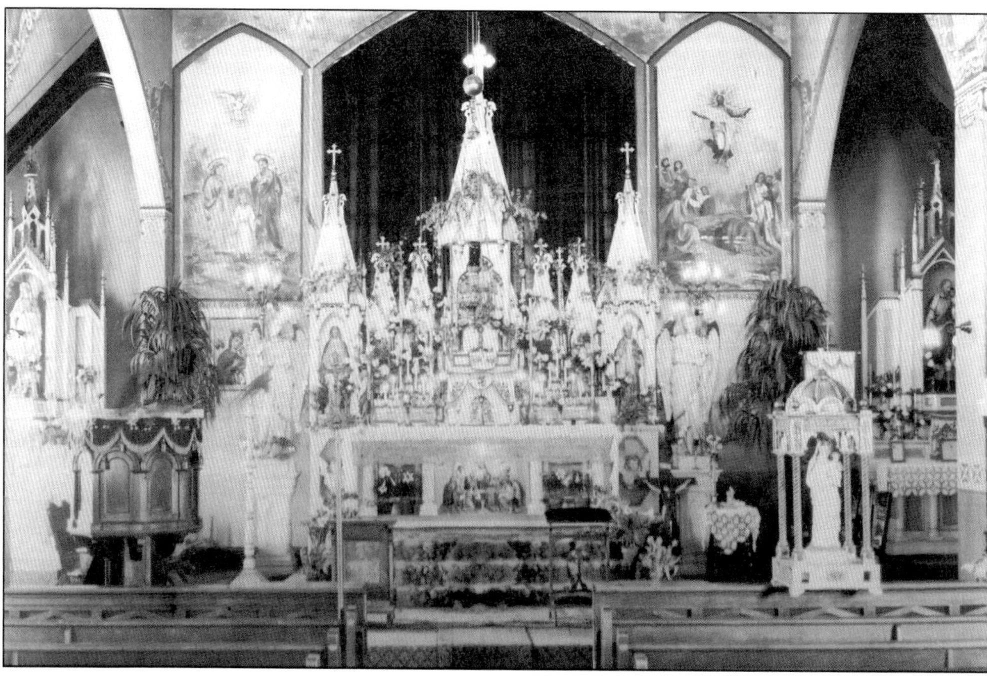

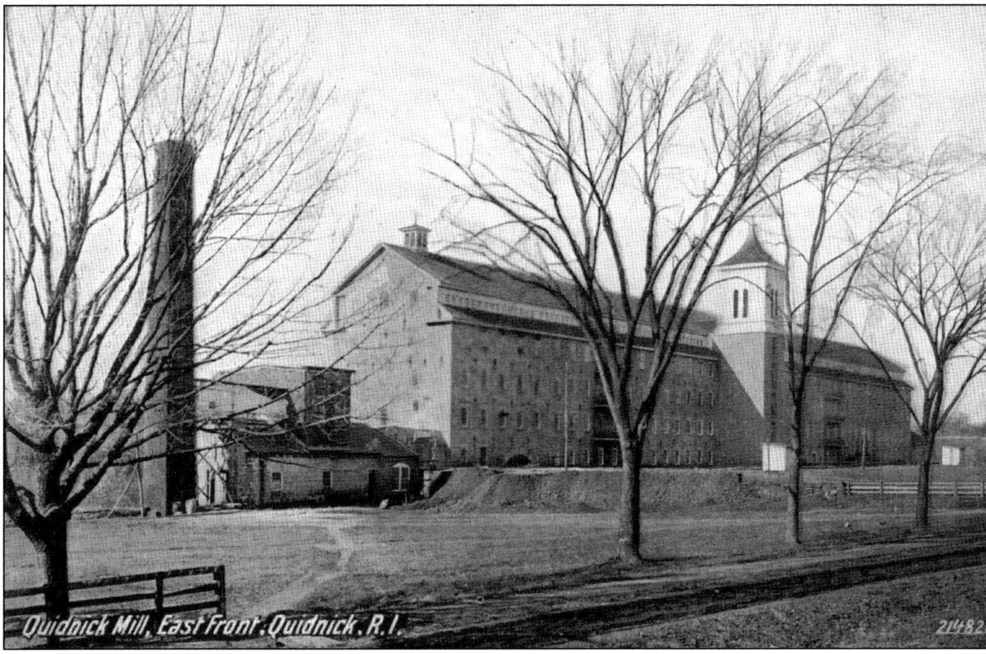

The Quidnick Lower Mill (or No. 2 Mill) was built in 1869 by Horace Foster for Amasa and William Sprague. Foster also constructed the Upper Mill (or No. 1 Mill) for the Spragues in 1848. The site is now occupied by American Hoechst.

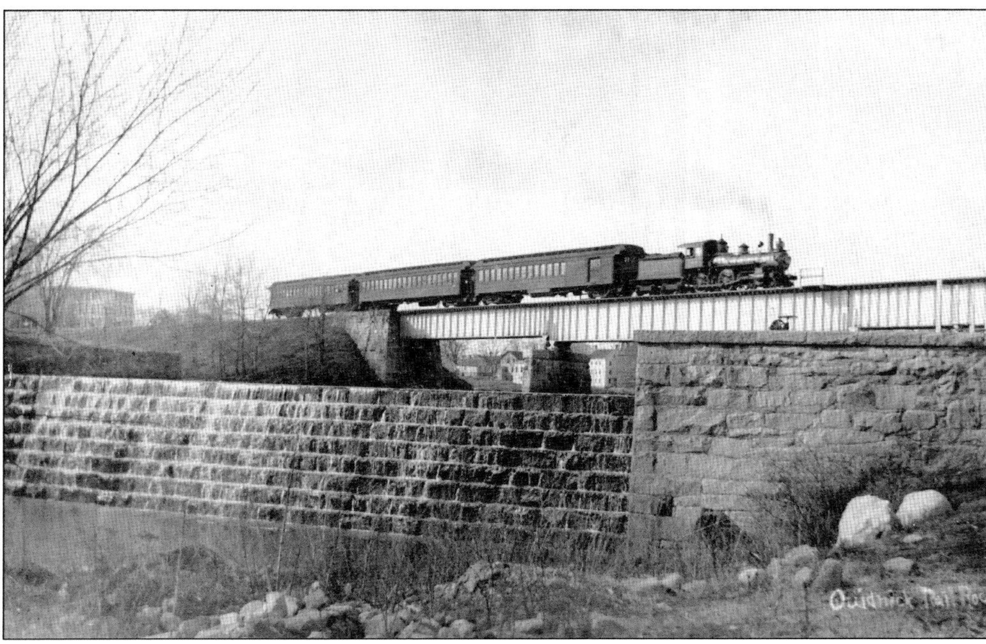

On this photograph, a passenger train leaves the Anthony Train Station. It passes the Quidnick Dam on its way to Arctic and beyond. This bridge is now part of a rails-to-trails path. The goal of the East Coast Greenway Alliance is to create a continuous, 3,000-mile, off-road trail connecting cities from Canada to Key West. Nearly 25 percent of the project has been completed. (Courtesy of Richard Siembab.)

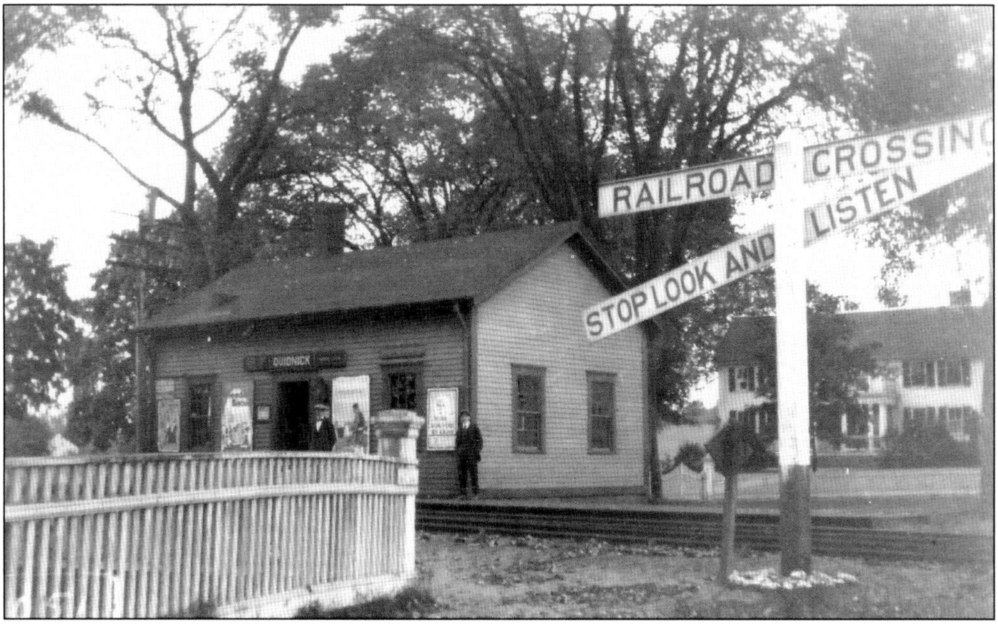

This postcard shows the Quidnick Railroad Station. Washington Street is between the station and the house in the rear. The station is gone, and the tracks are gone; however, the railroad bed is now part of the East Coast Greenway Alliance. (Courtesy of Richard Siembab.)

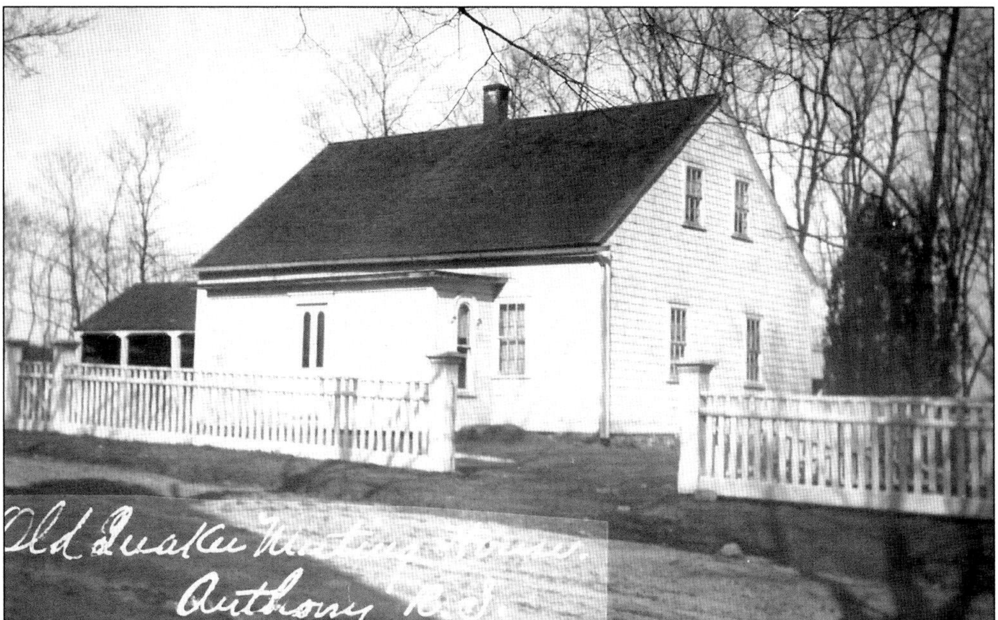

This is an early postcard view of the Quaker Meetinghouse. The Quakers began worship in a schoolhouse in 1813. They obtained this lot in 1821 and constructed this building four years later. The structure was sold in 1926, after worship had been discontinued for over 10 years. The building still stands. (Courtesy of Foster Historical Society.)

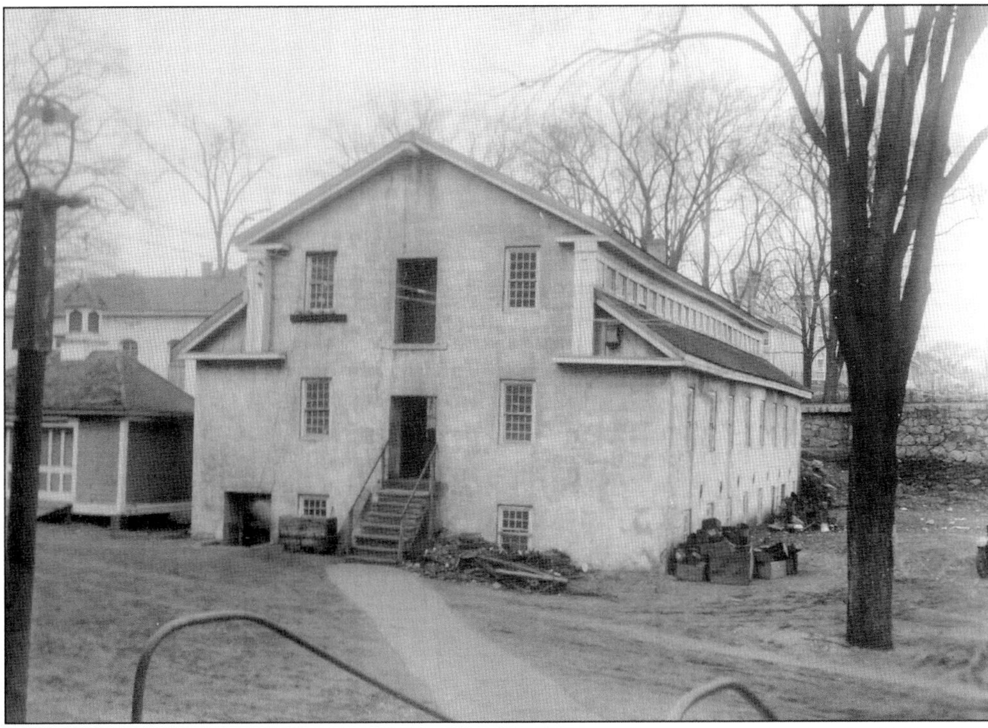

This mill, located somewhere on Washington Street, was damaged in the flood of 1920. The photograph below was taken on Easter Sunday in 1920. This area of Washington Street was flooded when the middle dam gave way from the floodwaters of the storm. Below, Homidas "Tom" Gladu floats down the middle of Washington Street. He was gateman for the mill for over 50 years, controlling the amount of water that went through the gates to operate the mill. The building on the right is the Anthony Mill Company Store (see page 106). (Below, courtesy of Richard Siembab.)

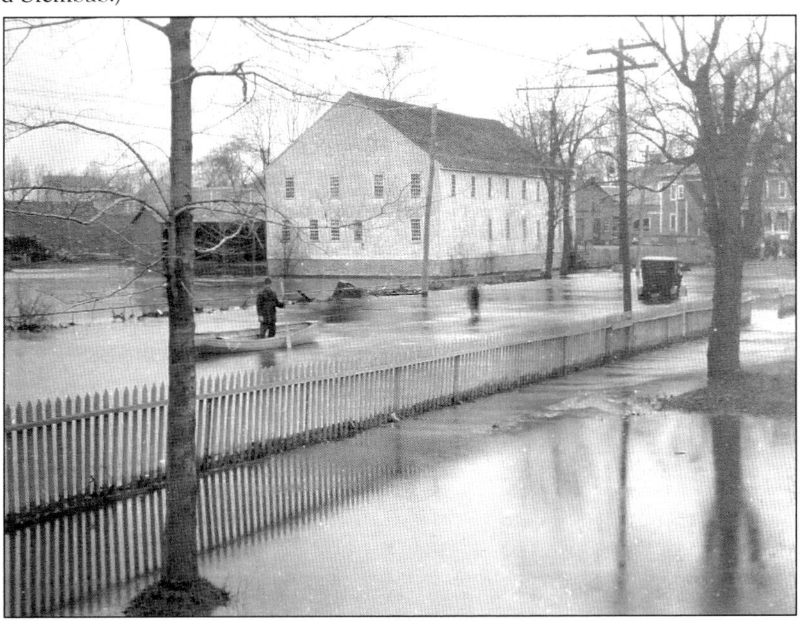

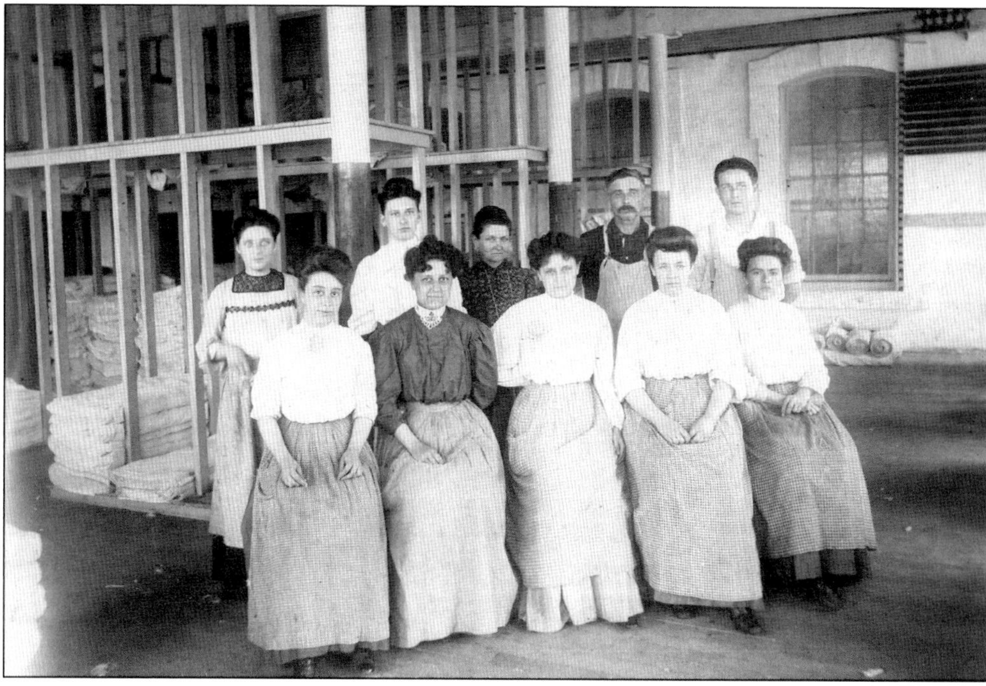

The Coventry Company was established in 1805 by brothers Richard and William Anthony. In 1806, they constructed their first mill, an 80-foot-long wooden structure. A new stone mill was built in 1810, and another five-story stone mill was erected in 1873. Cloth inspectors are pictured here in the 1890s.

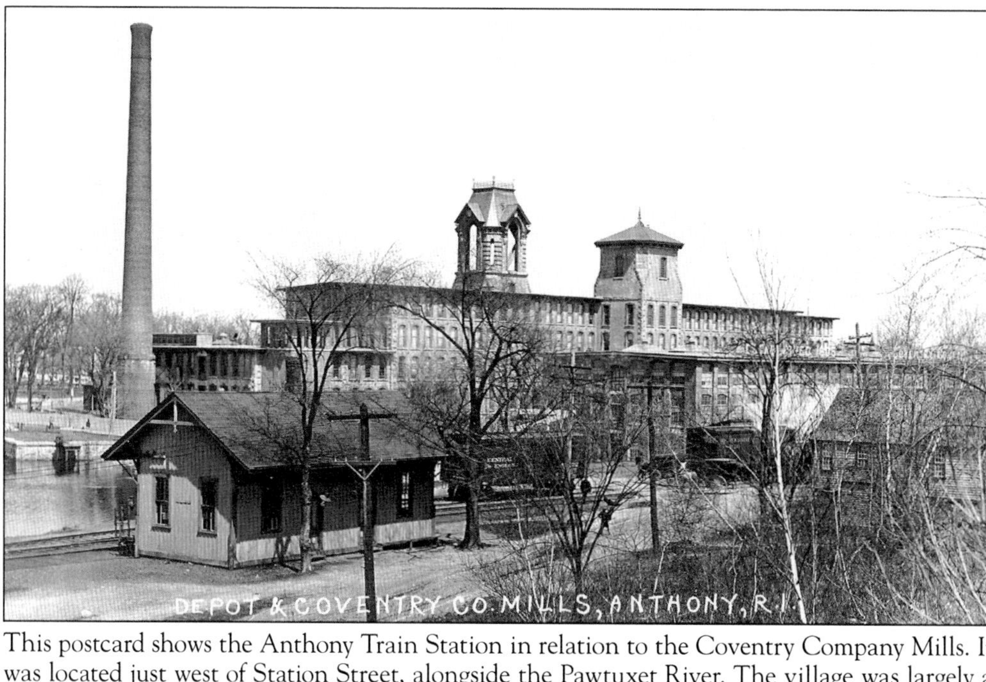

This postcard shows the Anthony Train Station in relation to the Coventry Company Mills. It was located just west of Station Street, alongside the Pawtuxet River. The village was largely a Quaker settlement and referred to as Quaker Village. The 1825 Quaker Meetinghouse still stands. Richard and William Anthony soon officially named the village Anthony.

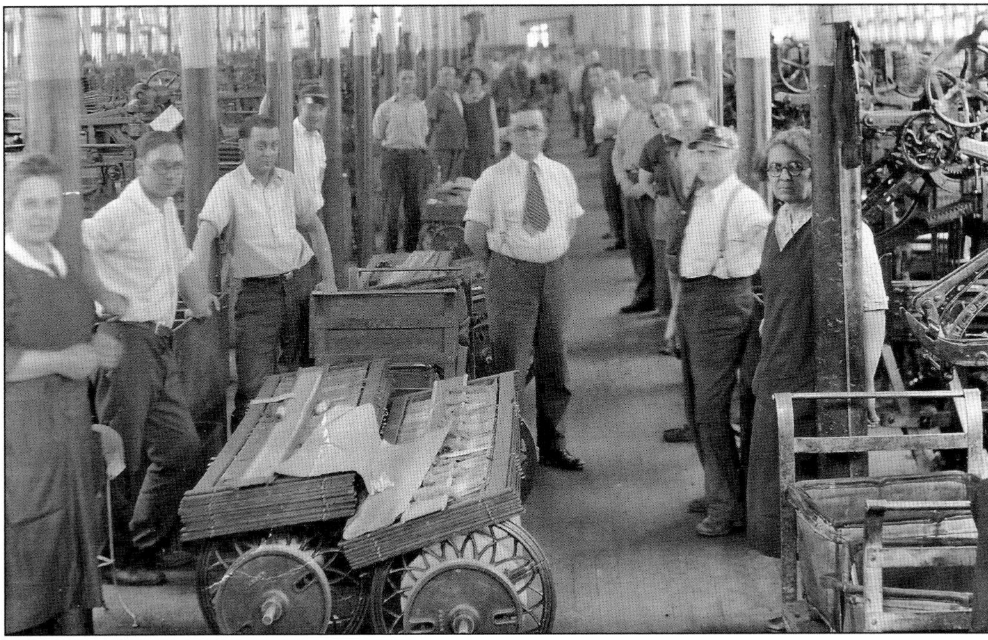

The Anthony Mill weave shop is pictured here in the 1930s. Eva Frenette is the 19-year-old girl standing in center to the rear. Alpherie Frenette is the man in the suit beside her; he is her father and the manager of the weave shop. (Courtesy of Richard Siembab.)

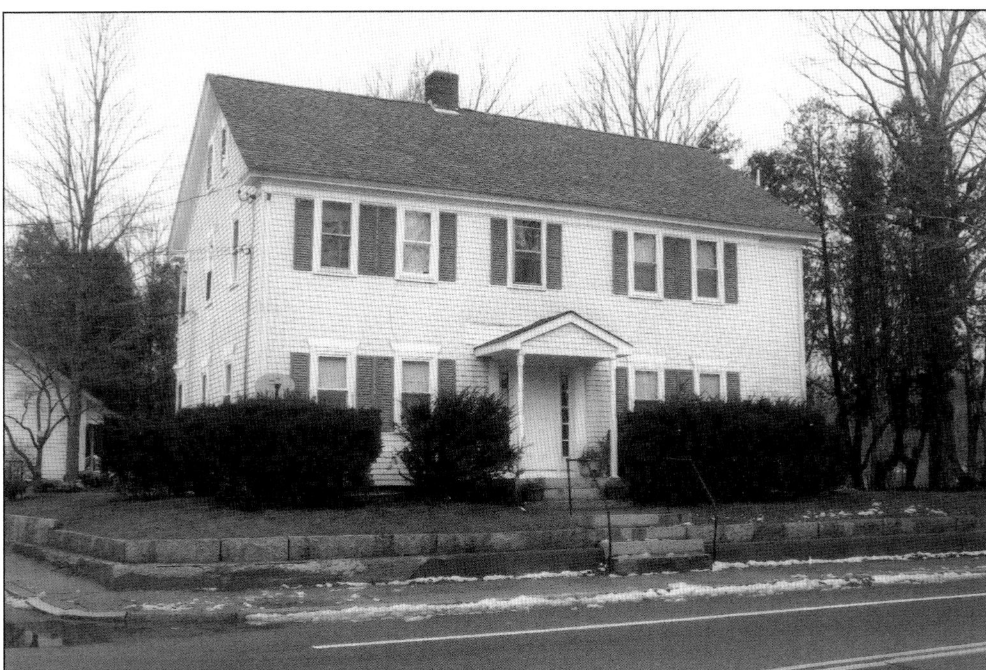

This 16-room house is located directly across from the mill on the corner of Washington and Boston Streets. It was built for Richard Anthony in 1807. Ten years later, he sold his interest in the property to his brother William. Later, it became the home of John Warner, the mill superintendent for 25 years. (Author's collection.)

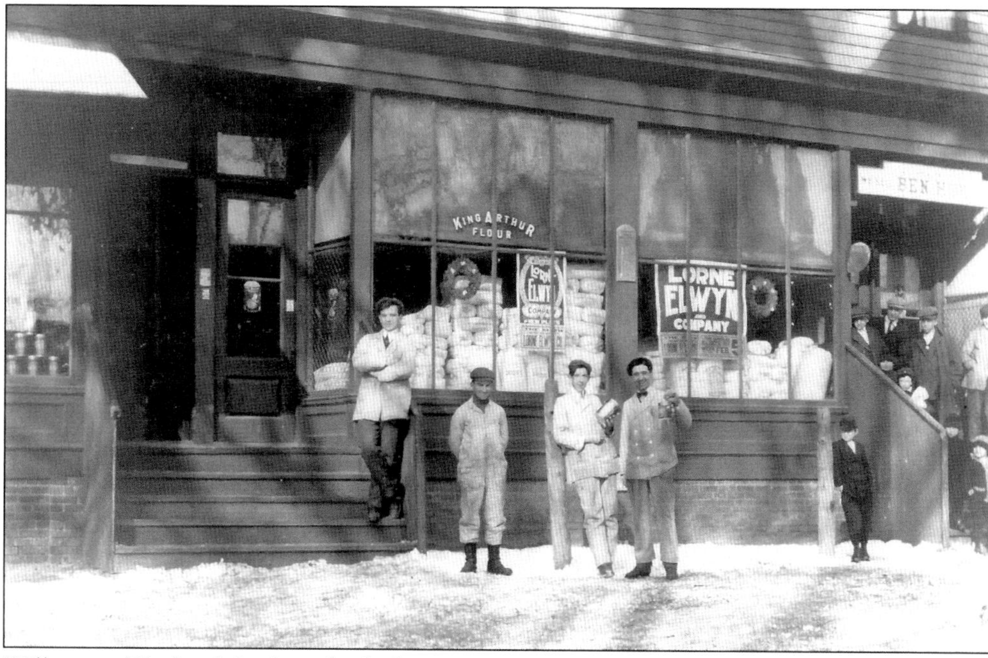

William and Richard Anthony built this company store across the street from their mill on the corner of Anthony Street in 1807. Cleophase Benoit ran the store when this photograph was taken in the 1930s. The signs in the windows state: "Always Reliable, Lorne Elwyn and Co., in new plays, The Show, Majestic, one week, Feb. 5." Note the wreaths in the windows.

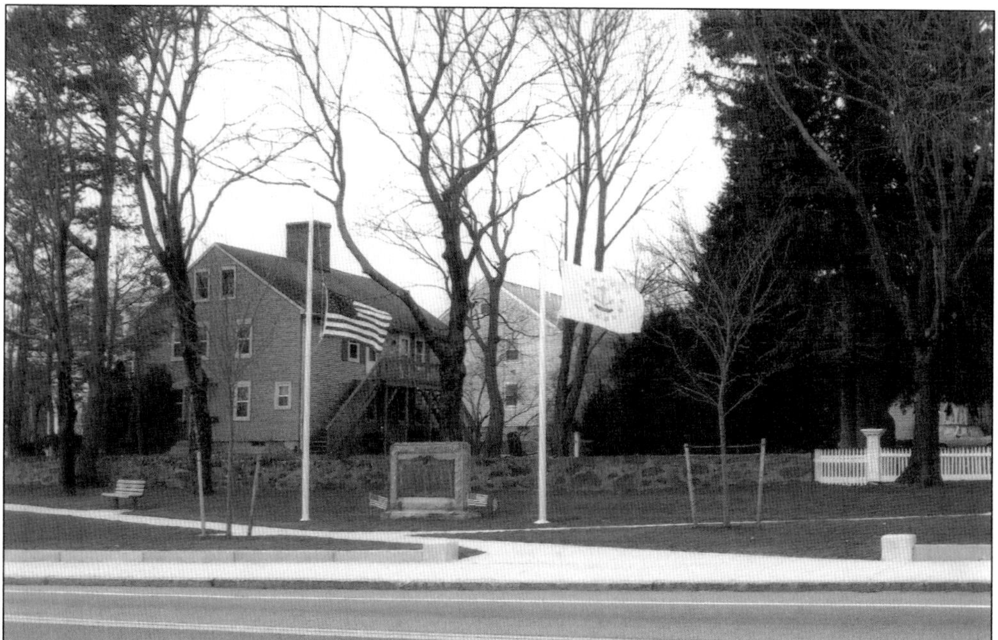

This January 16, 2012, image was captured on Martin Luther King Day. A World War I monument occupies center stage of this park where the Coventry Company's Mill Store used to be. It reads, "Dedicated to the Citizens of The Town of Coventry, who served their country in the WW, 1914–1918." There are 217 names listed. (Author's collection.)

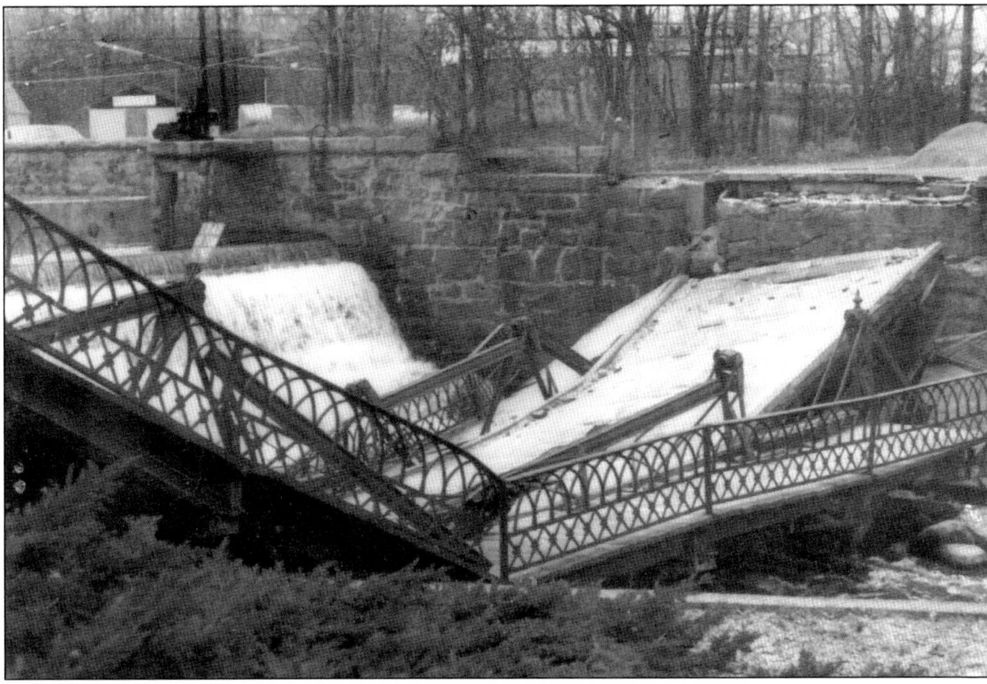

The Anthony Mill Dam, pictured above, created the pond that fed the headrace to the mill. The headrace trench was one of the shortest on the Pawtuxet River. The dam, built in 1873 using granite blocks, is about 80 feet long. The Laurel Avenue Bridge collapsed in 1983 and was replaced with a concrete one. After the floods of March 2010, it was determined the abutments had been weakened and the bridge was unsafe to drive over. It has been closed to traffic since. Below is a view of the Anthony Railroad Station from the mill side of the river. Laurel Avenue runs behind it to the homes on the hill. (Above, courtesy of Donald Carpenter: below, courtesy of Richard Siembab.)

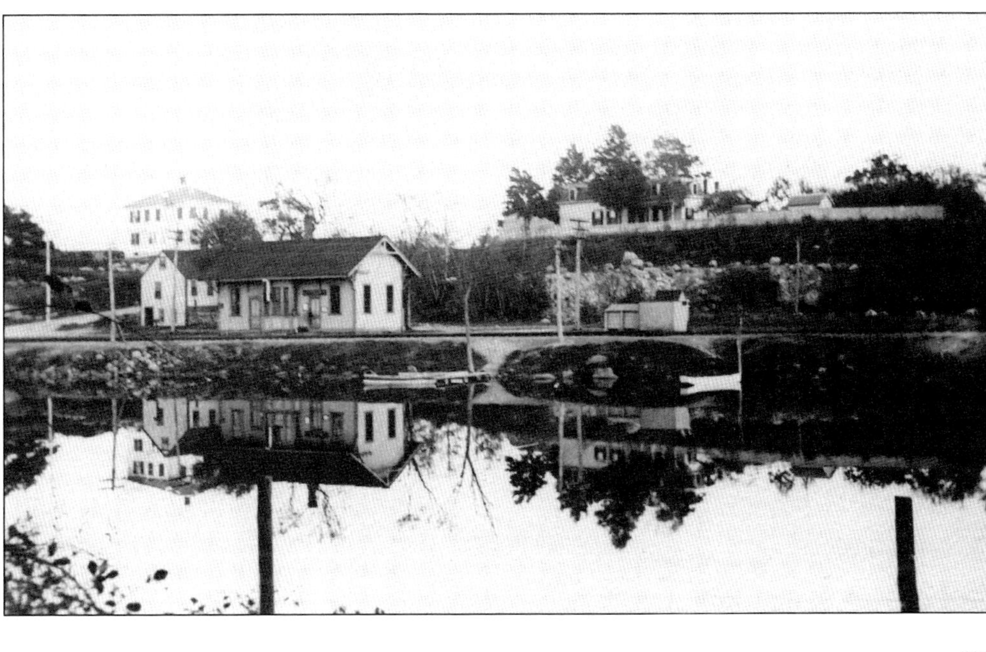

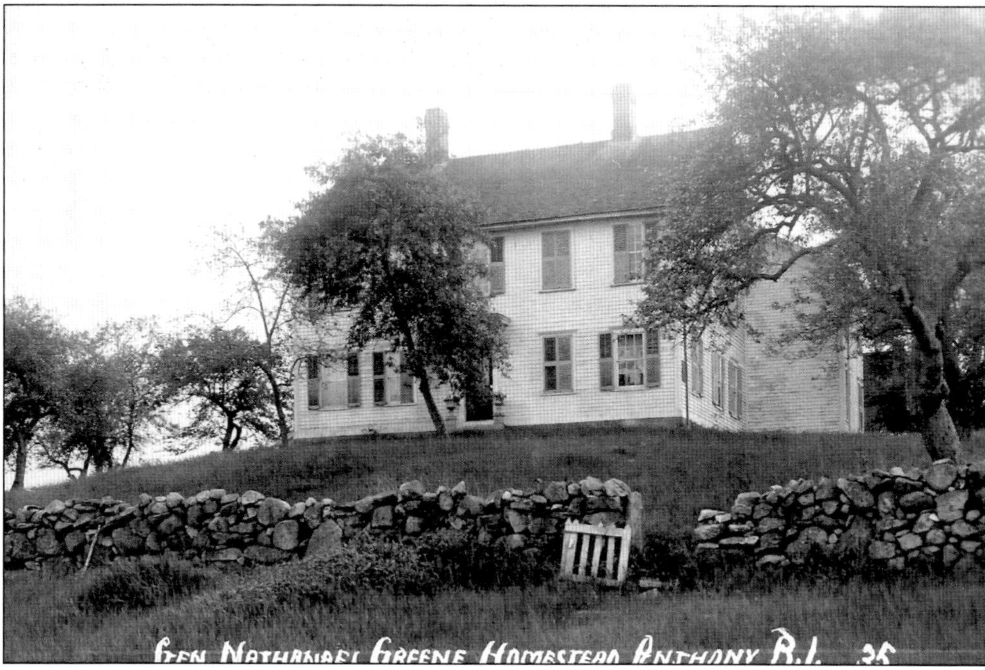

This postcard shows Gen. Nathanael Greene's homestead. He built it in 1770 after he came to Greeneville (later changed to Anthony) to take over management of the Greene forge. He was a major Revolutionary War figure, working closely with Gen. George Washington. (Courtesy of Foster Historical Society.)

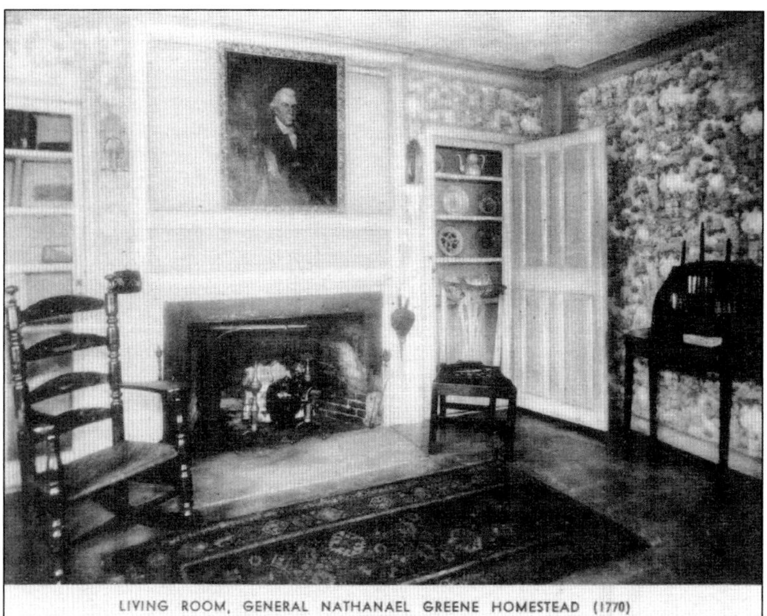

The interior of the homestead is visible in this c. 1930 postcard. It was totally restored and is now a National Historic Landmark, open to the public by the Nathanael Greene Homestead Association. It is listed in the National Register of Historic Places. (Courtesy of Richard Siembab.)

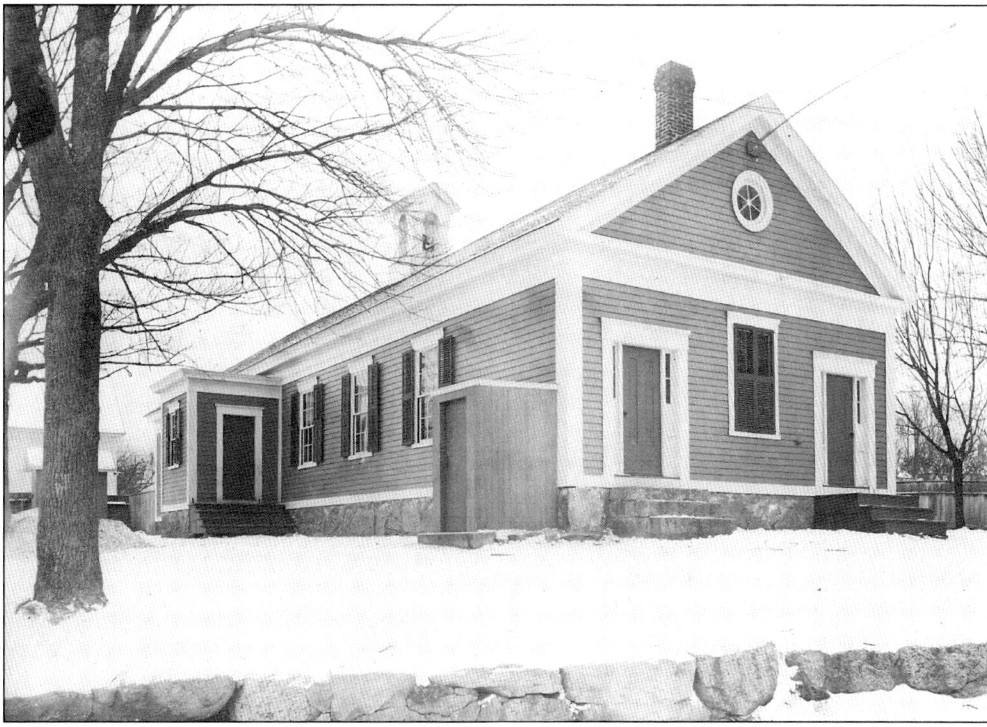

The Anthony Village School was built in 1844. The boys and girls had separate entrances in the front of the building and a third entrance on the side. The following verse is from "My School" by Helen O. Larson, age 88: "I loved the children that went there, they were all friends of mine / And it will stay with me, for all time."

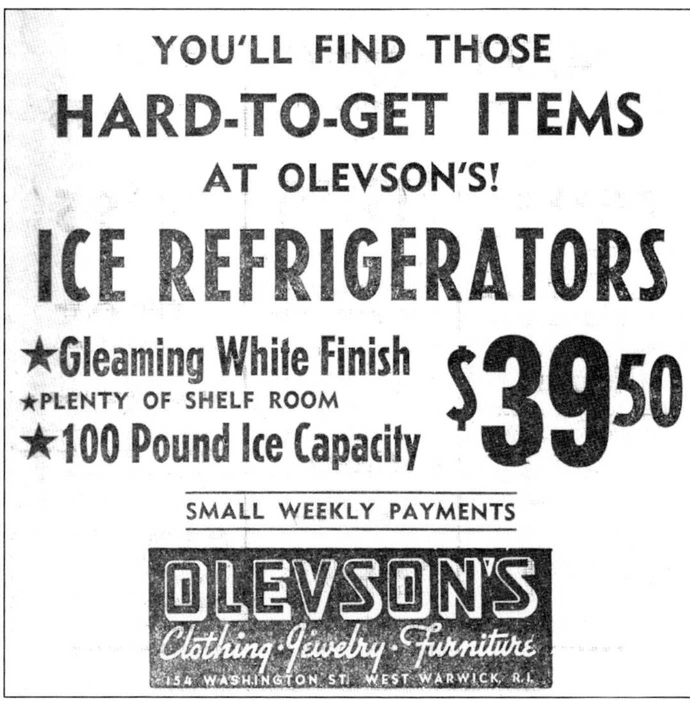

Capwell's Garage, located on Washington Street, later became an icehouse, where they sold blocks of ice to be used in iceboxes. Thus, the building is now used by Ice House Flowers. This advertisement, which appeared in the *Pawtuxet Valley Times* on September 30, 1943, promotes ice refrigerators for sale that could hold 100-pound blocks of ice supplied by the icehouse. (Author's collection.)

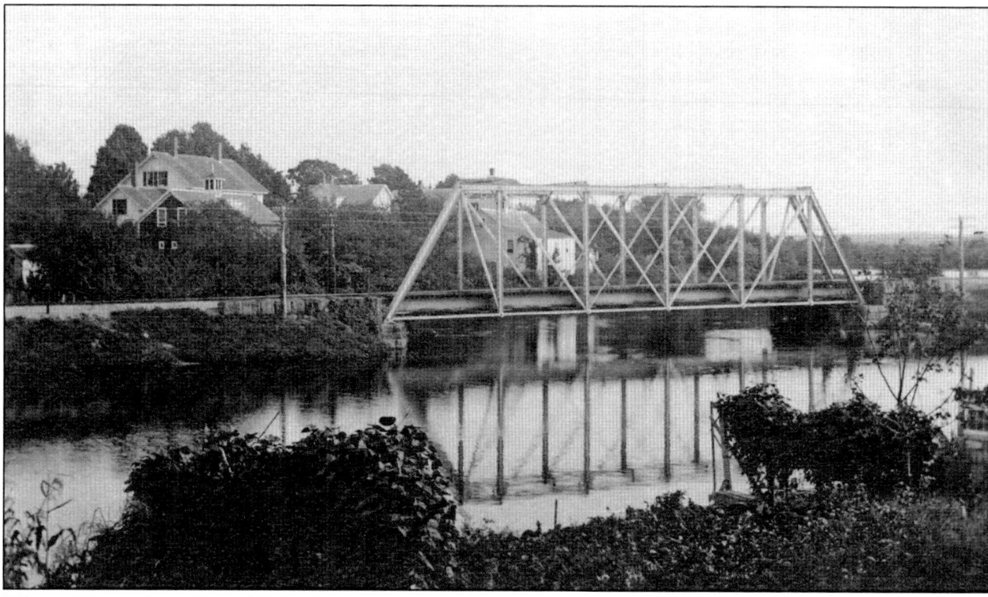

This is an early-1900s photograph of the Anthony railroad bridge. The bridge has been totally restored and is now a rails-to-trails bike path and a fraction of the East Coast Greenway. (Courtesy of Richard Siembab.)

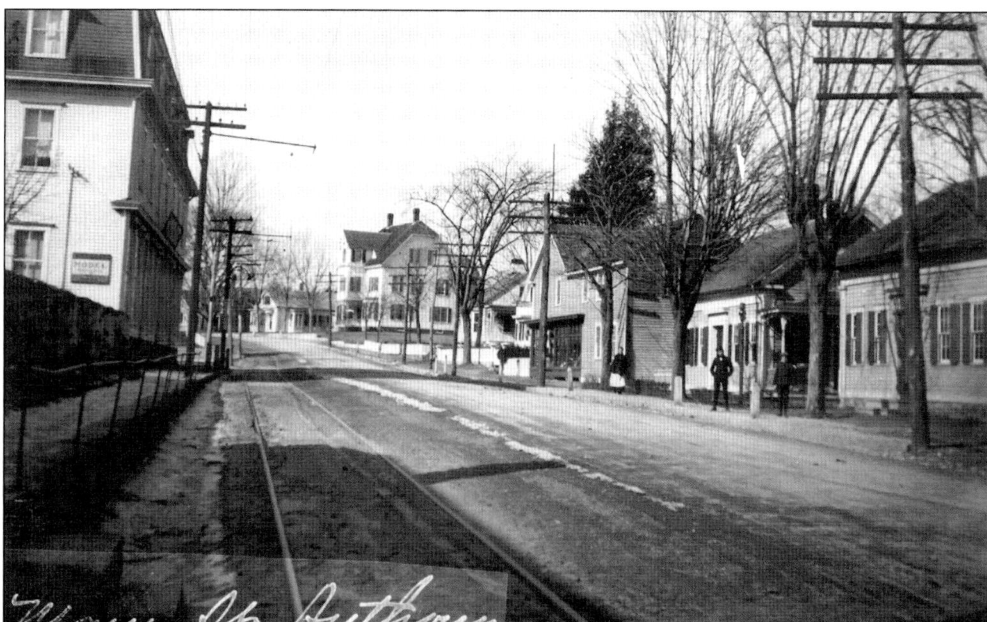

This postcard shows Washington Street, also known as Main Street in Anthony, to the west. The Byron Read building, constructed in 1882, is the large structure on the left. It has been a furniture store, hardware store, and funeral home. Currently, it is for sale and in need of total restoration. (Courtesy of Richard Siembab.)

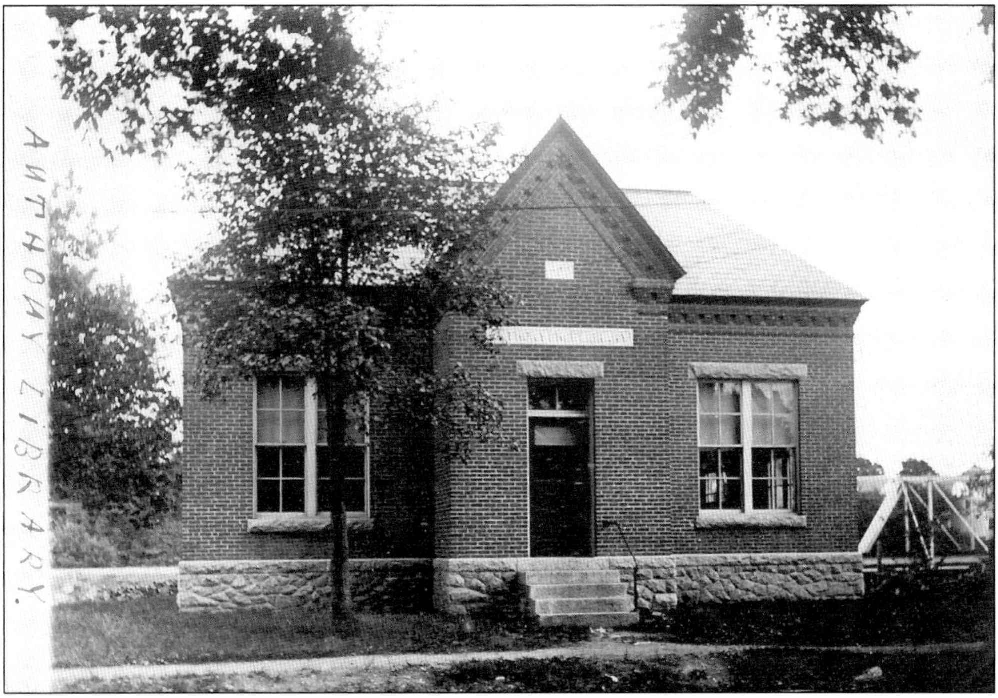

The Anthony Free Library was built in 1902 on Washington Street. There was a fire on January 3, 1918, that destroyed the roof. The building with a new roof can be seen on page 112. (Courtesy of Foster Historical Society.)

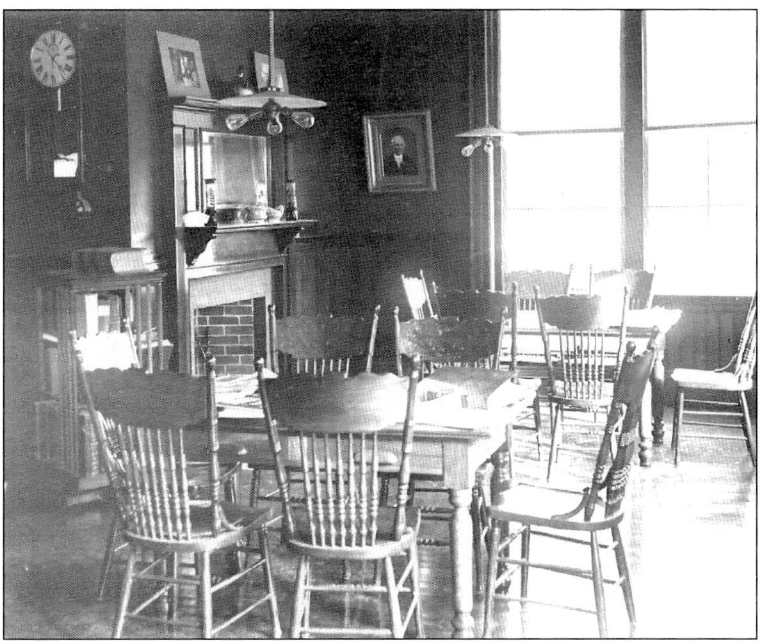

This postcard shows the interior of the Anthony Free Library reading room. Note the fireplace. (Courtesy of Lawrence G. Soucy.)

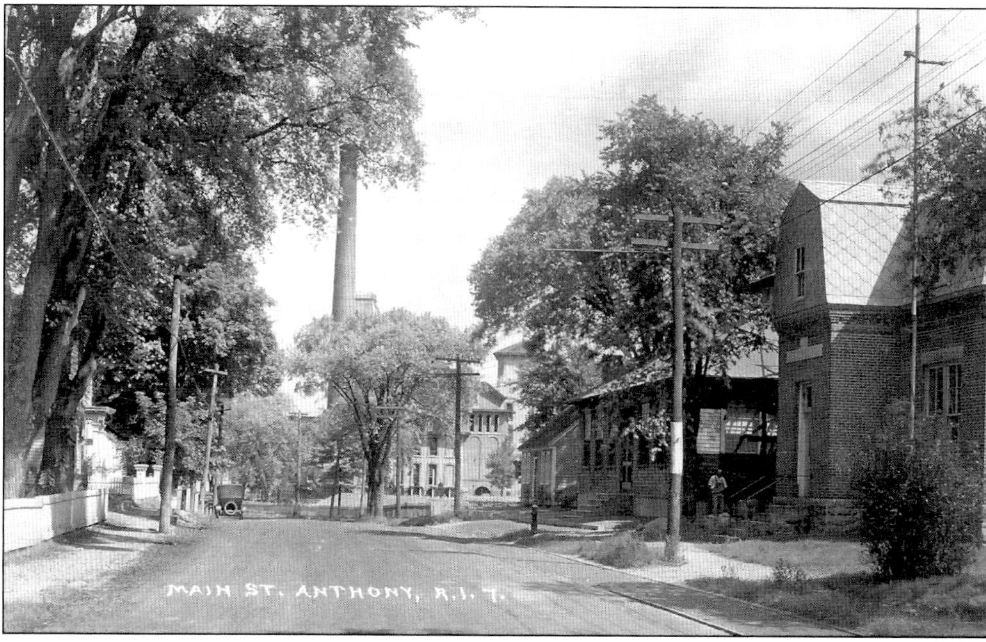

This postcard of Anthony shows Main Street to the east, now Washington Street, in the early 1900s. The Anthony Free Library is the building on the right after the fire of 1918. The Anthony Mill smoke stack rises to the sky. (Courtesy of Foster Historical Society.)

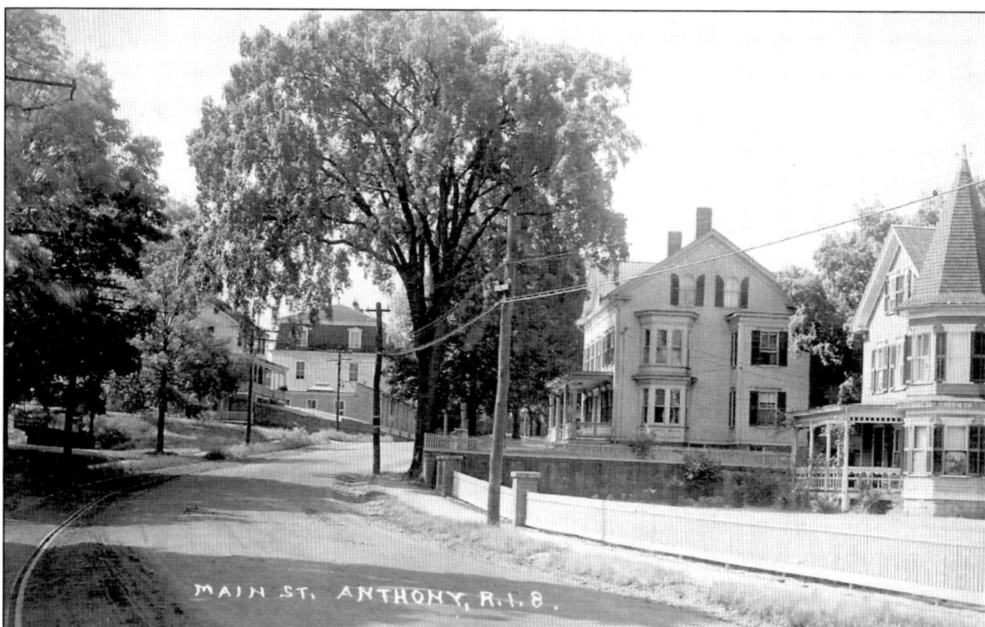

This photograph was taken from the same location as the image above, only facing west. Nina Nichols's house is the furthest house located on the right. The Byron Read Building is the last one seen at the top of the hill on the left. The trolley tracks are also running on the left. (Courtesy of Foster Historical Society.)

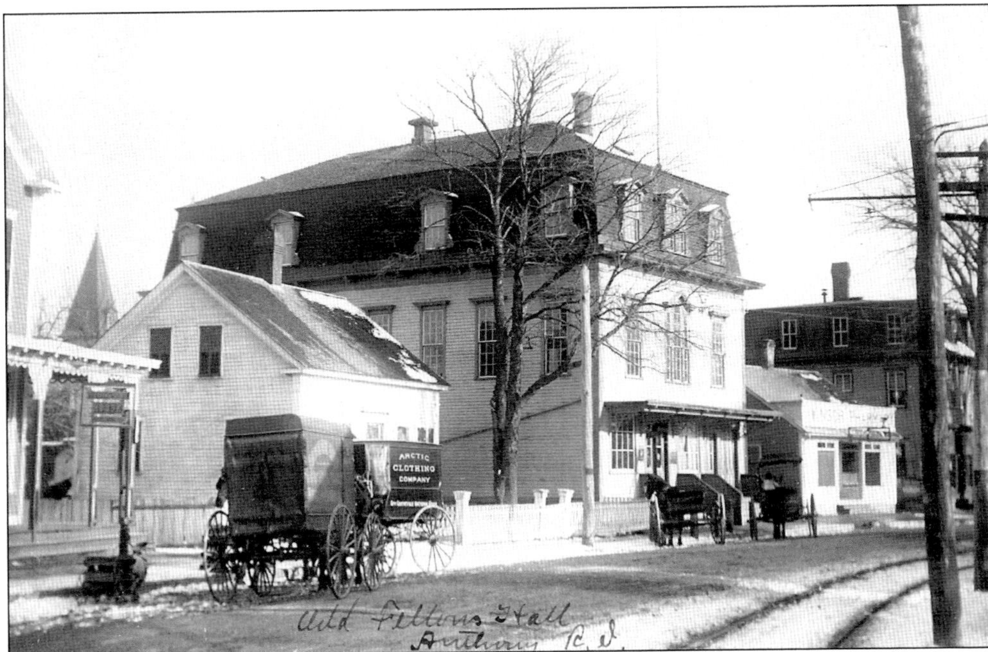

The large building in the center of this postcard was home to the IOOF. The small structure to the right of it is advertised as the Winsor Pharmacy. One of the delivery carriages in the foreground advertises, "Arctic Clothing Company." The photograph below shows the IOOF building completely destroyed by a fire in 1916. The following verse is from "Dedicated to Firemen" by Helen O. Larson, age 70: "Let's line both sides of the street, let's applaud as they go by / Because while fighting fires, some of them could die." (Above, courtesy of Foster Historical Society; below, courtesy of Richard Siembab.)

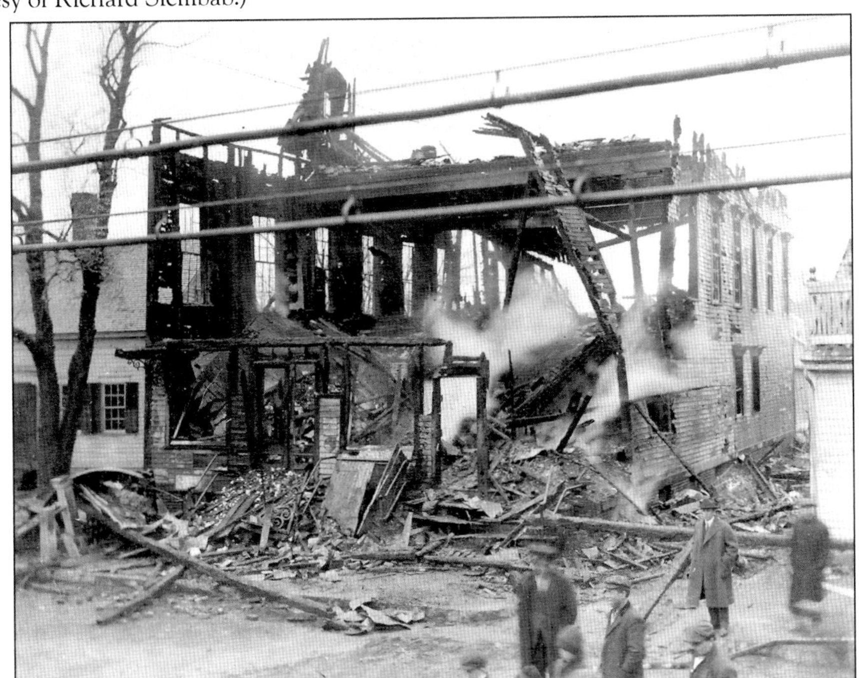

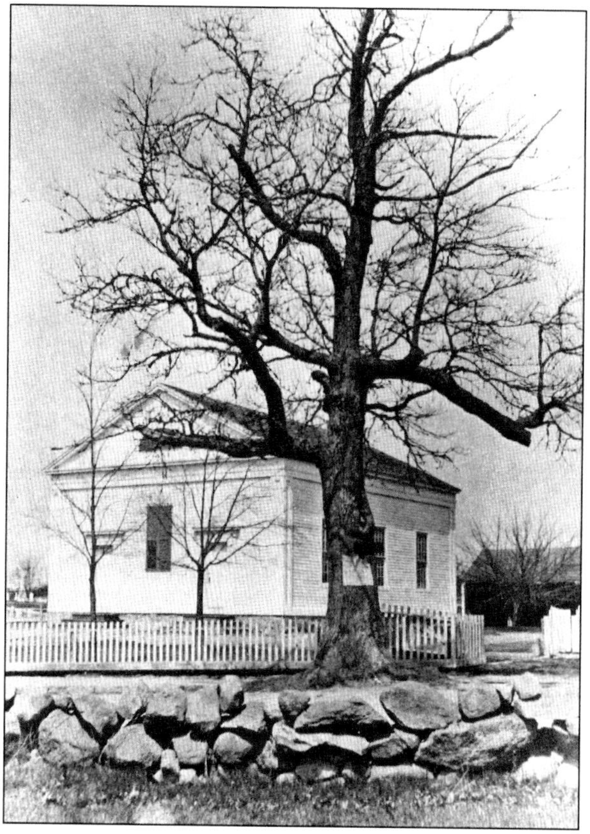

The Knotty Oak Baptist Church is pictured left in 1915. The church was known early on as the Coventry Six Principle Baptist Church, established in 1840. It received the name "Knotty Oak" because a large oak stood in front. Originally, the church was a simple Greek Revival meetinghouse. The church, shown below, has been transformed by the addition of a central entrance tower with a steeple and belfry. Also, fancier windows have replaced the plain ones on the sides to match the tower. Later, a canopy was added to the entrance. The following verse is from "Chapel in the Moonlight" by Helen O. Larson at age 80: "The bronze bell in the belfry, used to toll each night / To alert the people to come to, the chapel in the moonlight."

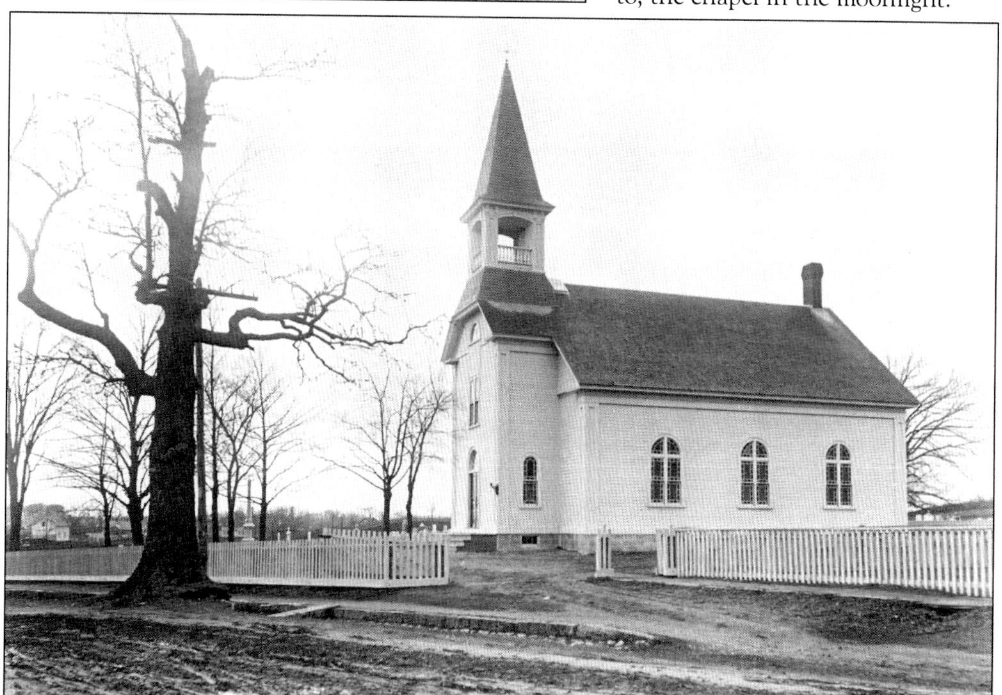

Nine

Black Rock and Washington

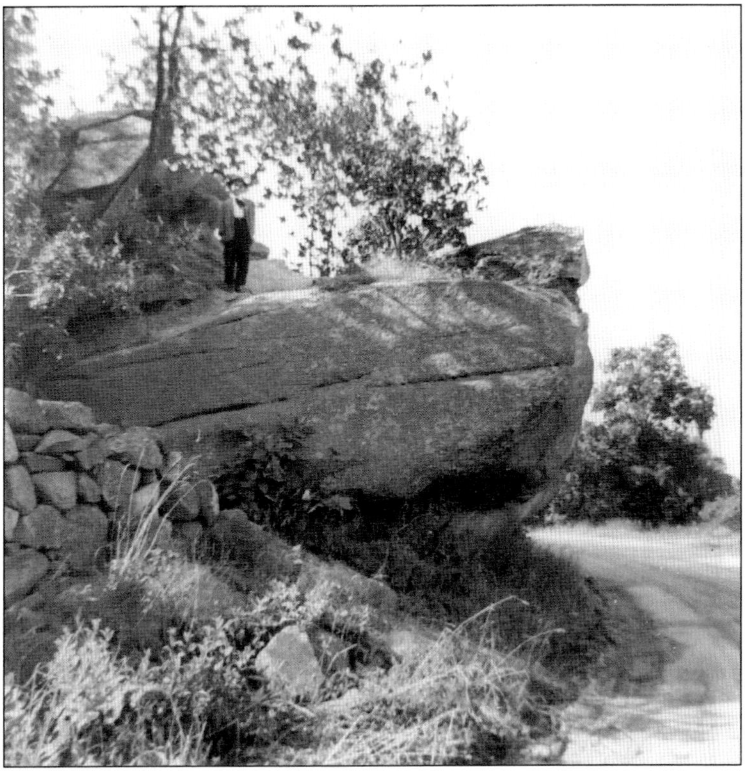

The author stands atop Black Rock during a break from the customary Sunday drive after church in the 1950s. Black Rock Village, as well as Black Rock Road, seen here, was named after this large granite boulder. Black Rock is said to have been a ceremonial meeting place for Indians who once lived in the area. (Author's collection.)

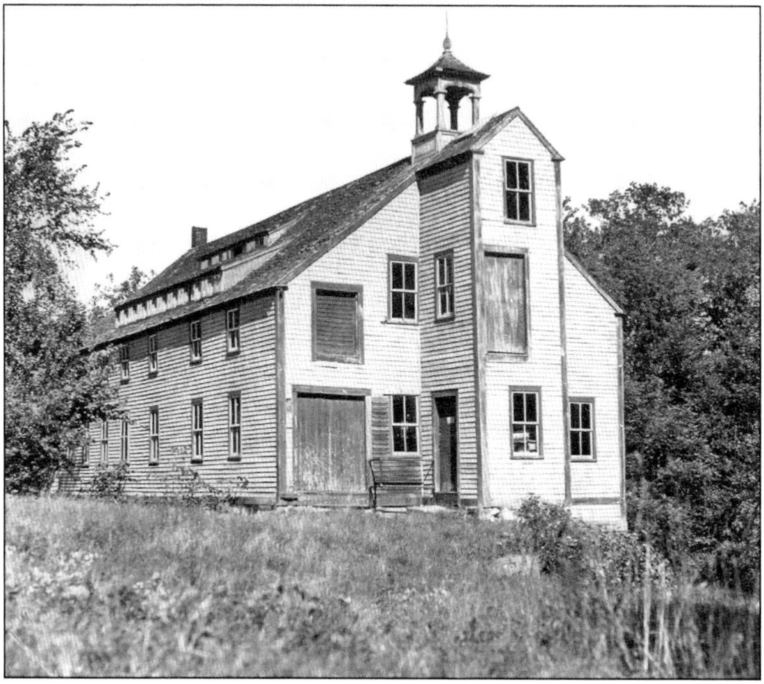

The Blackrock Mill was built in 1814 by Greene family members William, William F., Daniel, William Jr., and James. It was constructed of wood for the manufacture of cotton and located near Fones Pond. Their short-lived venture was sold to Nicholas Potter, who transformed it into a machine shop. No evidence of the mill remains. A house now occupies the site. (Courtesy of Donald Carpenter.)

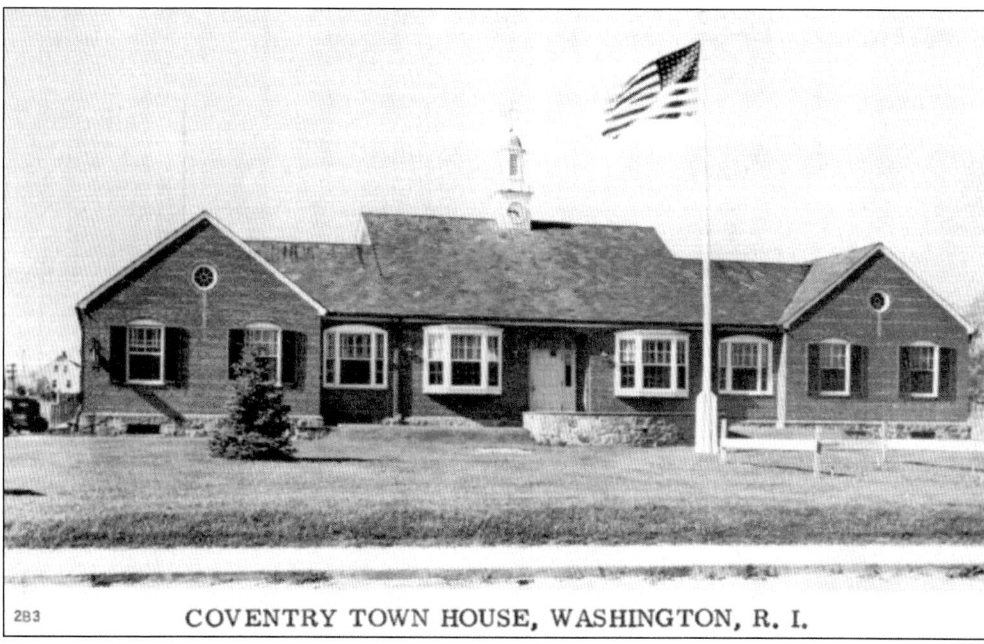

The town of Coventry built a new town hall on Main Street in 1941. The cornerstone was laid by Bertha E. Parker on August 23. The building was turned over to the Coventry Police Department for their headquarters in 1978. (Courtesy of Lawrence G. Soucy.)

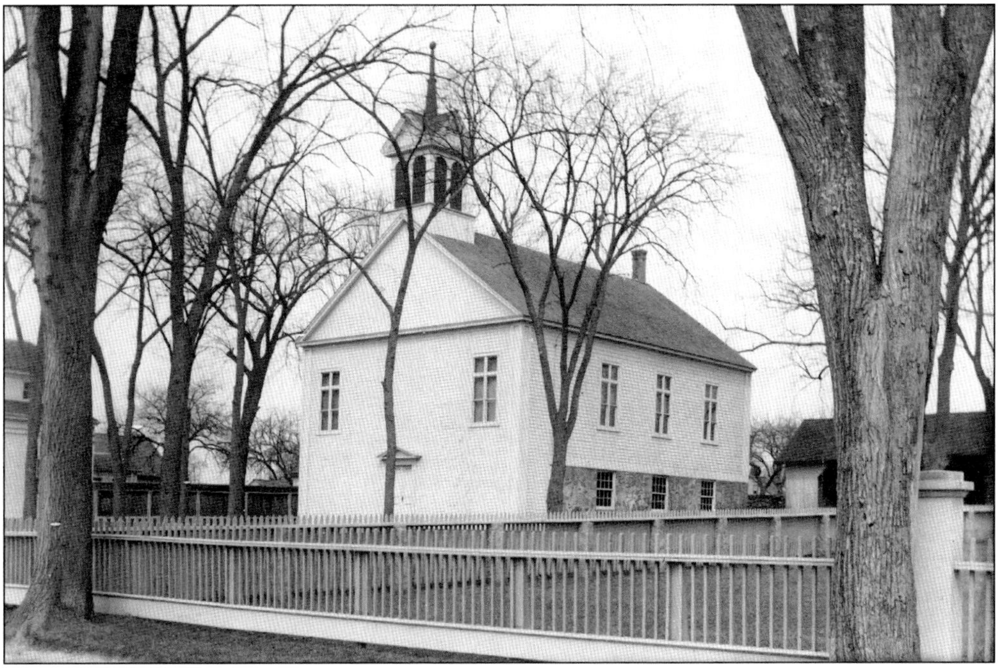

The Washington Methodist Church, located on Main Street and originally built in 1831 as a First Congregational Church, is where the author was baptized over 100 years later in 1942. Today, it is the Cornerstone of Faith United Methodist Church. (Author's collection.)

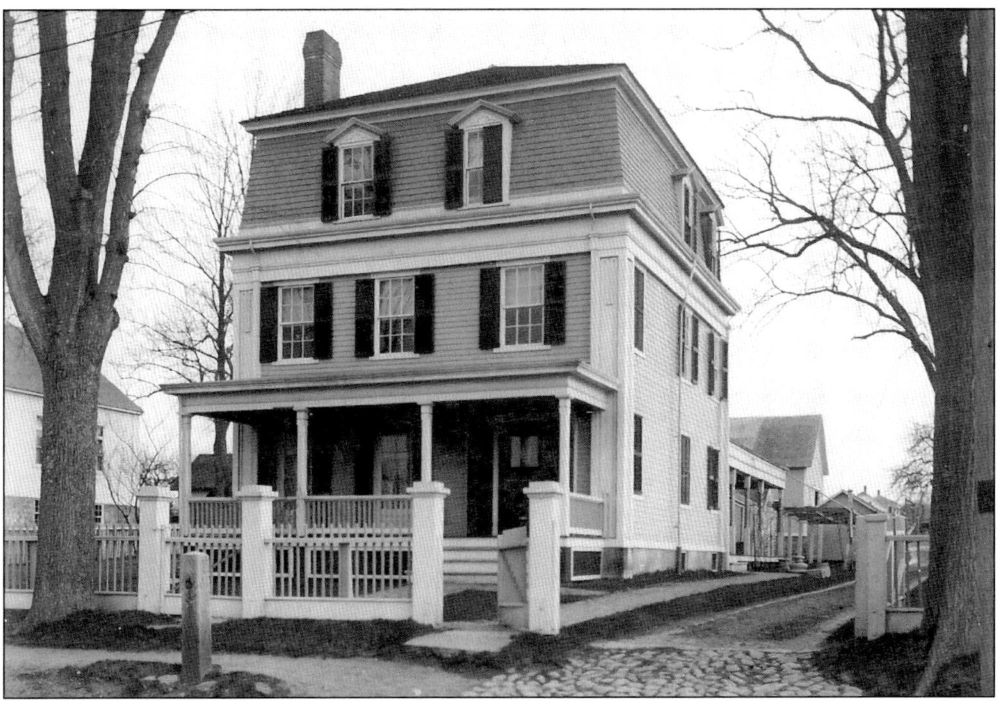

The minister of the Washington Methodist Church resided in the three-story Tyler House, torn down in 1940 in preparation of the construction of the new town hall, seen on the opposite page. (Courtesy of Donald Carpenter.)

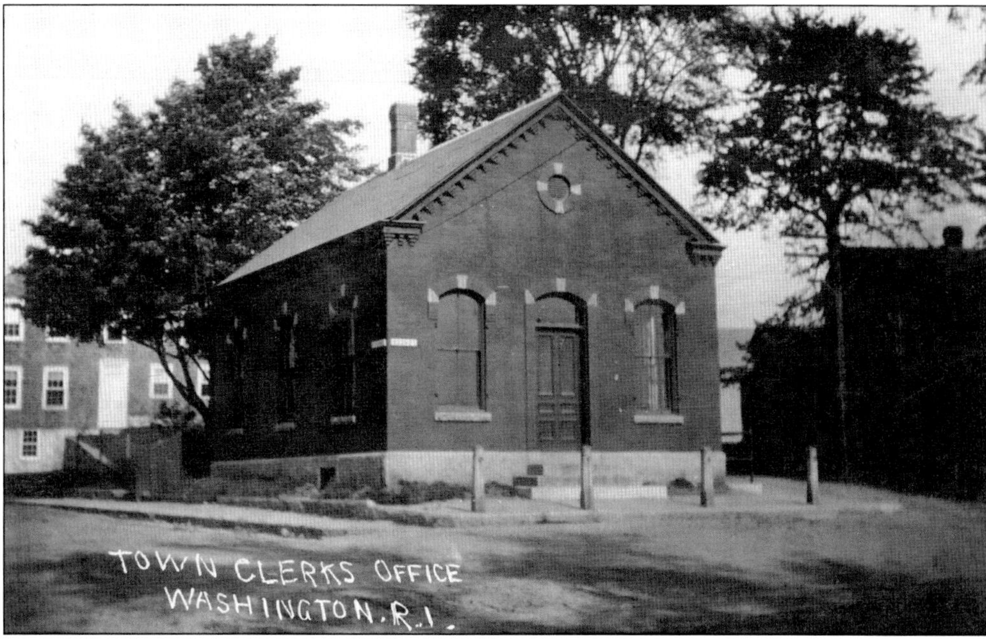

The village of Washington was chosen as the government center of the town. In 1881, this small brick building was constructed as the town clerk's office. It served the town until more space was needed; a larger structure was erected for this purpose in 1941, as seen on page 116. (Courtesy of Richard Siembab.)

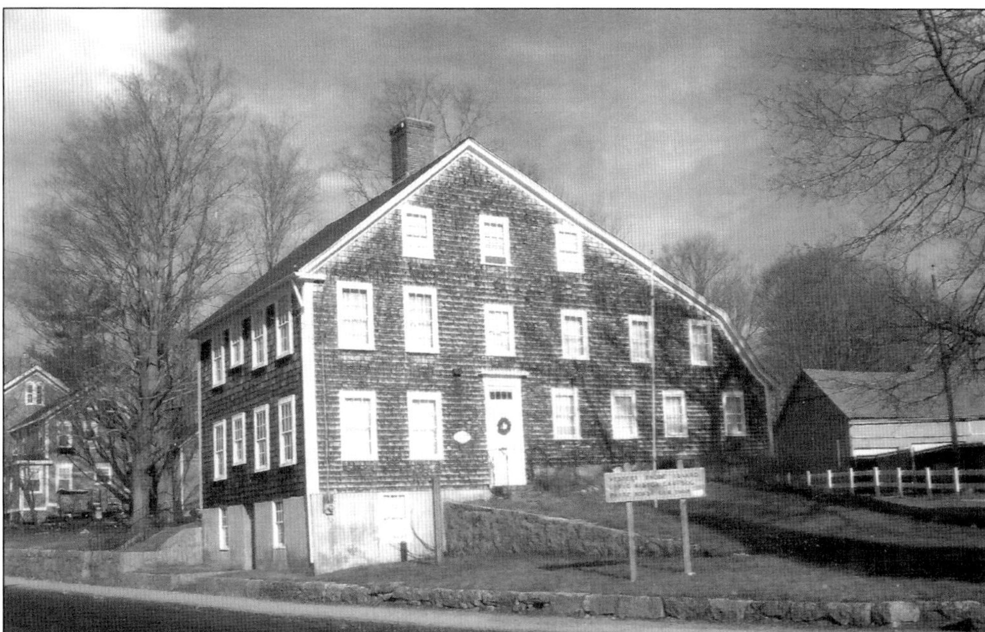

The Paine House, pictured here in 2012, is located on Station Street behind the old town clerk's office. Originally, it was much smaller and known as the Holden Tavern. A sign over the door once read, "Entertainment for travelers and good stabling for horses by A. Holden." It is believed to have been constructed in 1668, making it the oldest building in Coventry. (Author's collection.)

Pictured here on Cady Street in 1900, the Washington Village School, built in 1844, contained three rooms and a belfry tower. As the practice was, the girls and boys entrances were separated, and in this case, the entrances appear to be as far apart from each other as possible.

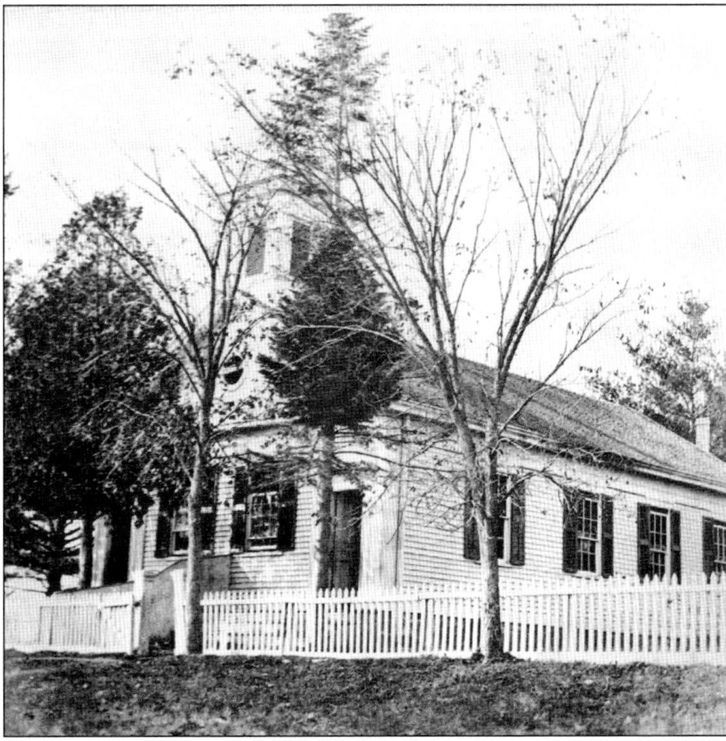

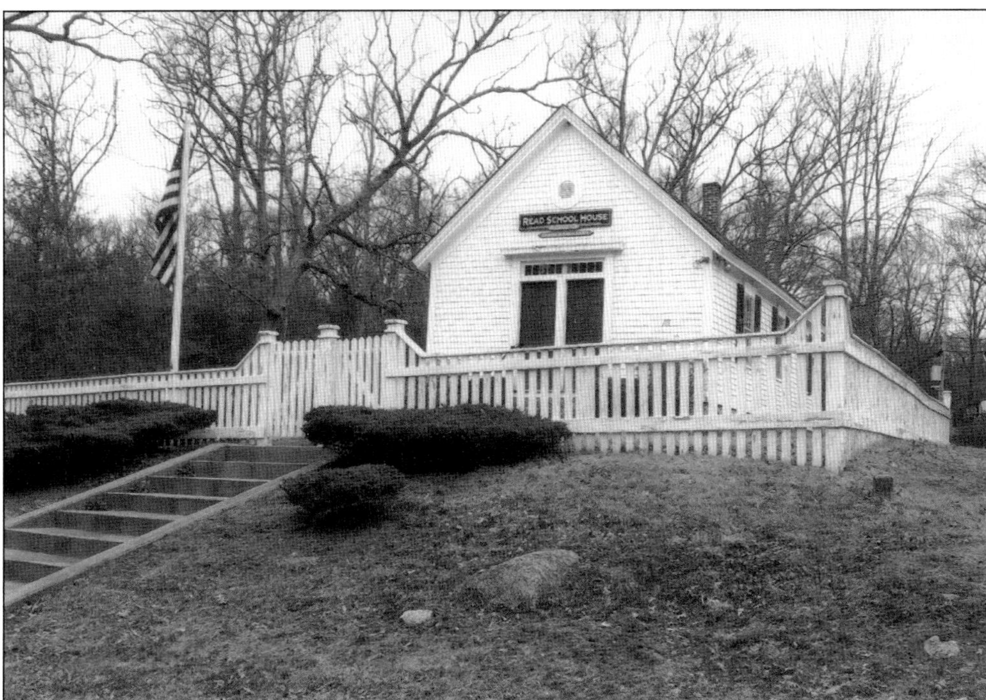

The Read School House is pictured here on February 29, 2012. The structure, built in 1831, was the last one-room schoolhouse used in Coventry when it closed in 1951. It is in excellent condition since its restoration. Note the separate entrances for girls and boys. (Author's collection.)

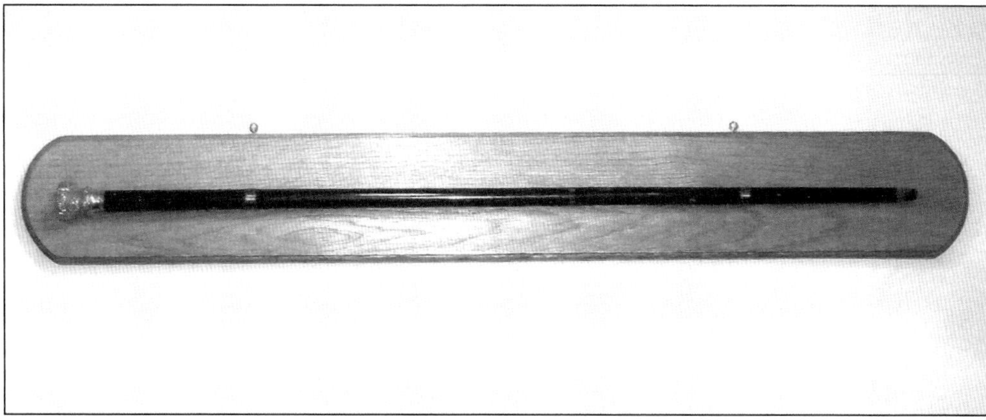

In 1909, Edwin Atkins Grozier, publisher of the *Boston Post*, initiated a campaign to recognize the oldest resident in many New England towns. Approximately 700 canes were distributed to the selectmen of these various towns throughout Maine, Massachusetts, New Hampshire, and Rhode Island. Upon the holder's passing, the cane was to be transferred to the next oldest resident. The canes were made by J.F. Fradley and Company of New York out of African ebony imported from the Congo. The wood was first lacquered and finished with French varnish, and then an ornate, engraved 14-carat gold head was affixed to the top; hence, it is also referred to as the gold-headed cane. The *Boston Post* ceased publication in October 1956. Below is a list of Coventry recipients that received the Boston Post Cane. It is now mounted and displayed on a wall in the town hall, as seen above.

Coventry Recipients of the Boston Post Cane with Year and Age when Received

Name	Year	Age	Name	Year	Age
Samuel Edmund	1909	87	Senator Felix Hebert	1969	95
Pardon Peckham	1916	94	12 year break		
Triphena Harkness	1922	93	Annie Andrews	1981	102
Electra Corp	1931	90	Sarah Ashworth	1982	95
Jerry Hopkins	1932	91	Leslie S. Daly	1984	95
26 year break			Elizabeth Brimacombe	1988	100
Charles A. Foster	1958	95	Cyril Herbert Place	1992	97
Phebe J. Love	1961	99	Herman Rusack	1994	98
Charlotte Spencer	1968	94	Cane Retired		

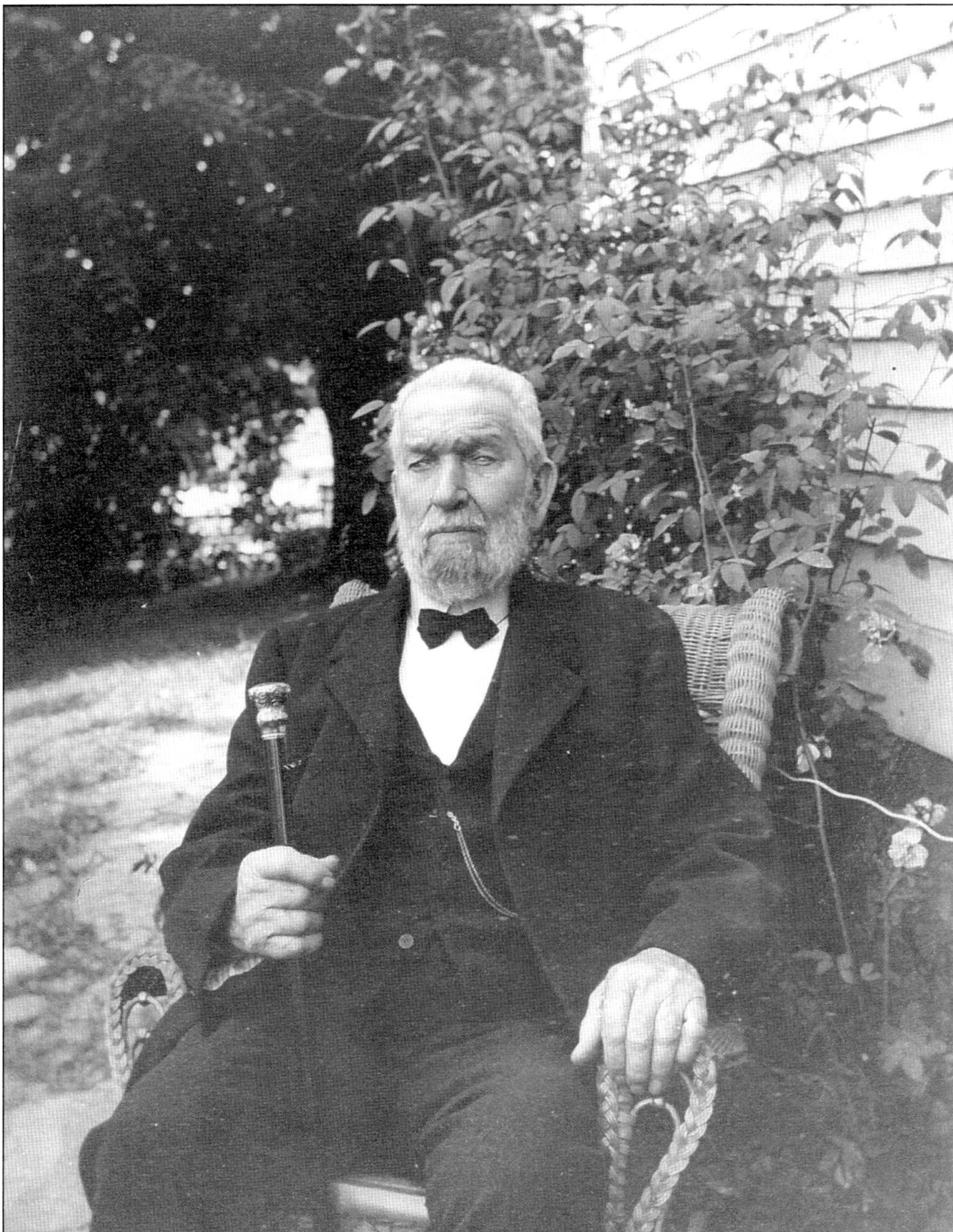

This photograph of Samuel A. Edmund was taken at a Fourth of July celebration in 1912. At the time, he was 91 years and 4 months old and resided in Washington. Abel Cornell of the town council presented the cane to him in 1909, when he was honored to be the first holder of the cane. Edmund passed away February 28, 1916. He would have been 95 in five days (it being a leap year) on March 4. H.N. Foster then presented the cane to Parden S. Peckham on March 18, 1916. Across the top of the gold head of the cane was the engraved inscription, "Presented by, the *Boston Post*, to the oldest citizen of [town and state] to be transmitted." Coventry retired their cane in 1994. (Courtesy of Richard Siembab.)

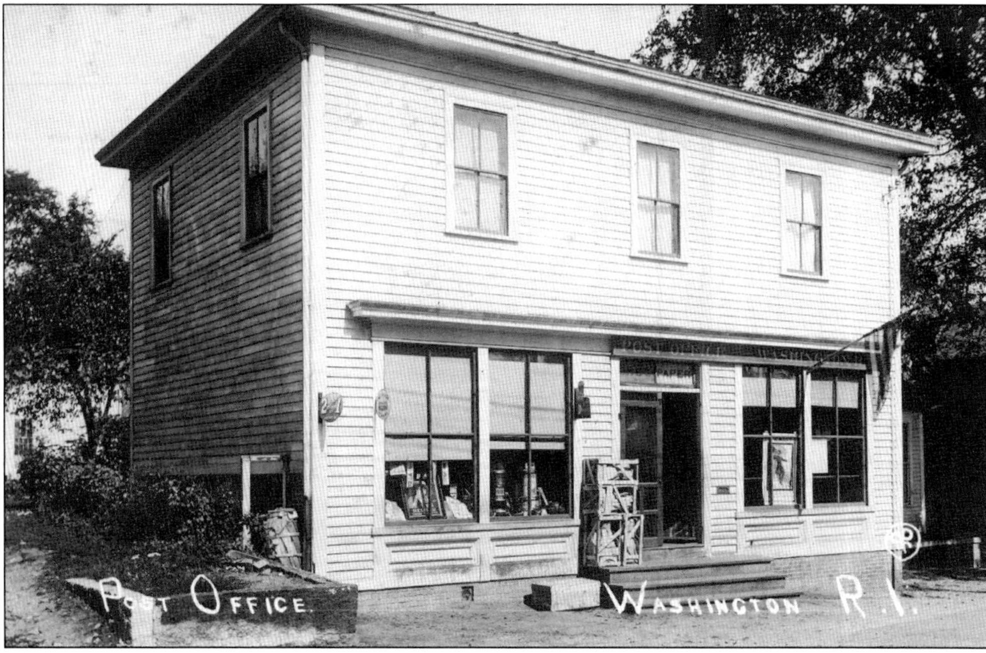

This is the hardware store in Washington Village. It was also the post office, but in later years, it became Duffy's Market. The building is seen below on the left in the 1940s photograph. This entire row of buildings has since been torn down, and the site is now occupied by the Coventry Shoppers Park. The blinking caution traffic light is for automobiles coming out of South Main Street located on the right. That also has been replaced with a new traffic light. (Above, courtesy of Richard Siembab.)

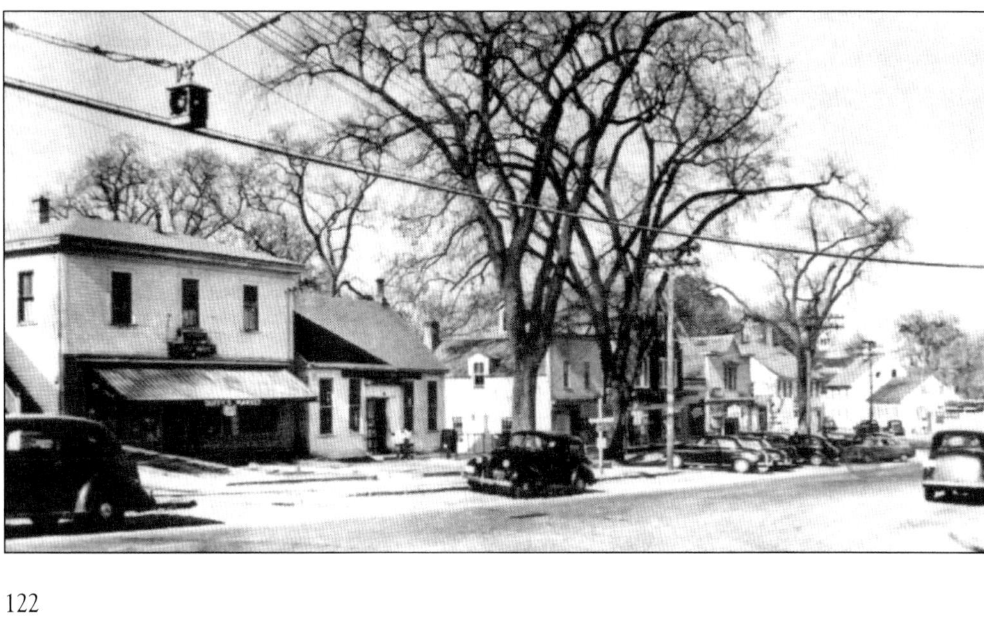

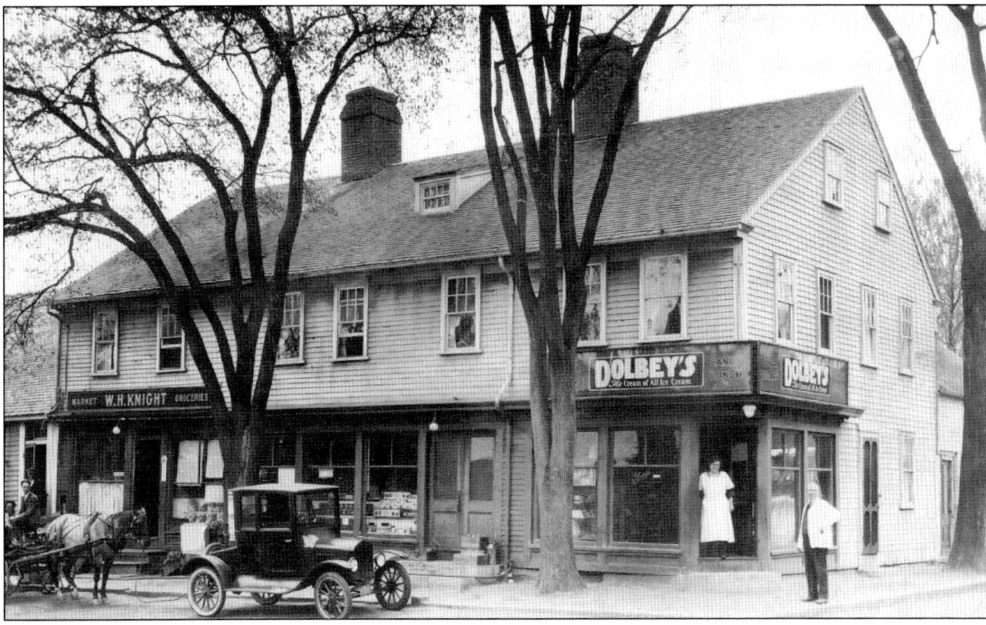

The building pictured above and below was located on the corner of Main and South Main Streets. W.H. Knight owned a market on the left of the building, while Dolby's on the right advertised, "The Cream of All Ice Cream." They also sold candy, soda, and cigars and served lunch. This was taken in the early 1900s, as transportation was either horse and buggy or the new-fangled automobile. The Washington Woolen Mill is shown below. South Main Street is located on the left after the trees and between the buildings. The South Branch of the Pawtuxet River flowed behind the mill. (Above, courtesy of Richard Siembab; below, courtesy of Lawrence G. Soucy.)

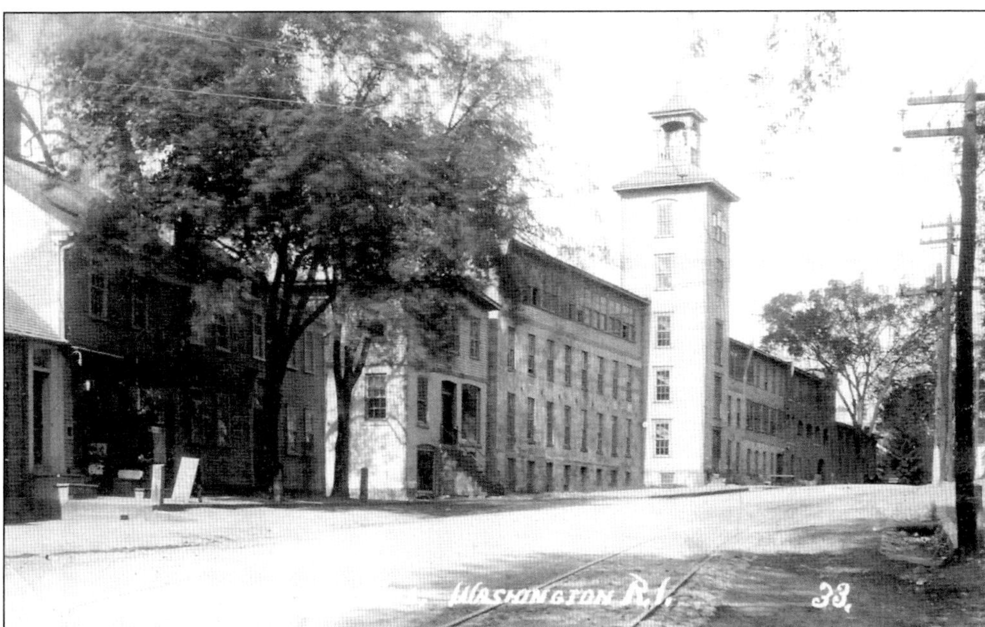

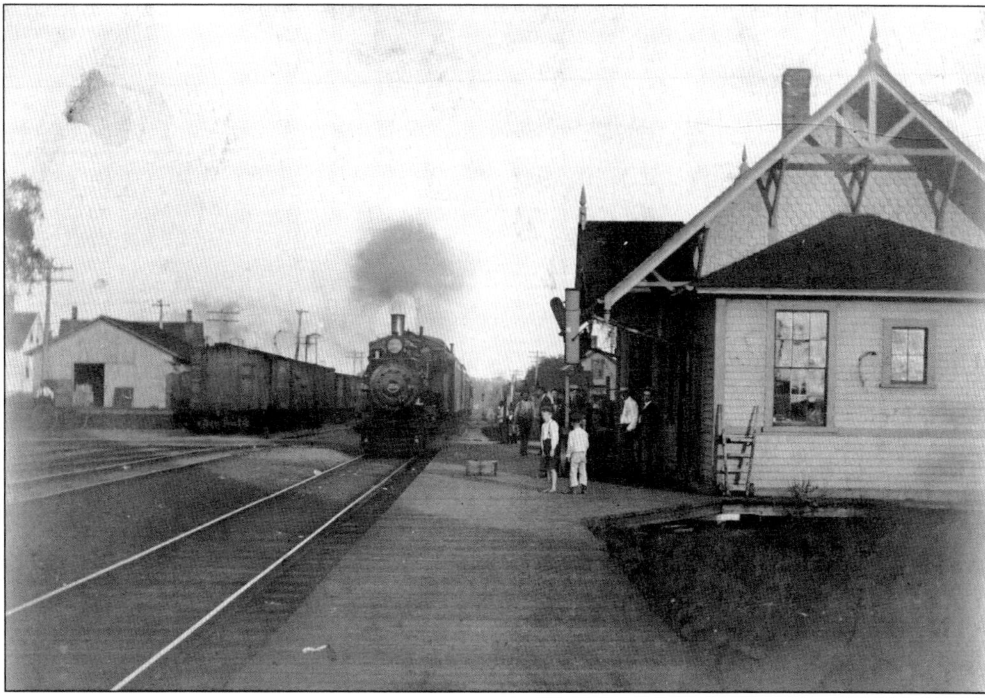

The Hartford, Providence, & Fishkill Railroad train pulls into the Washington Station on its way to Hartford. Passengers waiting to board are likely eager for it to stop. The postcard above, mailed on October 4, 1905, was signed, "Zilpha." She writes, "George has the card for you. Please call and get it. Will be home Saturday." The railroad company built this attractive station on Station Street. They also built an engine house, freight house, roundhouse (see above), and water tank. All of these buildings were constructed around 1854, the same time as the railroad came through. None of the buildings have survived the test of time. Below, the old Coventry High School, located on Knotty Oak Road, no longer exists. (Both, courtesy of Richard Siembab.)

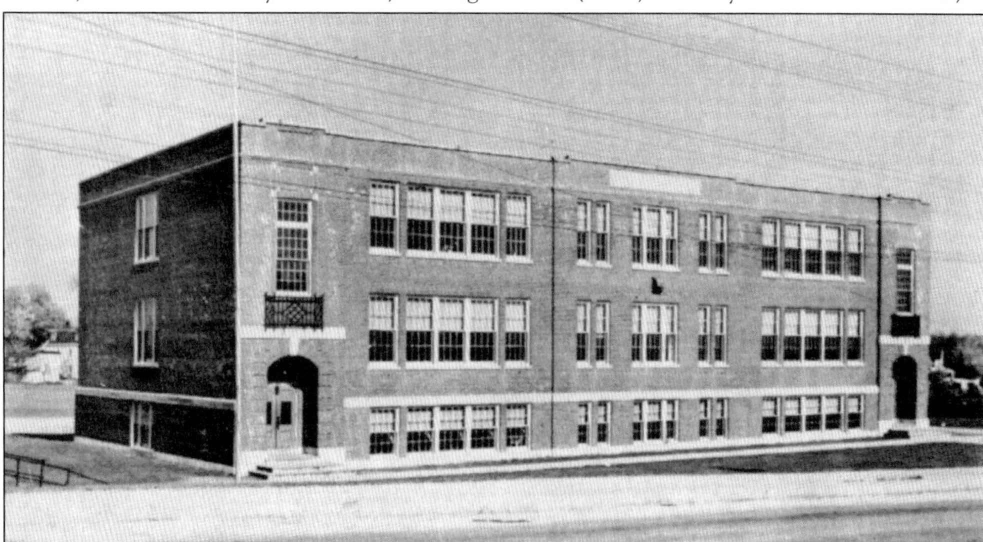

2C7 COVENTRY HIGH SCHOOL, WASHINGTON, R. I.

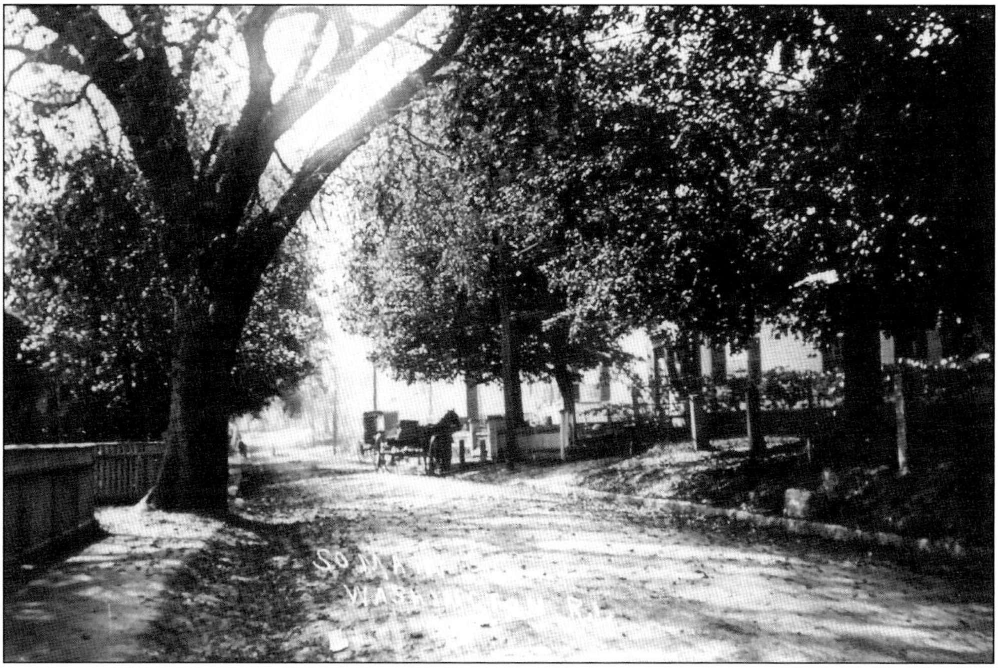

A tree-lined South Main Street is visible in this postcard, which faces south past the center of Washington. This area was placed in the National Register of Historic Places on July 10, 1987. There are 28 historic buildings included in the district and two that are not historic. The district also includes Cady and Wood Streets. Dawber's Cabins on Tiogue Lake are advertised in the postcard below. It is interesting that their post office box was in West Warwick. The following verses are from "I Walked the Dusty Roads," written by Helen O. Larson on June 30, 1999, at the age of 88: "I used to walk the dusty roads, many miles each day / I had to go to the store for groceries, and the store was far away." (Below, courtesy of Richard Siembab.)

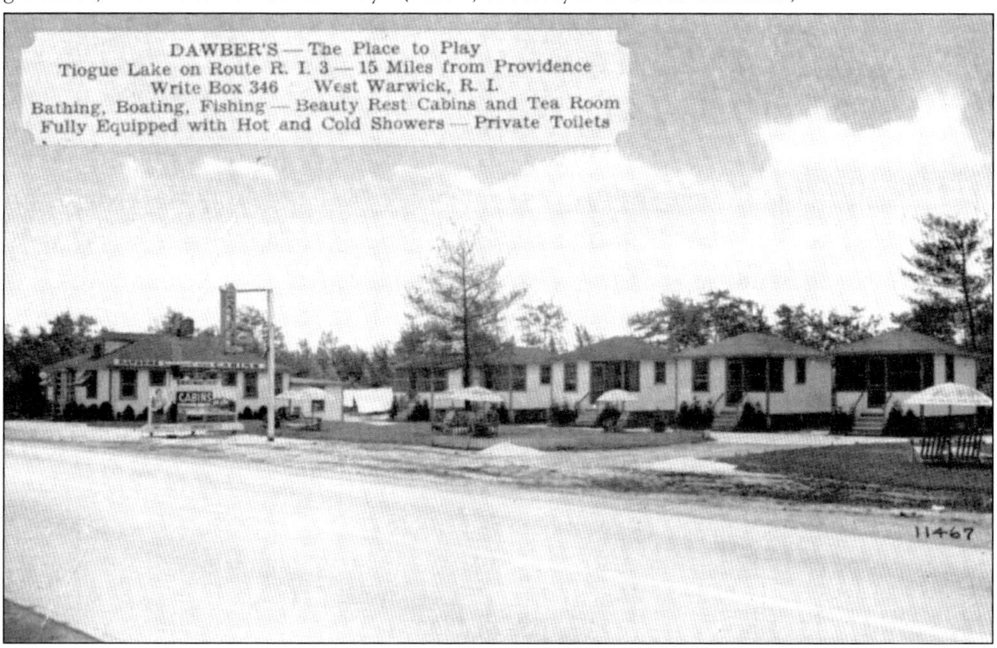

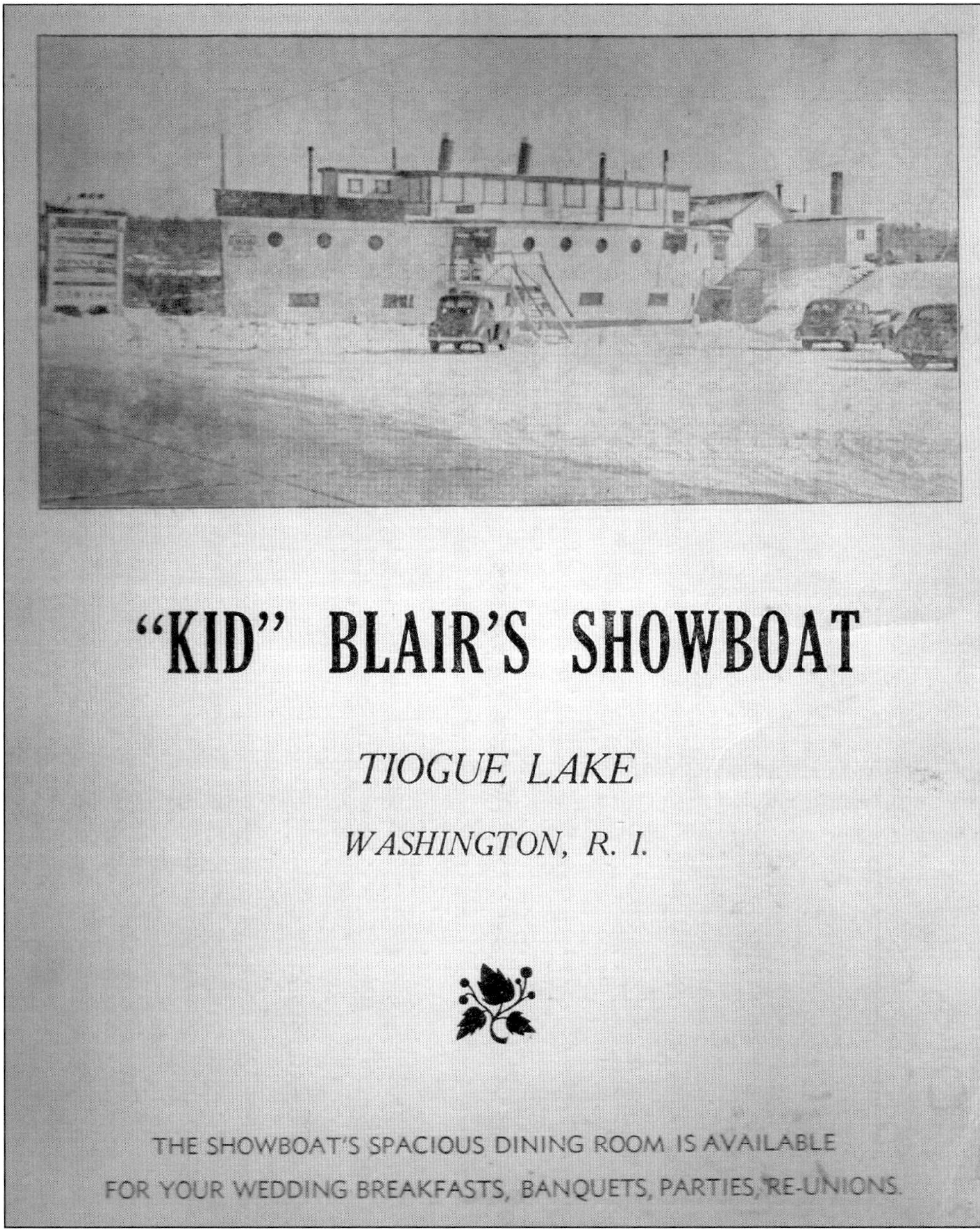

Alphee "The Kid" Blair was a former light heavyweight champion of New England. He traveled from coast to coast, meeting and defeating opponents. After his wrestling career, he opened "Kid" Blair's Log Cabin Restaurant on Washington Street in Arctic. The building can be seen in *West Warwick* on page 34. In 1935, he moved to Coventry and opened the Showboat Restaurant, pictured here. Built in the shape of a boat and against the dike holding Lake Tiogue, it was located on Tiogue Avenue, Route 3, which was the direct route between Boston and New York at the time. A menu from the early days offers T-bone, tenderloin, or sirloin steak for $2.50. It came with soup, little neck cocktail, hot rolls, vegetables, side salad, and potatoes. It also included tea or coffee and, of course, dessert. The Showboat burned down January 16, 1976.

Alphee "Kid" Blair traveled the country wrestling, frequently visiting the Pawtuxet Valley Fair in Fiskeville. During one contest, as he entered the ring, he tossed his robe to the crowd, and Opalma Jacques caught it. After the bout, he marched in victory down to her, took the robe, thanked her for holding it, and started a conversation. This led to courtship and, on January 25, 1925, marriage. Blair was quoted as saying, "The people of the Pawtuxet Valley were so nice to me that I just could not move out of this locality." The happy couple is pictured here in 1925. Blair's son Norman took over the business, and in the 1950s and 1960s, he added the beautiful bar seen below in a new cocktail lounge. He then renovated the Annex to offer additional dance space, making it one of the largest dining halls in the state.

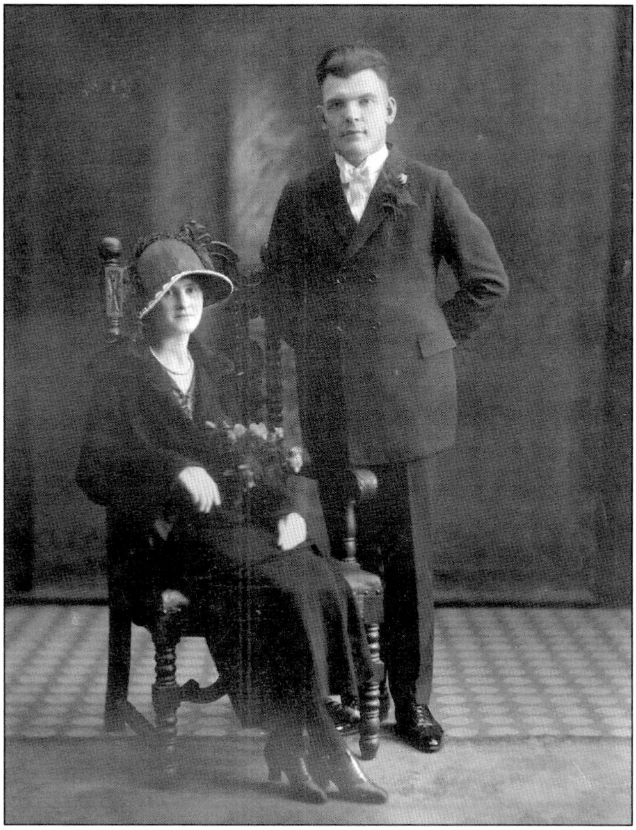

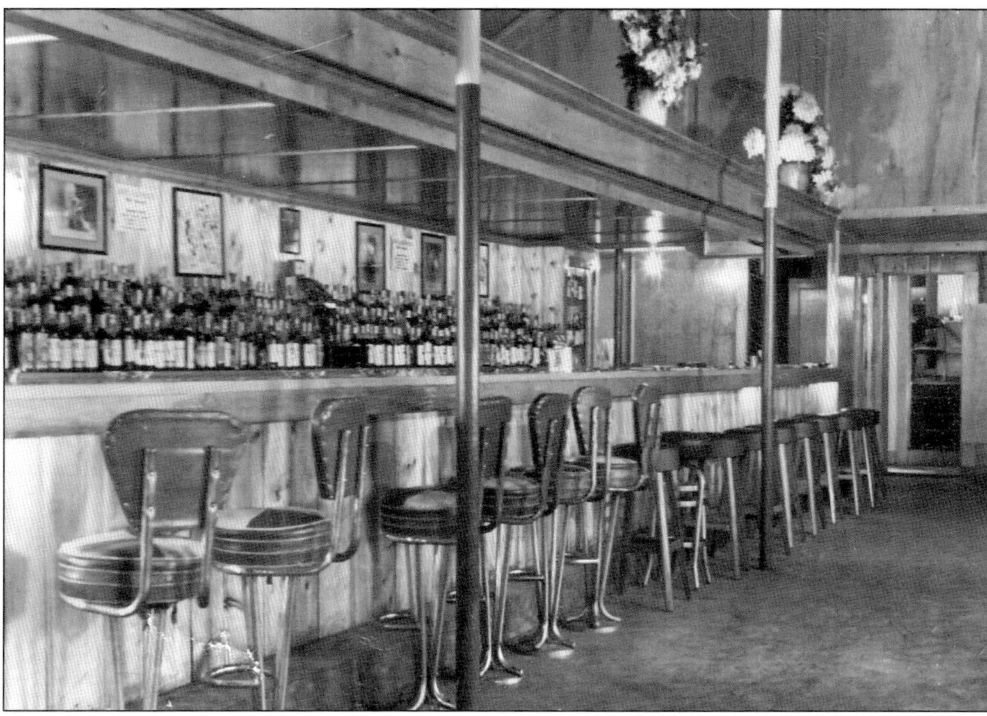